100
65.—

Hollywood Highbrow

PRINCETON STUDIES IN CULTURAL SOCIOLOGY

Paul J. DiMaggio, Michèle Lamont, Robert J. Wuthnow, and Viviana A. Zelizer, Series Editors

A list of titles in this series appears at the back of the book.

Hollywood Highbrow

FROM ENTERTAINMENT TO ART

Shyon Baumann

PRINCETON UNIVERSITY PRESS

PRINCETON AND OXFORD

Copyright © 2007 by Princeton University Press
Published by Princeton University Press, 41 William Street, Princeton, New Jersey 08540
In the United Kingdom: Princeton University Press, 3 Market Place,
Woodstock, Oxfordshire OX20 1SY

Library of Congress Cataloging-in-Publication Data

Baumann, Shyon, 1971–
Hollywood highbrow : from entertainment to art / Shyon Baumann.
p.   cm. — (Princeton studies in cultural sociology)
Includes bibliographical references and index.
ISBN 978-0-691-12527-5 (cloth : alk. paper)
1. Motion pictures—United States—History. 2. Motion pictures—Aesthetics.
3. Film criticism—United States—History. I. Title.
PN1993.5.U6B319 2007
791.430973—dc22   2007018558

British Library Cataloging-in-Publication Data is available

This book has been composed in Sabon

Printed on acid-free paper. ∞

press.princeton.edu

Printed in the United States of America

10   9   8   7   6   5   4   3   2

*This book is dedicated to Josée,
my favorite person*

Contents

Figures

List of Tables

Acknowledgments

THIS STUDY was supported by a Social Sciences and Humanities Research Council of Canada Doctoral Fellowship, as well as by research funds from the University of Toronto. I am grateful to have benefited from the advice, guidance, wonderings, conversations, criticisms, and encouragement of many helpful friends and colleagues: Susan Dumais, Seema Jayachandran, Miles Beller, Sara Michalak, Steve Morgan, Ziad Munson, Irene Bloemraad, Andy Andrews, and Ron Gillis. There were many other peers at Harvard, particularly participants in the 306R seminar where graduate students presented their work in progress, who provided constructive criticism and good ideas for how to best expand the project. In the early stages of this work, Aage Sørensen's unfailingly wise and insightful comments helped sort out key issues, and the stirring nature of his feedback made me all the more motivated to continue with the project (just what he was trying to do). I hope he would have approved of the final product. Gwedolyn Dordick's feedback is also gratefully acknowledged, as is the help of Peter Marsden, who really knows how research can be improved and is generous with his knowledge. In the later stages of the project, Alex Hicks provided a terrific set of suggestions for improvement. The later stages were also helped along by the excellent research assistance of Tara Hahmann, Afsoon Houshidari, Sasmita Rajaratnam, and Tara McMullen. I also wish to thank Ian Malcolm and Jill Harris at Princeton University Press for all their hard work; it is greatly appreciated.

Above all others, there are two people whose efforts deserve particular recognition. Stanley Lieberson advised me on this project from its inception to the point where it was accepted in partial fulfillment of the requirements for the degree of doctor of philosophy in the subject of sociology. The basic structure of the argument and the all-important links between theory and evidence were developed under his mentorship. I don't think there's anyone who can better sort out the right way to analyze and interpret data. I am thankful for the many intellectual contributions, large and small, he has made to this study. In the later stages of the project, as it expanded into book form, the intellectual leadership of Paul DiMaggio was extraordinary. If I were to go about things correctly, every page would have at least one footnote that reads, "I am thankful to Paul DiMaggio for this idea." For the sake of readability, I'll leave these out and just say here that his imprint is all over this book. Through several drafts, his feedback steered me clear of pitfalls, gave me useful directions for where to go next, provided valuable factual information (how does he know all that stuff?), and suggested ways to say what I wanted to say clearly and concisely. Everyone should be so lucky as to have Stanley Lieberson and Paul DiMaggio contribute to their scholarship. I could not have asked for more.

I want to say thanks to my mother for her moral support. She's always told me I could do anything. Although that's not true, it made me confident that I could at least write a book. And so I have. Finally, I want to thank Josée and Bram, for providing all the comforts and joys of home, a place where I could work hard to return to every day.

CHAPTER 1

Introduction: Drawing the Boundaries of Art

ALTHOUGH FILMS occupy a central place in American popular culture, that place is also, paradoxically, difficult to understand and characterize. Watching movies has been a major leisure and cultural activity for Americans for more than a hundred years. But for nearly the entire duration of their history, there has been an active debate about the movies and their merits. They have been criticized as dangerous, demeaning, dumb, and derivative, as regressive, blasphemous, sexist, racist, ageist, and ridiculous, among other things. But they have also been praised as enriching, enlightening, and enjoyable, as glorious, spectacular, ingenious, moving, and imaginative. Both the detractors and supporters of films have made their arguments well known.

The continuing disagreement concerning the place of films in American culture is a legacy of a number of monumental changes in the American film world over the last century. Some of these changes involve the methods of film production, while others involve the nature of the films themselves; still other changes involve the audiences for films. The primary subject of this book is the major historical change in the perception of films. By this I am not referring to revised opinions about particular films, though such revisions are also of interest. Instead, I mean *the creation of an understanding of the medium of film as a legitimate and serious artistic medium, and of a body of film works as being legitimate and serious works of art*. Moreover, in addition to this change in the perception of the medium of film, this book focuses more specifically on the changing perception of Hollywood films. Over time, a segment of the U.S. population developed and put forth a conventional (to them) understanding that many Hollywood films were serious works of art. This understanding stood in stark contrast to the prior conventional wisdom about the fundamental nature of Hollywood films, as a whole, as light entertainment.

It is thanks to this evolution in the perception of Hollywood films that we can now find among certain groups in society a willingness to intellectually engage with Hollywood films and to experience them as art. For example, the following paragraph led the review in the *New Yorker* for the film *Mystic River*:

> Clint Eastwood has directed good movies in the past ("Unforgiven," "A Perfect World"), but he has never directed anything that haunts

one's dreams the way "Mystic River" does. This extraordinary film, an outburst of tragic realism and grief, was shot in Catholic working-class Boston, a landscape of forlorn streets and brown shingle houses and battered cars. Yet there's nothing depressing about "Mystic River" as an experience of art. The movie has the bitter clarity and the heady exhilaration of new perceptions achieved after a long struggle, and one enjoys it not only for itself—it's fascinating from first shot to last—but as a breakthrough for Eastwood, who, at the age of seventy-three, may be just hitting his peak as a director. Based on a fine, scrupulous Dennis Lehane novel, "Mystic River" offers nothing less than a lucid detailing of malaise, a sense of fatality that slowly and stealthily expands its grasp throughout a community—a foul bloom taking over a garden. (Denby 2003:112)

Film critic David Denby was not alone in his praise for the film *Mystic River*, nor was he out of step with his approach to the film as a serious work of art. He was in agreement with many other film critics as well as with many audience members.

What makes this situation interesting historically, aesthetically, and so-ciologically is that there was a time when such a perspective would have been widely ridiculed by critics and public alike. Consider as examples the following passages. In a 1936 essay on the state of American films, William Allen White wrote about the place of movies in American society:

The best books, the best plays, the best music and the best poetry are written frankly for the discerning and the wise. The best in all other arts is conceived, produced, sold and lives or dies solely and with brutal frankness for the approval of the intelligent: in all the arts except in the movies. There, no artists, no directors, no writers, no theatres and no producers are set apart to please people of understanding. The Scarlet Muse of the silver screen sees only money, big money, quick money, the dirty money of her dupes. . . . [I]n all the movie world no place is pro-vided where persons of wit or gumption may go to find screen entertain-ment that is directed at the discriminating. (White 1936:5–6)

In addition to its alleged lack of intelligence, the film industry was also condemned as the cause of American society's moral deterioration. "The movies today are the most important single destructive force in our civili-zation" (Freeman 1926:115, quoted in Beman 1931:86), claimed an au-thor in the pages of *Educational Review*. It was the responsibility of art to ennoble. The movies, however, corrupted youth and molded society according to lascivious, shallow, vulgar, and materialistic standards and morals: "Socially pathological conditions are the result" (Young 1926:148), wrote one social scientist.

During the early decades of the twentieth century, there was a pervasive view of Hollywood resting near the bottom of a rigidly defined cultural hierarchy. Clearly, at some point the perception of Hollywood took a drastic turn. Understanding the reasons for this turn and its timing is the goal of this book.

THE CENTRAL ARGUMENT

The central argument of this book is that the legitimation of Hollywood film as art occurred mainly during the 1960s and was a process driven by three main factors. First, changes in American society over the course of the twentieth century opened up an opportunity space (DiMaggio 1992) in which an art world for film could develop. These changes occurred outside the field of film and include such social phenomena as the cultural consequences of the world wars and demographic, educational, and technological change within American society. The net effect of these developments was to create a social climate in which the cultural contradictions of film's claims to art were reduced and filmgoing could be practiced as an act of artistic appreciation.

Second, change from within the Hollywood film world brought that world more closely in line with other, established art worlds. Some of the most significant changes were the institutionalization of resources dedicated to film as art, such as the establishment of film festivals, the creation of the field of film studies, and the participation of directors in activities that advanced their standing as artists. Other crucial developments involved the evolution in film production and consumption practices such as a shift away from the studio system of production to a director-centered system, the growth of art house theaters, and the relaxation of film censorship. As a result of these changes, the production, distribution, teaching, and consumption of Hollywood film came to bear many important similarities to those of other legitimate art worlds.

Third, the art world for Hollywood film needed intellectual viability, and this requirement was met through the creation of a discourse of film as art and disseminated through film reviews, which were invented shortly after the invention of the cinema itself. But early film reviews employed a discourse of film in which reviewers evaluated films based on their entertainment value. During the 1960s, however, film reviewers began to employ a discourse of film as art that was characterized by a vocabulary and a set of critical devices that provided a way to talk about film as a sophisticated and powerful form of artistic communication.

This explanation fits squarely within the sociological perspective on art that emphasizes the social and collective nature of artistic production and consumption. In this view, most strongly associated with the pioneering work of Howard Becker (1982), the place of cultural productions in society and their status as art are dependent on the development, to varying degrees of robustness, of an art world. That is not to say that the artistic content of cultural productions does not play a part—content does matter and not all cultural production can succeed as the basis for an art world. But it is also to say that the relative merits of cultural productions do not become the basis for assessing artistic status without the collective contribution of an art world. What this case study of Hollywood film adds to our understanding of art worlds is that their development is connected to the opportunities offered by the wider social context. Furthermore, although it is well understood that art worlds are organizational and institutional achievements, this case study demonstrates that they are also intellectual achievements. Because art is an intellectual field, there must be a set of ideas to explain and justify filmic productions as legitimate art. Film criticism, therefore, is a key to understanding how Hollywood films could be accepted as art.

How Do We Know What Art Is?

Before we can go any further in answering the question of how Hollywood film became art, we first need to discuss the definition of art. No one has yet found a way to settle every dispute over this question. In some cases there is widespread agreement—classical music, Impressionist paintings, Italian opera. In many other cases there is disagreement, as with handcrafted pottery, rap music, and Broadway musicals. In each case, however, there is an absence of clear and precise principles for making a judgment, and no amount of consensus can hide that fact. Art, by its very nature as an essentially aesthetic construct, is difficult to define. This difficulty is reflected in legal rulings in free-speech cases. Art is a form of communication, and so must be protected as a form of speech. But obscenity is harmful, and communities deserve protection from it. Some photographs, literature, sculptures, and films contain material or messages that some people think are obscene. Who is to say which of these cultural products are art and which are not? As a defining principle "I know it when I see it" is clearly inadequate because we all see it differently.

In fact, we often leave decisions about what is art to "cultural experts"—critics, academics, and other intellectuals, granting them a certain amount of authority. However, they do not always agree with one another. Each group of critics can try to convince the other to see the matter as it does, but in the end, from a logical standpoint, there is no foolproof way to decide who is right. To further complicate matters, even in cases when critics do agree, there is no guarantee that the wider public will accept their judgment. Abstract art, for example, is clearly art in the minds of aestheticians and art critics. In the minds of many citizens, though, abstract art is fraudulent and worthless—it is painting, but it is not art. The question of how we decide what is art, then, becomes how cultural experts decide what is art, and why their judgments are accepted or resisted by the wider public.[1]

Before we address this question for the case of Hollywood films, we need first to describe and understand exactly what film got transformed into. How do we understand the category of art? What makes art special and worthy of our admiration and of prestige? What is the definition of art?

This question has been debated by aestheticians for many centuries. The debate has generated a number of definitions, none of which, it turns out, has been free from devastating criticism. Nevertheless, we can gain some insight into the core concerns of art by reviewing the debate. An early definition was put forth by Leo Tolstoy (1995 [1898], p. 40) in one of his philosophical writings, *What Is Art?*: "Art is that human activity which consists in one man's consciously conveying to others, by certain external signs, the feelings he has experienced, and in others being infected by those feelings and also experiencing them." The communicative and emotional elements of art are clearly important, but they do not provide an airtight definition. For instance, Tolstoy's definition seems to exclude those works that would inspire in audience members emotions unintended by the artist. It would also exclude works that were never exhibited to an audience—it appears that the potential for communication is not sufficient for Tolstoy. Such exclusions do not seem to square with intuitive notions of what art is.

More recently, philosopher Stephen Davies (1991:1) has distinguished between definitions that highlight what art does ("functionalist" definitions) and those that highlight the process by which art is created ("procedural" definitions). As he puts it succinctly, "The functionalist believes that, necessarily, an artwork performs a function or functions (usually, that of providing a rewarding aesthetic experience) distinctive to art. By contrast, the proceduralist believes that an artwork necessarily is created in accordance with certain rules and procedures." To illustrate the difference, we can take the common reaction to the Sistine Chapel as the heart of the functionalist definition. The awe, admiration, and even reverence that it inspires in audiences are characteristic of art. Because it provides this function, it qualifies as art. The example par excellence of the proceduralist definition is Marcel Duchamp's *Fountain*. Submitting for exhibition a ready-made urinal as art in 1917, Duchamp upended artistic conventions about what art should be. The key to its status and the status of other pieces like it as art is that they "are created by artists or others who have earned the authority to confer art status; they are discussed by critics; they are presented within the context of the Art world as objects for (aesthetic/artistic) appreciation; they are discussed by art historians; and so forth" (41).[2]

In addition to the philosophical approaches, the essence of art is variously claimed to be related to the biological aspects of its appreciation (see, e.g., Aiken 1998) and to psychological aspects of its appreciation (see, e.g., Arnheim 1986). The upshot of decades of work on nailing down a precise definition of art has been summarized by philosopher Nigel Warburton (2003:126): "We should probably stop wasting our time on the pursuit of some all-encompassing definition—there are better ways of spending a life, and the pursuit is almost certainly a futile one."

Lucky for us, we are not seeking to make a definitive statement on art as a category, nor are we seeking to make an airtight case that Hollywood films are art. Our task is much different. We begin with the fact that a certain body of American film work is widely recognized as legitimate art. Therefore, our understanding of art for the purposes of this book is that very same understanding put forth by the intellectuals and supporters of Hollywood films. Despite the fact that most films are considered entertainment, there is a body of Hollywood output that is consecrated on account of a set of characteristics that sets it apart as genuine art. Different film scholars have valorized Hollywood films for myriad reasons. In my reading of the literature, the perspective of those who have supported the view of Hollywood films as art can be characterized in the following way. What makes these films art is their beauty (in a purely aesthetic, and largely visual, sense); their innovation with or perfection of filmic conventions (dealing with all aspects of creation, such as editing, cinematography, art direction, screenwriting, acting, etc.); their communication of messages (advocating political views or philosophies of life, or raising questions); and their status as the expressive products of specific artists (mostly directors). They are art, therefore, because they succeed on one or more levels, concerning their aesthetic characteristics, their relationship to other films, their communicative dimension, or their place within a recognized oeuvre.

The acknowledgement of some Hollywood films as art is an act that transforms them into a special form of culture deserving honor and prestige. This category has a twofold relationship to high status. On the one hand, high status is a characteristic that art possesses. On the other hand, high status is also something that art bestows on its creators and audiences. Knowledge of and appreciation for good art can generate high status for individuals. That is to say, art lends itself to function as cultural capital (Bourdieu 1984). It is this special and powerful categorization of culture that Hollywood films can now aspire to, even if they often fail to achieve it.

The core question at this point is, *How* did a body of Hollywood films (though not all) gain this recognition as art? Depending on one's intellectual leanings, this question might be largely philosophical or sociological. From a philosophical standpoint, the question encourages a focus on the logical foundation for a categorization of Hollywood films as art. The quality of the films, therefore, is central to the explanation of their status as art. In contrast, a sociological standpoint encourages a focus on the social conditions of the production and consumption of Hollywood films. The social context, rather than the quality of the films, is privileged in the sociological explanation of their status as art.[3]

There is no denying that the changing characteristics of Hollywood films are relevant to understanding how an art world developed for them in the 1960s. Nevertheless, this book presents a sociological perspective, arguing that the coalescence of a novel perspective among a large group of people is a social process that lends itself more readily to sociological analysis than aesthetic analysis. To explain how an art world developed for Hollywood films, we need to consider the long-term evolution in the social conditions of film production and consumption. Rather than an examination of a snapshot in time, we are looking instead for the *story* of film's valorization as art, and that is a story that spans the full record of commercial cinema in the United States.

AMERICAN FILM HISTORY

In order to explain the recognition of art in Hollywood films, this book will draw on evidence from the entire historical period of American movies. Because of its youth relative to most other art forms, there are advantages to taking film as a case study to address the question of how we decide what is art. The information available for film is more complete (though certainly not entirely complete) than for other, older art forms. This brief description of film history will provide a time line of some of the most important events in the film world to give the reader an idea of the time period under review and the long-term nature of the development of artistic status.

Most sources trace the beginning of commercial cinema to 1896, the year when Thomas Edison first projected motion pictures for the paying public's consumption in New York City (for descriptions of the beginning of cinema see Mast 1981, Pearson 1996; Rhode 1976; Sklar 1994).[4] The many devices necessary for motion pictures had slowly developed over the previous decades, with innovations coming from both sides of the

Atlantic. Yet it was Edison who secured the key patents that allowed him to profit from the use of this new technology for public exhibitions. Just as innovations were slow in coming before commercial cinema, the nature of commercial cinema, at both the levels of technology and film content, evolved incrementally over the next few decades.

One of the first major developments in the film world occurred in the realm of exhibition. There was an explosion in the number of places of exhibition as public demand increased in the first several years of the twentieth century. Many small stores and restaurants were converted by their owners into nickelodeons, whose name came from the nickel price of admission. For reasons that will be explained later, nickelodeons were most common in working-class and immigrant neighborhoods, as filmgoing started off as a primarily working-class leisure activity. Demand outstripped supply of the one-reel films that the hundreds of individual producers were making, often with just a handful of technical and creative workers.

By the second decade of the twentieth century, certain groups, such as religious organizations and women's associations, were concerned about the potential for films to corrupt public morals. The popularity of the industry had continued to increase, and the power of visual imagery lent a sense of urgency to the movement to regulate the kind of material the public consumed. The first calls for censorship came from these groups who demanded that all films be screened and approved before gaining license for exhibition. In the first legal challenge to film censorship in 1915, the Supreme Court determined that films did not merit First Amendment protection, classifying them with shows and spectacles and outside of the realm of free speech. In order to gain some measure of control over the inevitable censorship, the film industry, which had begun to coalesce into a smaller number of major studios, offered to self-regulate its content. By the early 1920s the industry created the Motion Pictures Producers and Distributors Association, a semi-autonomous organization charged with ensuring that films would conform to a range of moral strictures.

Meanwhile, film content had evolved significantly. While the earliest films were short, often ten minutes or less, and had the purpose of showing images as a spectacle, films soon became lengthier and began to tell a story. David Wark Griffith is most often credited with having created a "film grammar," a set of technical innovations and dramatic techniques (e.g., the closeup shot and cross-cut editing) with his 1915 film *The Birth of a Nation*. By the 1920s the division of labor in filmmaking had become extensive. The technical expertise and financial capital required complex organizations to create efficiently and effectively the large number of films the market demanded. The studio system, which managed the large amount of required technical and creative expertise while keeping costs down, developed as the dominant mode of film production.

During this same decade the idea that film was a legitimate artistic medium became popular among a large number of European intellectuals. This sentiment was most intensively and widely held in France, where it was disseminated to the wider public. The acceptance at that time of film, specifically European films, as art was facilitated by the conditions of production and consumption in Europe. These conditions bore many similarities to those governing other art forms there. Such was not the case in the United States, where conditions of film production and consumption were strikingly dissimilar to those of high culture. Film started out as the new entertainment for the masses—it was inexpensive and concentrated in urban areas, often in working-class and immigrant neighborhoods. While there was limited recognition among a small number of American intellectuals that European films could be understood as art, this favor was not extended to Hollywood productions. The dominant discourse of American film appreciation was unequivocal—films were fun, but not challenging.

The introduction of sound into theaters in 1928 only added to the popularity of the cinema. Average weekly attendance estimates for that time generally range from 70 to 90 million. Filmgoing had become more common among the middle class, but the audience was still mostly working class. Attendance dropped during the Depression, but by the end of the 1930s was back in the range of 90 million per week. This level was maintained until the end of World War II. During the 1930s small advances in the status of Hollywood films were made as the major studios attempted to "upgrade" their product—through opulent theaters and through prestige, epic productions—in order to appeal to more of the middle class. These efforts helped to reposition Hollywood film as sometimes eligible for middlebrow artistic status.

By the 1950s the American film industry was undergoing enormous changes. Partly because of the growing popularity of television, and partly because of changing lifestyles associated with the baby boom, the audience for film was quickly shrinking and would continue to do so, irreversibly, for the next twenty years. This economic crisis for the film industry was compounded by a significant legal development. In 1948 the Supreme Court had found that the vertical integration of the industry, whereby five major studios produced, distributed, and exhibited most of the country's films, impeded competition. The studios were forced to divest themselves of their theater chains, a change that was to have far-reaching consequences for how films were made and financed over the following decades. In 1952 the Supreme Court decided a case in the film industry's favor when it reversed its 1915 censorship decision and declared that film was indeed a form of communication protected by the First Amendment. Over the next fifteen years, with help from a variety of court cases and from changing mores, the strict censorship governing American film production eroded, resulting in the basic labeling scheme that exists today.

Also in the 1950s, French intellectuals who were already comfortable with understanding film as art applied this aesthetic disposition to Hollywood films. They had developed a theory for explaining and evaluating film, auteur theory, and employed it to analyze Hollywood films. This theory holds that the director is the driving artistic force behind film production. In the early 1960s auteur theory and other elements of artistic analysis were imported into American film discourse.

The importation of auteur theory was one of a large number of radical changes in the American film world in the 1960s. It was a time of economic uncertainty, when attendance was decreasing dramatically and when the traditional production methods were being discarded as the film studios looked for ways to regain profitability. It was also a period during which the films being made changed, as they took on some European sensibilities and also reflected the social upheavals of American society. The 1960s were a crucial period of rapid and extensive growth of an art world for Hollywood films. Film scholarship is virtually unanimous in describing that decade as the time when the idea that Hollywood films could be art gained wide currency. This recognition meant that American films deserved to be approached with an open mind, not dismissed out of hand. Artists could work within the medium of film to create works of art that were due the respect and honor accorded to the fine arts. Writing for the National Association of Theatre Owners, Barbara Stones describes the transition in perceptions of film: "For most of the public, movies were pure entertainment, a chance to get out, relax and share in some on-screen excitement. Beginning in the 1960s a wholesale shift in attitude about American films occurred. Movies were somehow taken more seriously and elevated to the status of 'film literature' " (1993:201). It is the "shift" or "change in attitude," a growing agreement on whether film could be art, that needs to be explained, and it is the "somehow" that needs to be specified as factors that can be shown to have brought about the transformation.

The perception of European films as art had already taken hold, and I argue that they led the way for the intellectualization of Hollywood films. When the growth of television and other factors caused a dramatic decline in filmgoing, a "status vacuum" was created. The strong links to the working and middle classes were weakened, and films were available for cultural redefinition. The time was right for their consecration as art, and it was in the 1960s that an art world for Hollywood films developed in the United States. The perception that Hollywood films could be art gained currency among certain segments of the public at that time. Moreover, the institutionalization of a fine-art view of film created a feedback effect whereby filmmakers—and the studios that underwrote films—were encouraged to make the kinds of films that would win appreciation within the art world for film. The incentive structure had become more favorable for the production of artistic films and was also self-reinforcing.

The size of the film audience stabilized by 1970 at approximately 17 to 20 million average weekly attendances. Although the art world for Hollywood film was still vibrant into the mid-1970s, it was also at that time that film production entered the "blockbuster" era, when the predominant strategy involved spending vast sums of money to make a smaller number of films in a gamble that one incredibly successful film could make enough profit to more than compensate for the unsuccessful films. Despite the uncertainty and change that the film industry has experienced in recent decades, and especially in recent years, the blockbuster strategy still serves film studios, if not film exhibitors, quite well.

Two factors that have helped the film industry are favorable market regulations and technological advancements. During the 1990s, media regulations in the United States were relaxed to allow for greater concentration of ownership. While studio ownership by conglomerates is not new—Gulf+Western (now defunct) bought Paramount Pictures (since sold) in 1966—the industrywide concentration of media production into a few enormous media corporations is a more recent phenomenon. Moreover, these media giants have global reach. As one of the most profitable and important American export industries, media producers have successfully lobbied the federal government to negotiate advantageous international trade agreements. The protectionist strategies of previous decades, designed both to bolster domestic film industries and to defend national cultures, are largely eroded and no longer impede Hollywood profits. Recent figures from the Motion Picture Association of America (MPAA) (Motion Picture Association Worldwide Market Research 2006) indicate that domestic box-office receipts were $9.49 billion in 2006, and international box-office receipts were over $25.82 billion. Globalization appears to be working well for the film studios.

There is considerable uncertainty about the future health of theatrical exhibition on account of the technological innovations that have increased home film viewing. The growth of VCR ownership in the 1980s initially provoked fear and suspicion among the major film studios. Although they had been afraid that watching of videocassettes at home would erode theatrical admissions, they eventually found that the home-video market added to, rather than detracted from, their profits. The market for DVDs has proved to be more profitable yet, and while theatrical admissions appear to be declining—probably for the long term—the revenues from licensing films for the home-entertainment market now provide the majority of profits for the studios (Epstein 2005:19; Weinberg 2005:166) and have made studios more profitable than before (Manly 2005). So, while some *exhibitors* are encountering financial difficulties, likely due to consumers' increasing reliance on other modes of film viewing such as VHS, DVD, and cable television, the *film studios* appear to be benefiting from an increase in the ways that consumers can see films.

This beneficial relationship with technological advances does not hold, of course, for those technologies that allow viewers to break intellectual property laws. From counterfeit DVDs to theatrical camcorder piracy to illegal downloading over the Internet, there are many ways that viewers can see films without the studios receiving any revenue. There studios are naturally gravely concerned, and they are vigorously fighting piracy through copy protection technologies, successful lobbying for strong intellectual property laws, and aggressive prosecution of companies and individuals who test the boundaries of those laws. In addition, they are participating in new online business ventures to provide legal downloads of movies. If these ventures are successful, they will have taken a potentially threatening technology and turned it into a powerful tool to contribute to revenues.

Fighting piracy has risen to the top of the agenda of the Motion Picture Association of America. While the challenges presented by piracy are significant, the MPAA clearly believes that the movie business can remain viable for its member studios if they continue to protect their revenue streams.

THE SOCIAL CONSTRUCTION OF ART

Social constructionism is a perspective that holds that the categories and definitions we use to perceive and to understand the world are molded by cultural forces. Rather than objectively representing enduring truths and realities, the concepts we routinely employ to organize our thoughts and to communicate are shaped through social processes.

This view is not tantamount to a denial of objective reality. To say that art—the concept that this book happens to be about—is socially constructed is not to question whether it truly exists. Art exists; there are things in the world that are art and things in the world that are not art. This distinction, however, between art and non-art is frequently understood as obvious and is taken for granted. The fact that Shakespeare's *Othello*, for example, is real art is a given for us, as is the given that the messages inside store-bought greeting cards are not art.

A social constructionist perspective throws into question the taken-for-granted status of *Othello* as art and greeting cards as non-art. It encourages us to question why we draw the line where we do. Is distinguishing between art and non-art as simple as recognizing *Othello*'s innate qualities as inherently superior? Few would dispute that *Othello* has many qualities that are superior to a greeting card. However, the judging of qualities as better or worse is a normative exercise, not a logical one. Something is better than something else only in reference to a set of standards, and the particular standards we employ to judge culture are arbitrary. And so we judge *Othello* to be art in part because it makes smart and sophisticated comments about human nature in language that shows a formidable mastery of poetic conventions. But *must* these be the standards for identifying art? Could we not just as easily insist on others? The accessibility of the greeting card and the precision of its mechanical production generate negative evaluations, but why could we not just as easily view these qualities as positive instead? There is no logical reason why not, but the fact is, our culture arbitrarily assigns a negative value to these qualities in order to distinguish art from non-art.

The merit of the social constructionist viewpoint is clear when we try to understand why art is different across space and time. The line between art and non-art is drawn in very different places in different societies, and at different times within a single society. These different understandings of art reflect different standards for distinguishing art from non-art. When European explorers first encountered tribal masks in Africa, they did not consider them art. Today there is a vibrant market for African art as a fine art genre (Rawlings 2001). The art did not change, but the standards did.

To take a social constructionist viewpoint at all times would be mentally exhausting. Everyday thinking would be unbearably inefficient because we would be caught up in examining the various possible alternative ways that we could be thinking about the world. For the sake of efficiency, then, the concepts we use every day assume the guise of objective reality. It then becomes very easy to forget that the ways we understand the world are not perfect reflections of an independent truth. When we employ a concept like "art," it is useful for how it distinguishes those relatively few things in the world that are art from the vastly larger number of things that are not. It is the difference we focus on, and we ignore the fuzziness of the boundary. With a social constructionist viewpoint it is relatively easy to put the focus back on the fuzziness. The average store-bought greeting card, for example, is not art, but what if the card quotes a rhyming couplet from Shakespeare? Or what if the front of the card reproduces one of Monet's paintings? What if the card is handmade rather than mechanically produced?

A corollary of a social constructionist view of art is that cultural hierarchy—or the divisions between highbrow, middlebrow, and lowbrow culture—is also socially constructed. Our concept of art is complex enough to allow for these rankings, but these distinctions are equally arbitrary. Their existence begs the question of how various cultural productions are ranked. Why is opera highbrow while comic books are lowbrow? To answer the question of how rankings are created and maintained, it is necessary to look past the content of cultural productions to the conditions under which art is created, distributed, evaluated, and consumed. This stance within the sociology of art is called the "production perspective" (Peterson 1994). Only by examining artistic production and reception as social processes can we understand the socially constructed nature of cultural hierarchy and of artistic status. DiMaggio puts it succinctly: "even though systems of cultural classification present themselves as based on natural and enduring judgments of value, they are products of human action, continually subject to accretion and erosion, selection and change" (1992:43).

The Creation of Artistic Status: Opportunity, Institutions, and Ideology

With the above intellectual orientation in mind, what is the explanation for how an art world for film developed? Previous research on cultural hierarchy and artistic status provides a starting point for explaining film's redefinition as art, or what Peterson (1994:179) would call film's "aesthetic mobility." I propose a framework for explaining the creation of artistic status for film that is based on a synthesis of findings from an array of previous studies. Within this literature I identify three main factors that sociologists of culture rely on to explain the public acceptance of a cultural product as art—(1) an opportunity space, (2) institutionalized resources and activities, and (3) intellectualization through discourse.

The first factor is *the creation of an opportunity space through social change outside the art world in question*. DiMaggio (1992:44) contends that whether a cultural genre succeeds in earning recognition as art "has depended on the shape of the opportunity space (the existence of competitors, commercial substitutes, or publics and patrons of new wealth) and the point in time at which such projects take shape, which determines the preexisting discursive and organizational resources available for imitation." He applies the concept of opportunity space to the case of theater, opera, and the dance. In the case of theater, DiMaggio claims that the advent of film altered the market conditions for dramatic entertainment. Film quickly grew into a popular form of drama, a role the theater had served. With the increased competition at the lowbrow end of the spectrum, theater was encouraged to change its format and to serve as a higher form of drama, a change that was facilitated by the presence of the models established by operas, museums, and symphonies available for emulation. DiMaggio acknowledges that an explanation for aesthetic mobility must consider not only events within an art world, but also events that occur outside an art world, for the timing of these events helps to define what an art world can accomplish. Other authors have cited the importance of a favorable opportunity space, created by events outside of art worlds, in explaining the aesthetic mobility of opera and Shakespearean plays (Levine 1988), literature (Beisel 1992), and "serious" classical music in Vienna (De Nora 1991) and the United States (Mueller 1951).

In the case of Hollywood film, the opportunity space for an art world for film grew enormously during the 1960s. Just as the advent of film changed the opportunity space for dramatic theater, the advent of television did the same for film. Television took on the mantle of the entertainment for the masses that had previously been worn by film. Moreover, television siphoned off disproportionately high numbers of the working-class audience for film. Many audience members also abandoned film when the baby boom began in the 1940s and continued into the 1960s. Some audience members dropped out while they exploited other leisure options made available through rising national levels of prosperity. At the same time, the number of young people in college was growing rapidly, providing a pool of highly educated patrons who would become the "film generation." Through these changes outside the film world, a new context for film appreciation emerged. By the 1960s, filmgoing was no longer just an easy way to pass the evening hours. Because society had evolved in certain ways, filmgoing had become a significant cultural activity.

The second of these factors is *the institutional arrangements underlying the production, exhibition, and appreciation of art, as well as the various activities and practices carried out in those institutional settings.* Perhaps the best illustration of such factors can be found in Becker's (1982) thorough analysis of the importance of organizations and networks in art worlds. He views the creation of art as collective action. For art to succeed, a coordinated effort is necessary on the part of a large number of people performing different functions. While the artist is at the center of the art world, the participation of collaborators of many different kinds is essential for art to maintain its status as art. For example, a novelist's work is edited by an editor, promoted by a publisher, reviewed by book reviewers, and taught by literature professors. In this light, he explains the creation of an art world as an instance of successful collective action. "The history of art deals with innovators and innovations that won organizational victories, succeeding in creating around themselves the apparatus of an art world, mobilizing enough people to cooperate in regular ways that sustained and furthered their idea" (Becker 1982:301).

A number of authors have found that creating institutions and mobilizing resources are integral to art world formation. Levine (1988) argues that the establishment of separate groups of performers and separate theaters and halls for drama, opera, and symphonic music was a necessary step in the elevation of these entertainments to the status of art. DiMaggio (1982) argues that a group of "cultural entrepreneurs" in nineteenth-century Boston acted on behalf of the upper and upper-middle classes to create a high culture of symphonic music, painting, and sculpture separate from popular culture. Through trustee-governed nonprofit enterprises, the Boston Symphony Orchestra and the Museum of Fine Arts, these well-placed "cultural capitalists" and artistic "experts" achieved the organizational separation of high from popular culture. DiMaggio also argues that the model established by classical music and the visual arts was adopted by practitioners and patrons of theater, opera, and aesthetic dance (1992). Each genre embraced the trustee-governed nonprofit organizational form. White and White (1965) argue that the development of a new system of artistic distribution and appreciation, that of dealers and critics in opposition to the existing "academic system," enabled the ascendance of the Impressionist movement in France.

In a similar fashion, the art world for American film was founded on a complex arrangement of institutional supports, film production, and consumption practices. This arrangement organized the American film world into a field where film could be produced and exhibited as an art form in its own right. For example, the economic pressures that led to the creation of hundreds of small, independent art-house theaters helped to nurture avant-garde and controversial film production. The establishment of film festivals in the 1960s such as the New York Film Festival and the Chicago International Film Festival provided prestige and visibility for film as art. Likewise, the creation of academic programs of study at such places as New York University and UCLA provided status and resources for framing film as art. Moreover, the changing economics of film production in the 1960s shifted the mode of filmmaking away from the assembly line of big studio productions toward a director-centered model that resembles the production of other art forms.

While institution building is an activity common to a wide range of fields, the third and final main factor I identify is specific to cultural or symbol-producing fields. This factor is *the grounding of value and legitimacy in critical discourse*.[5] Ferguson (1998) makes the case for the crucial role of the intellectualization of a cultural product in the development of a cultural field.[6] The explanation for the role of intellectualization relies on Bourdieu's (1993) concept of a "field" of cultural production, which focuses on the relations between cultural producers and consumers, who are sometimes one and the same. A cultural field (also applicable to intellectual endeavors outside the boundaries of art) comes into being when cultural production begins to enjoy autonomy from other existing fields in terms of the type of capital available to cultural producers. In any given field, actors engage in competition for capital. To the extent that there is a distinct form of symbolic capital available to consecrate cultural products of a particular genre, the field is autonomous. For example, the literary field has achieved a high degree of autonomy; it offers prestigious prizes and critical success that constitute the symbolic capital that may serve as an alternative to economic capital for authors. Ferguson (1998:600) persuasively argues that it is through texts that the field of cultural production is extended "well beyond immediate producers and consumers" and is transformed into an "intellectual phenomenon." The development of a field-specific aesthetic both provides a rationale for accepting the definition of a cultural product as art and offers analyses for particular products.

The ideological component of the creation of artistic status is cited by some of the same authors who recognize the institutional and organizational factors. Both Levine (1988) and DiMaggio (1982; 1992) argue that academics and aesthetes developed a sacralizing ideology to legitimate various forms of high culture. Peterson (1972) and Lopes (2002) both cite the development of a group of professional jazz critics and academic students of jazz as a driving factor behind the elevation of jazz. White and White (1965) argue that the development of a new system of artistic distribution and appreciation enabled the ascendance of the Impressionist movement in France. A system of dealers and critics arose to challenge the existing academic system. The critics provided a new ideology for evaluating the careers of Impressionist painters that legitimated claims of genius in their work. DeNora (1991) contends that an ideology of "serious" classical music was formulated by the Viennese aristocracy when the bourgeoisie became wealthy enough to threaten the aristocracy's monopoly on classical music concerts.

In each of these studies, there is a compelling argument that intellectualization by cultural specialists helps to legitimate cultural products that entertain as art. However, there is very little systematic data evinced to support these arguments. Such evidence would take the form of a content analysis of the ideas and language that intellectuals and art experts employ to explain and interpret the cultural products under study. This evidence is available for film, and the analysis offered below will show how film critics in the 1960s adopted a discourse that treated film as art. The intellectualization of film involved referring to select directors as "masters" of film, interpreting the messages inherent in even the most popular of films, and contextualizing the evaluation of films through genre or oeuvre comparisons, as well as other linguistic and critical devices.

Elements of the tripartite explanatory framework outlined above—opportunity space, institutionalized resources and activities, and intellectualizing discourse—can be found in previous case studies of transitions from entertainment to art. However, no author has previously articulated a general schema that can be widely applied to cases of the creation of artistic status. I call the above schema *the legitimation framework* and I argue that it can explain the artistic legitimation of not only Hollywood film but of other artistic media as well.

The aim of this book, however, is to explain how Hollywood films became widely viewed as art. The significance of the legitimation framework is to organize the historical forces at play so that we can understand their respective contributions to the art world for Hollywood film.

As a researchable phenomenon, the perceptions of film over the century, like many historical events and developments, are complex in origin and their changes involve reference to a wide array of developments, actions, and events. The legitimation of film as art involves not simply a shift from entertainment to art, but several related social processes. These include upward status mobility of the entire genre of film; the retrospective canonization of old Hollywood; the differentiation of various strains of production (European, serious Hollywood, experimental, blockbuster); and the creation of critical communities around restricted "cult" genres.

This book seeks to tell as complete as possible a story of the most important developments in the social history of film as found in film history scholarship. There is bound to be disagreement over which elements of American film history should be accorded the greatest significance in helping chart a course toward acceptance as art. Nonetheless, I hope readers find the plot of this story, to borrow the terms of the industry itself, original, compelling, and, most of all, convincing.

OUTLINE OF THE CHAPTERS

There are many ways to tell a story, chronologically being the most common because it corresponds to everyone's personal experiences—we live chronologically. However, it is not always the best way to make a convincing argument, especially when the argument is complicated. Because I want to show how various factors were important to the legitimation of film in very different ways, this book tells the story of the art world for American film according to an analytical sequence, specifically a legitimation framework.

The first part of the analysis, presented in chapter 2, considers the historical events that contributed to the changing of the opportunity space for film. Drawing on the large body of film history scholarship, comparisons are drawn between the American context and several European contexts. Among the cases I review, there is covariation between the timing, on the one hand, of the acceptance of film as art, and, on the other hand, of key developments outside the field of film. The evidence suggests that these changes in opportunity space influenced the perception of film as art. The argument also relies on information gained from historical statistics. The focus in this chapter is on developments outside the film world, particularly the development of competitors to and substitutes for filmgoing, the growing pool of educated film viewers, and changing intellectual currents.

The study continues in the third chapter with a review of the changing institutional arrangements and practices through which film was created, exhibited, and evaluated. Drawing again on both film history scholarship and historical statistics, and also compiling statistics from electronic archives, chapter 3 focuses primarily on changes within the film world. The major changes examined are film production practices, exhibition venues, censorship restrictions, film festivals, ties to academia, and directors' self-promotion. This chapter also draws comparisons between the American case and several European cases and capitalizes on the differences between them to better understand the influence of specific changes within the film world.

The fourth chapter examines the role that intellectuals, primarily film critics, played in the redefinition of film as art. This issue encourages a different methodological strategy. Content analyses of film and book reviews and film and book advertisements provide systematic data for assessing the influence of critics on common understanding of film as well as for identifying and measuring the constitutive elements of an intellectualizing discourse. Comparisons between film and literature help us to see how discourse can influence artistic status by justifying aesthetic claims and conventions to the wider public. By providing the vocabulary and analytic techniques, film critics made an artistic approach to Hollywood films possible for the reading public.

The final chapter sets out the argument in an integrated fashion and then explores the implications of this study for several strands of research in the sociology of culture. First, it points to key concerns for the social construction of artistic status and offers an explanation for why film does not enjoy the same degree of legitimacy as highbrow genres such as opera or painting. Second, it discusses film consumption practices as a form of cultural capital, linking film appreciation and class politics. Third, it elaborates on the significance of an intellectualizing discourse in artistic

legitimation. Fourth, it draws together the causal factors, which were arti-
ficially disentangled for the sake of analysis, in Hollywood's legitimation.
Fifth, it discusses the applicability of the lessons learned here for understanding processes of legitimation in other cultural realms, such as science
and law. Last, it evaluates theories of cultural hierarchy and the dynamics
of cultural fields in light of the findings for film. I argue that the redefinition of Hollywood films must be understood as a product of both the
focused activities of particular actors and larger structural change. Part
of the explanation for the changing status of Hollywood films lies with the
concerted (and sincere) efforts to change people's minds about whether
Hollywood films were art. But the explanation must also be found with
a complex course of events that were unrelated to questions of the status
of Hollywood films. In essence, historical accidents are key to understanding the story.

Through film history scholarship, much is known about the historical
facts of American film production and reception. This book adds little to
our knowledge of facts and so it is not a work of history per se. Rather,
it is a work of analysis—the major goal is to uncover the significance of
already known facts and to fashion an explanation for the question of
how films became art. This book, then, explores the relationships between
these facts and cultural hierarchy. Some historical work was required,
however. The investigation of changes in film reviews and advertisements
required archival work with primary sources. This data collection was
necessitated by the need for systematic samples for quantitative analysis.
All other parts of the analysis were accomplished through reference to
the vast body of existing film history scholarship. Despite this robust
and fascinating literature, the sociology of art in general has neglected
the social history of American film and film criticism. This book is an
effort to increase, from a sociological perspective, our understanding of
the classification of film in the United States over the past century and
hence to understand the ideological and organizational foundations of
the valuation of art.

CHAPTER 2

The Changing Opportunity Space: Developments in the Wider Social Context

THE SAME ACTION taken at two different times can have quite different meanings and consequences. This is true for trivial events, such as a greeting, as well as for actions involving large numbers of people and the mobilization of vast resources. Temporal context matters. We cannot understand how the actions of groups and individuals bring about social change without examining how the social environment helped or hindered that change. Moreover, long-term changes in the larger social context suggest an explanation for the timing of those actions. Changing social conditions tell us not only why the actions of groups and individuals are effective, but also why they happened when they did.

Applying this line of reasoning to the case of the change in status of Hollywood films, it is clear that we need to think about how American culture and society influenced the development of an art world for film. In particular, given that we know that the art world for film developed in the 1960s, we need to identify those general features of American society that might have worked against this development before the 1960s. In addition, we need to understand how changing social conditions in the 1960s could have opened an opportunity space for the legitimation of Hollywood films. How did the wider society change during the 1960s in ways that made possible the consecration of American film as art?

In this chapter we focus on the interaction between the film world and the wider social space, including broader intellectual and aesthetic trends, within which the film world operated. In doing so we see how the legitimation of Hollywood film was facilitated by events that were seemingly far removed from the film industry. I identify several key historical events and circumstances that each helped to shape the opportunity space for the legitimation of Hollywood films in the 1960s. Earlier events and conditions had shrunk that space in the United States and enlarged it in various European countries. This difference is reflected in the earlier legitimation of film as an artistic medium in Europe. Later events then opened the opportunity space in the United States in the 1960s.

Among the early historical states of affair and events of most importance are (1) *World War I* and its economic, political, and social ramifications, which were naturally markedly different in the United States and in Europe; and (2) American urban conditions, both demographic and geographic. Later developments of significance include (1) *World War II* and its economic, political, and social ramifications; (2) technological innovations that created *competing leisure options*; (3) the post–World War II *increase in the birthrate* in the United States; (4) rising *levels of education* in the general population; and (5) *changing intellectual currents*—most importantly the Pop Art movement—that favored consecration of popular cultural forms.[1] I argue that each of these developments, independently and in concert, influenced perceptions of film in surprising and unforeseen ways. While subsequent chapters are primarily concerned with the internal workings of the film world, a focus on the opportunity space for Hollywood film turns our attention away from the film world to events in the wider society and especially to events in other cultural realms.[2]

This chapter first discusses the various national circumstances in the United States, England, Germany, Italy, and France in the first several decades of the twentieth century that influenced the *nature of film audiences*. As will be discussed, the status of art is intimately—though not exclusively—tied to the status of its patrons. The early patronage by European intellectuals and upper-middle-class filmgoers facilitated the legitimation of the relatively small film industries in Europe. In the United States, the working-class nature of film attendance and intellectuals' aversion to Hollywood militated against legitimation. Through comparisons with several European film industries, we will see how certain features of American society promoted trends in filmgoing that were strikingly divergent from trends in Europe. These trends were tied to the consequences of World War I in Europe, and to the characteristics of a working-class urban immigrant lifestyle in the United States. The historical evidence shows that social conditions in Europe were more amenable to the development of an art world for film than they were in the United States.

The chapter progresses to a discussion of the circumstances that led to the opening of the opportunity space for film as art in the United States in the 1960s. The nature and size of the American film audience were altered by a confluence of technological, demographic, and cultural factors. The dramatic post–World War II decrease in the popularity of film in the United States created new possibilities for the valuation of film within the cultural hierarchy.

The core idea of the opportunity space is that at certain times historical events become more likely through the emergence of a favorable setting. The set of social forces that composed the opportunity space were influential despite seeming to have been distantly related to the phenomenon itself. Causally speaking, the opportunity space is necessary although not sufficient. A full accounting of the story of that legitimation needs to explain the connection between the elements of that space and Hollywood films' status as art.[3]

THE FIRST WORLD WAR AND URBAN-AMERICAN LIFE: TWO DISPARATE INFLUENCES ON FILM ATTENDANCE IN EUROPE AND THE UNITED STATES

Social conditions in France, Italy, Germany, and, to a lesser extent, England made available a pool of patrons who could effectively support the idea that film was a legitimate medium for artistic expression. To varying degrees, European audiences incorporated intellectuals and proportionately more middle- and upper-middle-class members. The affiliation with these segments of society proved beneficial for film's prestige and legitimacy in Europe. The early European support for film as art is an important historical precedent because it provided an example and a rationale for the claims that were to follow for Hollywood films as art.

The social conditions in the United States, however, created an audience for film that was neither of the best *size* nor of the best *composition* for the development of an art world. In the United States, the predominant affiliation of filmgoing with the working class worked against film's consecration.

The Composition of Film Audiences: The United States, England, Germany, Italy, and France, 1900–1930s

Contemporary audience analysis involves a sophisticated measuring of an array of demographic variables. Such analyses help the profit-oriented culture industries to more effectively produce and market their products. These studies, however, did not exist during the first decades of the twentieth century. Even after their invention, the film industry was relatively slow in adopting them, relying more often than not on conventional wisdom until approximately the 1960s. As a result, data on the composition of early film audiences is based only rarely on quantitative assessments of demographics. Instead, the best evidence to characterize these audiences comes from qualitative historical studies. Based on such studies, a comparison of the American film audience with the audiences of England, Germany, Italy, and France in the period prior to World War II illustrates the significant differences that existed.

From the beginning, commercial films were extremely popular with the working classes in the United States (Stones 1993:22). Critics of the film industry in the United States called film "the cheap show for cheap people" (quoted in Hampton 1970:61). Filmgoing was indeed inexpensive, costing only a nickel initially, then a dime, and averaging less than a quarter by the end of the 1930s (Brown 1995:Ch.2). Ross (1998:15) explains the economics that underlay the association between filmgoing and the working classes: "With millions of people effectively excluded from expensive entertainments, cultural entrepreneurs created an alternative world of cheaper amusements aimed largely at blue-collar audiences and the rapidly expanding ranks of low-level white-collar workers." The result is that many working-class people went to enjoy one of the few forms of entertainment that they could afford. Ross (1998:19) reports that a survey of Manhattan audiences in 1910 "found that 72 percent of audiences came from the blue-collar sector, 25 percent from the clerical workforce, and 3 percent from what surveyors called the 'leisure class.' "[4]

And what effect did this strong class association have for stereotypes about films and filmgoing? Snobbery about films was prevalent. Mast (1981:4) reports that the wealthy or well-educated viewed filmgoing as an opportunity to go "slumming" but generally "shunned" films, while H. L. Mencken called films "the appropriate attainment of the American 'booboisie.' " Generally speaking, educated or wealthy people felt disdain for films because they saw in them a lack of sophistication or aesthetic value. Similes linking movies with tastelessness, and movie patrons with morons, continually popped up in fiction and articles of the 1920s and 1930s. Filmgoing was frowned upon, and so the status-conscious stayed away.

Tackiness, however, was not the only image problem facing movies. They were also characterized as corrupting and immoral, an "urban vice" (de Grazia and Newman 1982:8), by religious authorities and some intellectuals and social commentators. This charge was based on the content of films, which, although quite tame by today's standards, was relatively violent and risqué in early twentieth-century America. These concerns were greatly heightened by fear that moving images had a powerful influence on people—especially working-class people, children, and ethnic minorities (Butsch 2001)—provoking antisocial or criminal behavior. Sklar (1994:18) claims that for "respectable" society films "belonged in the same class as brothels, gambling dens and the hangouts of criminal gangs."

The film industry was further denigrated by the uncomfortable, unseemly, and sometimes hazardous (from a public health perspective) conditions of the nickelodeons (Uricchio and Pearson 1993:30). To meet the fast-growing demand for movies, many store and restaurant owners converted their establishments into small movie houses. These nickelodeons represented an opportunity for large profits with a minimal capital investment. As Hampton describes it, "[m]any of the store-show owners were immigrants who had been operating cheap lunch rooms and restaurants, candy and cigar stores, and similar small retail shops when the film frenzy began to inundate America" (1970:58).

Nickelodeons quickly grew in number. Gomery (1992:21) attributes the speed of their growth first to a healthy national economy at the time of their introduction, and second to a rapidly expanding population base. The population growth was largely fueled by immigration, and these new immigrants were largely urban, poor, and able to enjoy early film, which was silent and did not demand fluency in English.

As Thompson and Bordwell (1994:36) explain, the movies offered a constellation of objectionables—the content, the audience members, and the venues. Nickelodeons were "sinister" in their potential to socialize youth to lives of depravity and crime.

Not incidental to the discussion is the fact that a large number of nickelodeon owners and patrons were immigrants. Unlike in European countries of the time, the dynamic of a WASP establishment that looked down with condescension on a poor, urban immigrant class was woven into perceptions of the place of film in American society. And that place was with the immigrants themselves, near the bottom of the social hierarchy. Moreover, some film historians have documented that the ethnicity of films' producers, in addition to films' consumers, played a part in generating antipathy toward the industry. Many early filmmakers and film executives were Jewish, including executives within the major studios. Among the various dimensions of anti-Semitism existed the idea that "the entertainment Jew polluted high culture" (Carr 2001:34), and that Hollywood was in essence a Jewish oligopoly (Vaughn 1990:40). Among social critics who both decried Hollywood and held anti-Semitic views, the predominant view of the consequence of Jewish influence on Hollywood was that the film industry generated profits through appealing to society's basest instincts and impulses—such was the modus operandi of Jews (Gabler 1989:278). There is ample historical evidence that part of the prestige problem in the early decades of Hollywood was a result of the transfer of antagonistic attitudes toward the filmmakers to the films themselves and the entire film industry.

Hampton argues that proliferation of nickelodeons in the United States started the film industry off on a different trajectory from what was to occur in Europe. Rather than creating inexpensive makeshift theaters from stores and restaurants, European films "became a part of variety theater and music-hall programs," with prices similar to those other forms of entertainment (1970:62). Consequently, there were far fewer outlets for exhibition, which in general was more expensive for populations with less disposable income. Hence, cinema was not a mass entertainment phenomenon to the same degree that it was in the United States. The disparity was exacerbated during World War I, when production in European countries fell sharply.

The loss of the American market, combined with the absence of cheap theaters, brought the industry in Europe face to face with economic conditions that never obtained here. Some of the producers withdrew from the business. Others proceeded on entirely different lines, turning their energies to the making of photoplays for the classes rather than the masses, and thereby initiated a development which has been wholly different from the course of the American movie. (1970:63)

Of the European countries, film patronage most resembled that of the United States in England, where the rate of attendance was higher than elsewhere in Europe and was mostly a working-class activity.[5] In addition, "films continued to be despised by intellectuals" into the 1920s (Armes 1979:58). However, Napper maintains that intellectuals became interested in films in the late 1920s and that serious film criticism got its start in England in 1927 with the inception of the journal *Close Up* (1997:37). A drive for respectability and middle-class and upper-middle-class patronage began in the 1930s through the incorporation of the aesthetic conventions and talents in the London theater, which enjoyed a great amount of cultural prestige (Armes 1979:59).

In contrast, by the 1920s filmgoing in Germany was common among all classes. Abrams writes that the working class "formed the vast majority of cinema audiences at least until the 1920s, when movie-going became more respectable" (1996:648). At that time, "[c]lusters of downtown premiere cinemas appeared in major German cities . . . where films premiered before Germany's social and political elite" (Saunders 1994:21). The intelligentsia of the time was attentive to the role of cinema in society and engaged the cinema "at a high level of intellectual and philosophical sophistication" (Elsaesser 1996:144). What is more, German intellectuals had shown interest in films, writing about them and participating in the making of literary adaptations, even before the 1920s (Saunders 1994:23). Sklar writes that while in Germany theaters planned as important works of architecture had helped bring in the middle and leisure classes since 1911, opulent theaters were not constructed regularly in the United States until much later (1994:45). The German film scholar Siegfried Kracauer (1987:91–92) wrote in the 1920s about Berlin's film "palaces" that "to call them *movie theaters* (*Kinos*) would be disrespectful. . . . The architecture of the film palaces has evolved into a form that avoids stylistic excesses. Taste has presided over the dimensions and has spawned costly interior furnishing inspired by a refined artisanal fantasy. The *Gloria-Palast* presents itself as a baroque theater. The community of worshippers, numbering in the thousands, can be content, for its gathering places are a worthy abode."[6]

Filmgoing in Italy also crossed class barriers, and it had been taken seriously as an art form and patronized by intellectuals. "There had been little intellectual snobbery about silent cinema which . . . attracted the interest of leading writers (D'Annunzio) and was by the 1920s the object of attention in a wide range of specialized periodicals" (Buss 1989:10).

In France, too, in the very first years of the cinema, a large portion of the audience was working class. It was not long, though, before exhibitors and producers began to target middle- and upper-middle-class audience members through advertising and publicity that featured these classes as audiences and that emphasized the "morally uplifting nature of the film programme" (Ezra 2004:79). These efforts were successful at bringing in the targeted audiences who were subsequently socialized to behave in movie theaters as they did when watching live theater or formal music concerts (Ezra 2004:79).

Following World War I, French intellectuals took a tremendous amount of interest in the medium (Knight 1957:93). Beginning in the 1920s, the French art world for film flourished as intellectuals wrote and spoke about the art of film and developed organizations to welcome and nurture an educated audience. France became the model for an art world for film (Crisp 1993:214). Moreover, although French film producers would have appreciated a mass market for their films, they were more effective at developing an audience for film as art.

> This process began much earlier and was much more systematic in France than elsewhere. Basically the audience concerned was the middle-class intellectual and cultural elite; they saw themselves as working for the defense of French cinema and of cinema as a cultural form; and their means of operation were the cine-club, congresses and study groups, the concept of the cinematheque, a separate theater circuit committed to art films, and critical journals of a more reflective kind. (Crisp 1993:226–27)

It was Ricciotto Canudo who founded the Club des Amis du Septieme Art, the first cine-club, in 1921 (Temple and Witt 2004:14). It was an important catalyst for the cinephile movement, as cine-clubs sought to "educate" the tastes of mass audiences and from the early 1920s through the 1930s grew in size and number throughout France.

In sum, in the major European film-producing nations, filmgoing was popular among the middle and upper classes and accepted by intellectuals by the 1920s or 1930s. In contrast, filmgoing was primarily a working-class activity in the United States until at least the 1950s. While the differences in patronage between countries do not tell the whole story, there is a close parallel between the kinds of audiences associated with cinema attendance and attitudes toward the place of film in the cultural hierarchy. As will be discussed further in chapter 3, the recognition of film as art occurred far earlier in Europe. The appreciation of film as an art form was most prevalent in France, where film audiences also included a larger proportion of intellectuals invested in promoting film as an art form. France was also the source of the mode of film analysis that was eventually to be adopted in the United States. Intellectuals were virtually absent from American film audiences.

What is more, American audiences were also much more avid filmgoers. Although reliable statistics for attendance in Germany during the interwar period are lacking, the best estimates are that, among those over eighteen years of age, Germans went to the cinema on average approximately between 6.6 to 13 times annually (Saunders 1994:24).[7] An even lower level of cinema attendance existed in France, where, Crisp reports, per capita attendance was 3.6 per year in 1919, and had risen to 6 per year by 1937. These figures represented perhaps a European nadir: "the filmgoing public was still grotesquely small by international standards and incomparably small for a major film-producing country." While per capita annual attendance was much higher in England, 30, the rate in the United States was one-third higher yet, 40 attendances per person per year. One figure reported in 1929 claimed that in France "7% of the population goes to the cinema, whereas in the United States, 75% of the population goes" (Crisp 1993:12–13, 213).

A further possible complication to the relationship between audience composition and film's status arises from the relative ethnic homogeneity of European audiences. In the absence of much immigration, European working classes were ethnically similar to their middle- and upper-class counterparts. A resulting greater cultural similarity might have allowed respective European national cinemas to produce relatively more sophisticated films, engaging traditional cultural themes, metaphors, ideas, and issues of national history. In contrast, because of the cultural diversity of the American immigrant working class, films needed to be relatively less sophisticated in their appeal to a wide audience. Such a difference would have been a further disadvantage for an art world for film in the United States.

The historical evidence paints a clear picture of the differences between U.S. and European film audiences, both in their size and in their composition. In a variety of ways, audience characteristics were related to the potential for art world development in the countries studied above, and those characteristics favored film as art in Europe and film as entertainment in the United States.

Modernism, Nationalism, and Early European
Intellectual Involvement

In 1931 Jean-Paul Sartre wrote, "I submit that the cinema is a new art form which has its own rules and unique practices, that it cannot be reduced to a form of theater, and that it ought to be as useful to cultural understanding as Greek and philosophy are" (quoted in Abel 1988:xi). As an eminent French intellectual, Sartre was participating in the intellectualization of film. He was not the first of his countrymen to pro-claim film an art form on equal footing with the other high arts. But as we have seen, in making the above statement he had good company in France to share his view, as he had in Germany (Kaes 1987:9), Italy, and other European countries as well. Nevertheless, he would have been desperately out of synch with the American intellectual disposition when it came to film. The question is raised, Why were European intellectuals willing to perceive and discuss film as art so much earlier than their American counterparts?

There are two related primary reasons for this early involvement. Neither reason is based on a perception that European films were more artistic than American films. The first reason is based, rather, on the prevailing intellectual climate in Europe following the devastation of the First World War. After World War I, within European art worlds there was a widely held belief that existing conventions and aesthetic values needed to be discarded.[8] It was with this "tone of anxiety and pessimism" (Davies, 1996:952) that Modernist values in art and culture arrived in Europe to bring a radical aesthetic shift. Modernism's arrival was at least partially facilitated by the horrors of war; artists and other intellectuals working in an array of fields (visual arts, music, literature, theater, etc.) adopted themes and conventions that were dramatically different from prewar practices.

European cultural life in the postwar period, then, was characterized by a withdrawal from aesthetic traditions and a search for alternative models. In this climate, where a generation was "in search of new cultural models" (Saunders 1994:41) and "cultural elites tried to move beyond the postwar atmosphere of disillusionment, cynicism, and resentment" (Hake 2002:26), film could be readily embraced as a symbol of a new cultural order. Kaes (1987:21) maintains that in Germany "[t]he collapse of the Wilhelmine Reich in World War I brought an end to the bourgeois value system based on idealism and humanism. American mass culture could thus charge onto the disintegrating cultural field unopposed—especially since America also played a dominant role in politics and commerce." The intellectual environment allowed artists and intellectuals with an interest in film to indulge that interest relatively easily as there was a generalized acceptance of new modes of artistic production while the old were jettisoned. At the same time, because the film industries of Europe had fallen apart during the war, it was American film that occupied the vast majority of European screens.[9]

This fact leads to the second important reason why intellectuals in Europe became involved in film earlier than their American counterparts—the close link between national cinemas and national identities (see, e.g., de Grazia 1998; Ezra and Harris 2000; Lewis 2003; Reich 2002). Hay (1987:11) quotes the Italian critic Corrado Pavolini, who wrote in 1930, "Cinema is not a transposition onto the screen of a bourgeois theater that is equally shared among every civilized country; instead it is the only modern expression of a national collectivity, and therefore profoundly different from one people to another." Uricchio (1996:67) argues that this link was a direct result of World War I.

National cultures are of special significance to cultural commentators, and this was especially so during the interwar period of increasing nationalism in many European countries. The rapid growth of the cinema at that time focused attention on the potential influence of vast quantities of imported American cultural product. Films, in particular, were believed to be enormously powerful in their ability to shape public attitudes, values, and beliefs. The fear was that, along with American films, European audiences were subtly being Americanized. Kaes (1987:21) argues that the cinema "was the most important factor in the European process of Americanization in the period of relative stabilization between 1924 and 1929." This belief was widely enough held to merit legal sanctions, not only to protect native film industries, but also to protect the native *mentalité*. The Bavarian state government held at the time that "any foreign film was a threat to German culture" (Monaco 1976:44). Hay (1987:66) reports that the "alien" values that films disseminated were seen at the time to have "corrupted the traditional foundation of Italian culture." These reports reflect the emerging contemporary view of film as "a national resource" (Saunders 1994:9).

The combination of a belief in the cinema's transformative effects, a belief in the cinema's ability to "convey the crucial concept of the nation" (Buss 1989:26), and the fact of the rapid Americanization of European film exhibition created a special circumstance that called for the attention of cultural commentators. Intellectual involvement was encouraged by the perceived need for Italy to "preserve and at times assert its own cultural identity" (Hay 1987:67) through film; in Germany this translated into "a concerted campaign by the trustees of German *Kultur* to adapt the motion picture to their social and political purposes" (Saunders 1994:23); and during the 1920s "an unspoken opposition to the American cinema now fueled something close to a collective effort to establish distinctly French theories of cinema" (Abel 1984:xvii).

It appears, then, that the First World War created an environment for the reception of film in Europe that was dramatically different from that in the United States, and that this different environment can help explain why film was intellectualized earlier in Europe. While the United States did participate in WWI, it did not experience firsthand the death and devastation on a national scale that was typical in much of Europe. The American film industry became dominant after the war, such that international trade in film was overwhelmingly one-way. There was no crisis of American national identity and national culture linked to film. There was so little foreign content on American screens that there was no connection in the minds of intellectuals or the public between cinema and nationalism. Film production was at the time the backbone of American cultural imperialism and was both a source and expression of American solipsism.

While I argue that the Modernist movement and the link between nationalism and film production are the keys to understanding early European intellectualization of film, it would be disingenuous to completely deny the importance of differences in film content. Although there are more similarities than differences in the content of American and French, Italian, and German films of the interwar period, it is true nonetheless that production conditions differed sufficiently to permit an early differentiation of film product. Kaes (1987:17) notes that German filmmakers "made use of high-brow literature as subject matter in order to gain cultural legitimation," resulting in the adoption of a high-brow/low-brow dichotomy (1987:18). Saunders supports this characterization, noting that "the line between high and low cinema culture remained fluid" (1994:34).[10]

No film historian points to an analogous differentiation of film in the United States in the interwar period, although some rather unsuccessful attempts to differentiate film were made. The early existence of an aesthetic vanguard in German and other European cinemas was another factor that facilitated intellectual involvement. However, it should be emphasized here that such an aesthetic development in film content was in no way necessary for intellectualization to take place. While some kinds of content are more readily intellectualized, it is clear that there is only a loose relationship between cultural substance and the creation of a validating discourse. The content of early European films cannot explain how they became regarded as art while American films did not. As we will see, the retrospective intellectualization of early American films renders suspect any assertion that content is the answer.

POST–WORLD WAR II CHANGES IN THE SIZE
   AND COMPOSITION OF AMERICAN FILM AUDIENCES

While the differences between American and European film audiences
were large prior to World War II, in the following decades American audiences came to more closely parallel their European counterparts. In the
following sections we will review the various social forces that changed
the place of filmgoing in American society, and the concomitant changes
in the composition and size of American audiences. A further significant
source of change was evolution in the larger intellectual environment of
the 1960s. This development was central in bringing in the intellectual
component of the audience that had only previously been a part of European filmgoing.

Rising Educational Levels and the New Film Generation

In a mid-1990s article assessing the state of the American film industry,
Susan Sontag (1996) recalls of the late 1960s, "It was at this specific moment in the 100-year history of cinema that going to movies, thinking
about movies, talking about movies became a passion among university
students and other young people. You fell in love not just with actors but
with cinema itself." The reference to university students is important—the
role of higher education is central to understanding how film audiences
changed in the 1960s.

   Higher education has greatly expanded over the course of this century.
Particularly large gains were made after World War II when returning
veterans went on to college, and further gains were made as baby boomers
entered college in the 1960s. Figure 2.1 shows the total enrollment in
institutions of postsecondary education in the United States, and figure
2.2 shows the percentage of eighteen- to twenty-four-year-old people enrolled in postsecondary education. Both graphs show upward trends beginning immediately after World War II and continuing through to the
end of the time period under study.

   By the end of the 1940s, television was quickly growing in popularity
among middle- and low-income households. Boddy quotes from a 1949
Business Week article that claimed that "TV is becoming the poor man's
theater," and cites a study of 1950 TV-set owners that showed that "ownership declined with incomes and educational levels beyond moderate levels" (Boddy 1998:27). Simultaneously, film declined in popularity, and
film's shrunken audience was less heavily working class. Sklar notes that
studios first became aware in the late 1940s that educational attainment
was positively correlated with cinema attendance (1994:270), and that

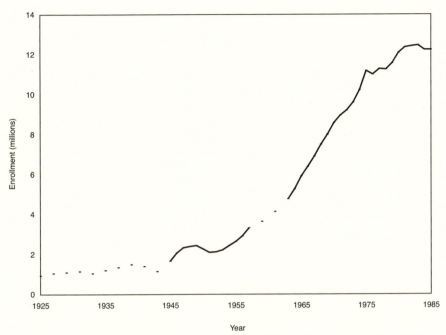

Figure 2.1. Total Enrollment in Institutions of Higher Education, 1925–1985 (dotted lines indicate missing data)

1960s film audiences, students who were "primed for artistic rebellion," became known as the "film generation" (1994:325).[11] Writing for the *New York Times Magazine* in 1969, film critic Richard Schickel (1969:32) commented on recent survey results that showed that movie audiences were disproportionately young and that those who attended most frequently were either college students or college graduates.[12] Schickel hypothesized that the most frequent attenders among high school students were those who planned to go on to college.[13]

The film history literature is rife with assertions that the audience for film in the 1960s was qualitatively different from previous decades. Solomon maintains that filmgoing became less of a family activity in the 1960s and that studios then had to satisfy "a narrower, more sophisticated, and more particular audience" (1988:148). Cook (1998:12) concurs, writing that the American film audience in the late 1960s and later "was younger, better-educated, and more affluent than Hollywood's traditional audience."[14]

The film history scholarship is clear about the matter of the changing nature of film audiences. Having established this historical trend, the question becomes, How is this qualitative difference significant for the

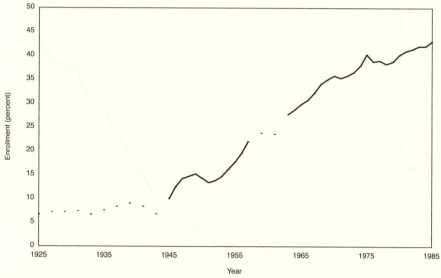

Figure 2.2. Percentage of 18- to 24-Year-Olds Enrolled in Insitutions of Higher Education, 1925–1985 (dotted lines indicate missing data)

changing status of Hollywood films as art? There are at least three mechanisms through which the increase in postsecondary education influenced the status of film as art. First, as DiMaggio (1982; 1992) and Levine (1988) have noted, associations with the status of audience members have in many cases contributed to the rise and fall in prestige of various art forms. Both authors argue that the development of the existing cultural hierarchy in the United States occurred in the nineteenth and early twentieth centuries and that those art forms that are at or near the top of the hierarchy benefited from strong associations with the upper and upper-middle classes.[15] Similarly, when the composition of film audiences began to include fewer members from lower socioeconomic strata and relatively more from higher socioeconomic strata, film itself may have experienced "symbolic enhancement" (Lieberson 2000:126–30) from the association with a higher status audience. Consequently, claims of film's artistic status could enjoy more credibility with the increase in the prestige of film.

The second mechanism posits an increase in the audience's capacity to treat film in a sophisticated manner, as art rather than as entertainment. This explanation is informed by the theory of cultural capital that claims that arts appreciation is trained both through educational institutions and through familial socialization (Bourdieu 1984; DiMaggio and Useem 1978). These authors claim that a taste for high arts is facilitated by the educational system that teaches individuals how to approach and to understand high art. This is particularly true of postsecondary education. Through extensive intellectual and experiential training, individuals learn how to decode and make sense of the sophisticated aesthetics of high art. It is plausible, however, that once this training has occurred, individuals will bring it to bear not only on high art, but on all forms of culture that they consume. The acts of analysis and interpretation will not simply manifest themselves as activities tied to high cultural experiences, but will be expressed as a general disposition toward all culture. Bourdieu makes this argument explicitly when he writes that

> the legitimate disposition . . . comes to be extended to other, less legiti-
> mate works, such as avant-garde literature, or to areas enjoying less
> academic recognition, such as the cinema. The generalizing tendency is
> inscribed in the very principle of the disposition to recognize legitimate
> works, a propensity and capacity to recognize their legitimacy and per-
> ceive them as worthy of admiration in themselves. (1984:26)

The proper audience, then, first had to be constituted before film could succeed as art. Rachlin (1993) argues that the formation of an audience with a preference for (disposition toward) particular genres of literature and other arts was a prerequisite for the success of the *nouvelle vague* cinema in France. Similarly, it might have been the case in the United States that the success of an artistic approach to film in general first required the formation of a receptive audience that was appropriately predisposed.

It is not, however, necessary to accept the argument that higher educa-tion fundamentally shapes one's aesthetic disposition. The third mecha-nism that may account for the impact of changing educational levels in film audiences is the desire of an expanding middle class to be informed about current critical thinking. Halle's (1993) work, for instance, casts doubt on the theory that the highly educated actually experience art in a fundamentally different way from the less educated and suggests instead that the highly educated have a good sense of what tastes are suitable for people of their social positions. Instead of experiencing culture in a differ-ent way, perhaps individuals had, through the educational process, come to expect that there should be some critical comment, beyond the descrip-tive into the realm of analysis, of which it was important to be aware. A proponent of this view is Gans (1999), originally writing in 1974, who argues that an "upper-middle taste culture" has become prevalent in the United States. Taste cultures are

> shared or common aesthetic values and standards of taste. *Aesthetic* is
> used broadly, referring not only to standards of beauty and tastes but
> also to a variety of other emotional and intellectual values that people
> express or satisfy when they choose content from a taste culture. . . .

> Users who make similar choices among and within taste cultures [are] *taste publics* [emphasis in original]. (1999:6–7)

Gans identifies five publics and cultures: high culture, upper-middle culture, lower-middle culture, low culture, and quasi-folk low culture (1999:ch.2). It is the upper-middle taste public, Gans suggests, that has grown fastest since World War II due to the expansion of higher education. This taste public "relies extensively on critics and reviewers" to categorize culture and to validate its tastes, "goes to see foreign films and the 'independent' productions that now come out of Hollywood," and can be identified as the source of "the great popularity of foreign films" (1999:109). While some of Gans's empirical observations may seem out of date (hardly surprising as they were originally made thirty years ago), his analysis can still be helpful in establishing the connection between the growth of college-educated audiences who were attuned to critical approbation of foreign and independent films on the one hand, and the increasing acceptance of film as art on the other.

This line of argument raises questions about the source of the artistic approach to film. Rather than originating with audiences themselves, an intellectualizing discourse on film was developed by critics, filmmakers themselves, and other intellectuals who were members of the film world. The history of American film criticism and the development of a legitimating ideology of film as art are discussed in depth in chapter 4. Given that film critics were writing reviews that increasingly discussed films as art, the growth of an audience increasingly attuned to criticism and intellectual writing on film meant that large numbers of people were adopting the view that there was art in film.

The second and third mechanisms, those proposed by Bourdieu and by Gans, are alternate conceptions of what was happening among audiences. That does not mean, though, that they are mutually exclusive. It is possible that both mechanisms are operating simultaneously. The aesthetic dispositions of the audience may have genuinely changed, as Bourdieu's analyses would suggest, at the same time that they developed a heightened concern for critical opinions, as Gans would argue. Such a view seems to be supported by Mast, who, originally writing in 1971, notes how film audiences have changed over time.

> Only recent American audiences, the third generation of movie-goers, expect the film to be art and not formulaic entertainment. . . . The present movie audience takes its movies as seriously as it does the products of the novelist and poet. The new influence of the intellectual movie critics, who now exert more power and attract more attention than the critics of any other art, is merely a symptom of these new expectations. (1981:4–5)

Although we do not have the evidence necessary to arbitrate between these three alternative mechanisms that link the changing nature of film audiences with the legitimation of Hollywood films, we can nevertheless assert with reasonable confidence that this change in who was seeing films was historically significant. Among the myriad social forces at play, the makeup of the film audience must be acknowledged.

Leisure Substitutes, Technological Innovations, and Demography:
  The Shrinking of American Film Audiences

While the nature of the film audience evolved, so did its size—it shrank dramatically. This section analyzes the relationship between the introduction of competing and substitute leisure-time options and the drastic reduction in the scale of the post–World War II American film industry. This monumental change meant that film lost its standing as the most profitable and common form of entertainment in the United States and could be evaluated within a very different context of cultural options.

Although authors of the history of the American cinema generally acknowledge that many statistics concerning the film industry before the 1950s are contradictory or unreliable, there is widespread agreement about the most significant trends in cinema attendance. Soon after its introduction as a recreational activity, movie watching became enormously popular. Ross (1998:7) reports, "By 1910, nearly one-third of the population flocked to movie theaters each week; a decade later, nearly half the population did so."[16] According to figures from Brown (1995) and from the 1996 edition of *International Motion Picture Almanac*, there were on average 50 million cinema attendances per week in the United States in 1926, the earliest figure reported by these sources (see figure 2.3). Weekly attendances then rose sharply to 90 million before falling back to 60 million in the early 1930s, the time of the Depression. By 1945 weekly attendances again reached 90 million. Although there may be some question as to the accuracy of these numbers, especially concerning yearly differences, they are generally in agreement with numerous accounts (e.g., Mast 1981; Rhode 1976; Schatz 1996; Sklar 1994) of the enormous popularity of films during that time period.

The decrease in average weekly attendances following World War II was precipitous—in 1946 average weekly attendances fell to 78.2 million, in 1947 to 70.5 million, in 1948 to 65.8 million, in 1949 to 60.9 million, and in 1950 to 58 million. It was the beginning of a long period of decline. By 1960 average weekly attendances were 25.1 million, and by 1970 17.7 million. Attendances rose moderately thereafter, reaching 20.3 million in 1985.

Figure 2.3. Weekly U.S. Theater Attendance, 1926–1985

A natural place to begin looking for an explanation for the great de-crease in filmgoing is with the major competitor for dramatic entertain-ment—television. As many film historians have noted, the advent of televi-sion had a large negative impact on filmgoing (see, e.g., Balio 1987; Brown 1995; Hirschhorn 1983; Mast 1981; Sklar 1994; Solomon 1988; Stones 1993).[17] In fact, throughout the literature on film history, the de-cline in cinema attendance is attributed to television's rise more than to any other factor. Similarly, historians of American television lend support to the notion that television negatively affected film attendance (Boddy 1998; Kisseloff 1995; Winship 1988).

After beginning around the turn of the century, television technology took several decades to develop. Commercial television services were first offered in England by the BBC in 1936, and in the United States by NBC in 1939 (Winship 1988:ch.1). At that time, television viewing was an ex-tremely limited phenomenon. Not only was the programming scarce, but there were few manufacturers of television sets, which were inconve-niently large in size and had discouragingly high prices (Kisseloff 1995:120). Before advances could be made to change this situation, prog-ress was halted when researchers were required to work on radar and other military developments (Winship 1988:17).

Following the war, however, researchers for companies such as NBC, CBS, RCA, and DuMont made real progress in bringing more manage-ably sized and somewhat less expensive sets to consumers. In 1948 sixty-six companies were producing television sets (Boddy 1998:27). The increase in the number of companies working on television technology meant an increase in the number of sets produced and a concomitant decrease in prices. As NBC, CBS, and DuMont (and later ABC as well) began to offer more in the way of regular programming, demand increased further. Winship relays a journalistic account from the late 1940s that reports that "[s]hows like Milton Berle's Texaco Star Theater were emptying city streets on Tuesday nights. A movie house manager in Ohio placed a sign on his theater door: CLOSED TUESDAY—I WANT TO SEE BERLE TOO!" (1988:17).

There is some dispute within the literature concerning just how expensive television sets were and who could afford them. DiMaggio and Cohen (2003:57, n.3) cite Survey of Consumer Finance data that estimate the median price at $428 in 1948 and 1949, and $325 in 1950. They note that these prices would have made a television a very expensive purchase at that time. Another study by Gomery (2001:123) of television's early audiences finds slightly different figures—$400 on average in 1947, but a sharp decline to below $200 in 1948, with further declines thereafter. Gomery argues that although the very earliest television owners were members of the upper-middle class, that situation rapidly changed as middle-class families splurged for televisions that had also become more affordable. Because television was a one-time expense, the savings on tickets for movies, sports, theater, and other live events were often how families economically rationalized the purchase.[18] Despite the discrepancies found in the historical statistics, it is nonetheless clear that by the early 1950s televisions were to be found in all but the most privileged of homes, including most working-class homes.

The Statistical History of the United States from Colonial Times to the Present, published by the Department of Commerce and the Bureau of the Census, first reports figures for television use for 1946, in which year approximately 8,000 television were in use. There were 3.9 million televisions in use in 1950, and just one year later, there were 10 million. In 1960 46 million televisions were in use and 61.5 million in 1970, when 89.9 percent and 95.3 percent respectively of American households contained a television (*Statistical Abstract of the United States*).

The coincidence of television's rise in popularity and the decrease in the rate of filmgoing suggests strongly that television helped to erode the commercial success of the film industry (see figure 2.4). Just as film stole mass audiences away from theater, television lured mass audiences away from film. Stones writes that "[b]eginning in the 1950s Hollywood retrieved and reworked existing technology to give moviegoers an experience they couldn't replicate with television" (1993:165). These innova-

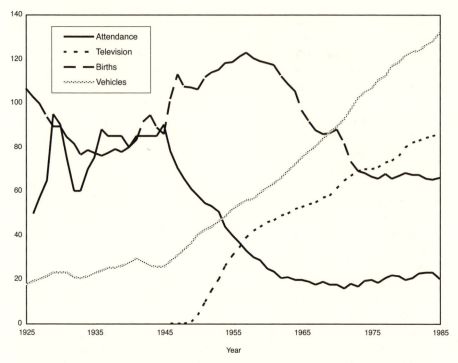

Figure 2.4. Weekly U.S. Theater Attendance (in millions), Television Sets in Use (in millions), Births per 1,000 Women 15 to 44, and Passenger Vehicle Ownership (in millions), 1925–1985

tions included color, wide-screen projection, and 3-D projection. Despite these efforts, "movie attendance continued to decline" (Stones 1993:179).

Although a number of authors have linked decreases in filmgoing with television's rise, there is a slight discrepancy in the timing of the two trends—filmgoing decreases significantly in 1946, before television ownership is widespread enough to account for the decrease. This fact is noted by Sklar (1994:274), who points to the commitment of "time and money to home and family building" that the baby boom necessitated.

In addition to television data, figure 2.4 allows us to compare cinema attendance with the birth rate per 1,000 women aged fifteen to forty-four. The historical statistics support Sklar's assertion that an increase in births contributed to a decrease in filmgoing. The increase occurred in 1945, upon return from World War II of a large number of military personnel. The link between the formation of new families and a change in cinema attendance habits seems clear—with very young children to take care of, many young couples were less disposed to go out of the home for their entertainment. This is because the difficulty of caring for very young children, or paying for a babysitter, would have made a trip to the cinema less appealing. Furthermore, because of strong norms against making disruptive noise in a theater, the prospect of bringing infants to the cinema would have been unattractive to many couples.

Such obstacles were irrelevant in the case of television. It appears that the changing demographic reality both prevented many young people from maintaining their habits of going out to see films and facilitated the adoption of television as a new source of entertainment. When the birth rate abates in the 1960s, there is no change in cinema attendance, which remains fairly stable at a low level. At that point television has become yet more popular, and it appears that habits of television viewing have largely supplanted filmgoing. An expectation that cinema attendance should rebound when the birth rate declines is unreasonable. Such an expectation would assume a symmetrical causal relationship (Lieberson 1985:ch.4). In this case, after the increase in the birth rate, the new leisure habit of television viewing obscured the need or desire for people to go to theaters, so that even when the birth rate declined there was no drive for increased cinema attendance. There was, therefore, an interaction of social forces—the coincidence of the beginning of the baby boom with the growth in television watching—contributing to the decline in filmgoing.[19] While the timing suggests that television alone did not cause a decrease in filmgoing, the sheer amount of time television watching consumes for the average American suggests that it detracts from filmgoing. Television has been fingered as a culprit in the decline of American group-joining and civic life (Putnam 2000:ch.13), and the same reasoning applies to movies: to paraphrase Putnam, a strong commitment to television is incompatible with a strong commitment to going out to the movies, such as the American public used to have.

In addition to television and birth rates, another major development in American society also might have helped to decrease the rate of filmgoing—the creation of new leisure opportunities through vehicle ownership. Crisp (1993:69–70) argues that the commercial success of the film industry in France was greatly hampered by an increase in the proportion of the population owning a motor vehicle. Motor vehicle ownership increased leisure opportunities—it became possible to attend many more events and to visit many more locations. Films were therefore neglected in favor of substitute leisure options. The data on passenger vehicle ownership in the United States support the view that a similar relationship existed here (see figure 2.4). While automobile ownership was more common in the United States than in France or elsewhere in Europe before World War II, there was stronger growth in ownership immediately following the war. The upturn in ownership parallels the downturn in cinema attendance. In fact,

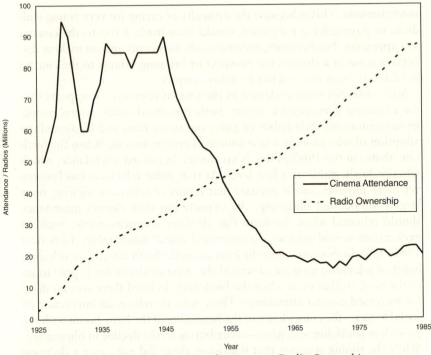

Figure 2.5. Weekly U.S. Cinema Attendance versus Radio Ownership, 1925–1985

like the increase in the birth rate, the coincidence appears closer than does the case for television and attendance.

A comparison with the history of another important electronic mass medium, radio, does not provide compelling evidence for a substantial influence of that medium on cinema attendance. Some film historians claim that the film industry suffered from competition with radio (see, e.g., Baxter 1993:27). Figure 2.5 shows that radio ownership grew at a fairly constant rate from the beginning of the data set, 1925, to the end of the data set, 1985.[20] There is, however, no coincidence between the growth in radio ownership and the point at which cinema attendance begins to decline. The apparent lack of an effect on cinema attendance might be surprising for those who would point to the vast popularity of many dramatic, narrative radio programs, some of which were even transferred to television later on.[21]

Although visual inspections of graphed data are quite useful for speculating about causal influences, a time-series regression analysis can better determine the relative importance of competing causal forces. Table 2.1

TABLE 2.1.
Prais-Winsten Time Series Regression of Influence of Television, the Birthrate, and Vehicle Ownership on Cinema Attendance

	β	S.E.	p
Television	−1.05	0.40	0.012
Birthrate	−0.40	0.15	0.008
Vehicles	0.21	0.43	0.62
Radio	−0.07	0.42	0.87
1936 Break	12.02	5.92	0.05
1957 Break	−1.81	6.37	0.78
Constant	98.40	18.87	0.000

R^2: 0.67
Durbin-Watson: 1.29

provides the results of such an analysis.[22] One of the problems with assessing the effects of the birth rate on cinema attendance, however, is the fact that the birth rate makes significant changes in direction during the time period in question. In 1936 the birth rate bottoms out and then increases until 1957, when it reverses again and begins to drop. In order to control statistically for these reversals, two dummy variables are introduced into the equation, one for 1936 and one for 1957.

Of most substantive interest is the fact that the coefficients for television ownership and the birth rate are both negative and highly likely to have a real link to cinema attendance. The time-series analysis supports the argument that these two factors jointly caused a decrease in filmgoing. In contrast, the coefficients for vehicle ownership and radio ownership are highly unlikely to have real associations with cinema attendance in this analysis. For the case of automobiles, one interpretation of this finding is that cars provided both alternative leisure opportunities and an alternative mode for filmgoing in drive-in theaters. As for radio, it appears that when radio ownership grew, people managed to fit into their schedules without influencing their filmgoing habits.

The variables analyzed here are probably not the only alternatives that people turned to in lieu of filmgoing. They are however, some of the most important developments in American society of the twentieth century, and so are likely the most important with respect to cinema attendance. Nonetheless, further entertainment options that might have also influenced cinema attendance include sports. Sklar (1994:274), however, cites a study of postwar recreation and entertainment expenditures that "indicates that spending on spectator and participation sports was less, on a percentage basis, in 1953 than in 1946." This decrease might be expected because many people purchased televisions in order to watch sports. In this way, sports might have had an influence on cinema attendance, but this effect is represented by television ownership.

The evidence strongly suggests that the popularity of film is influenced by the existence of a substitute cultural option—television—and the activities that come with building families. In this way, events and developments that were well outside the film world influenced some important features of that world. As we will see, these features were implicated in the growth of an art world for Hollywood films. The following section discusses how the changing nature of film audiences can best be interpreted as an arena for the interplay of class politics and cultural politics.

Audience Gentrification

Any analysis of the determinants of cultural hierarchy must pay close attention to the role of art consumption in creating and maintaining social status. An axiom of this perspective on cultural hierarchy is that high-status groups are loathe to risk symbolic contamination through consumption of cultural goods associated with lower-status groups. The exception to this rule occurs when the gap between high and low groups is sufficiently large that no confusion results regarding the distinctions between the groups. For example, high-status groups tend to enjoy the music of specific musicians who are relatively unknown. Those who are widely popular among the general public, the middle classes, are likely to be avoided by higher-status groups. Examples of popular singers and musicians who tend not only to be avoided but derided by high-status groups include Celine Dion and Kenny G. These musicians make easy-listening pop music, a "middle America" genre. Because of the power that our tastes have to represent our identity, expressing a taste for easy-listening pop puts one at risk of being identified as a member of the anonymous middle-American mass.

No such danger exists, though, for high-status group members who express a taste for musical forms associated with low-status subcultural groups of which they could never plausibly be members. This distance allowed upper-middle-class whites to enjoy jazz when it was predominantly a disreputable, African American musical genre. Although Lopes (2002:174) focuses on the enthusiasm for jazz of the "mostly white, male, college educated, and middle to upper class" group he calls "the righteous elite," I would argue that the status distance between them and blacks in the 1930s helped to fuel that enthusiasm. Lopes (2002:135) also cites Neil

Leonard's 1962 argument that early white jazz musicians saw themselves as "romantic outsiders" whose involvement in jazz was a way of opting out of the conservative middle-class culture. Again, choosing to affiliate with a low-status subgroup, while maintaining an obvious distance from that subgroup, in order to be an outsider of an undesirable middle group makes sense from a perspective that views cultural production and consumption in terms of concerns about status.

This same conception of the link between status concerns and taste informs Gans's (1999:136) claim regarding "cultural straddling." Cultural straddling can be upward, as in the case of lower-status group members' attendance at art museums when inspired by a sense of cultural duty. Status-seeking purposes can likewise be the root of downward cultural straddling. High-status groups are limited in the extent to which they can downward straddle because too much cultural borrowing risks blurring the cultural distinctions that they otherwise uphold. Gans (1999:136) notes how this has played a role in the art world for Hollywood film: "Because status considerations are important, higher culture publics frequently take up popular culture only after it has been dropped by its original users; during the 1960s and 1970s, for instance, the films of Humphrey Bogart and the Hollywood musicals of Busby Berkeley were popular with higher culture publics." In this way the commercial failures of Hollywood were allowed to become artistic successes. The difference with the case of jazz is that jazz was closely tied to a low-status subcultural group. Through a form of reverse snobbery, high-status groups could benefit from their own taste for jazz. In the case of Hollywood films, high status groups were instead picking up a dropped football and running with it. When Hollywood films were the default dramatic entertainment for the masses (not a low-status subculture as for jazz), before the 1960s, high-status groups would have risked a status demotion by articulating a belief in the artistic value of Hollywood films. This risk was diminished, however, by the mass abandonment of Hollywood production, making them safe for high-status sponsorship. Such sponsorship, as discussed earlier, is a key mechanism for cultural mobility, and an important factor in the growth of the art world for Hollywood films.[23]

The history of the audiences for Hollywood films is a story of collective behavior and particularly of conformity to group norms about class and status. The legitimation of Hollywood films as art could never simply be about legitimating the culture of the masses, because that would mean elevating the masses themselves relative to higher-status groups, which by definition cannot occur. Instead, the legitimation of Hollywood films was precisely about the *perpetuation* of audience segregation by class. Cultural gems can only look like lost treasure if they are not currently being worn by those who are thought to have bad taste.

Film, Television, and Social Functions

The advent and growth of television influenced film in another way that was not mediated by the nature of their audiences. The image of film is affected by what film does—its social function—as much as by who its audience is. For several decades film served the social function of default dramatic entertainment, even as a time killer, especially when cinemas were one of the few places one could find air-conditioning in the 1930s and 1940s (discussed further in chapter 3). Films were the primary source of amusement for the population. Because of this function, even those films that tried to serve a different, higher function went largely unrecognized.

But television altered film's social function. When television became the default entertainment medium and the primary source of amusement, film was eligible for redefinition and also compared favorably to television as an art form. Among the many other factors at work, the status of film was in part dependent on its assessment relative to this other, similar option.

The Weakening of Cultural Hierarchy and the Pop Art Movement

This chapter has so far dealt with demographic, technological, political, and social change in Europe and the United States to show how such changes facilitated the growth of an American art world for film in the 1960s. In the final section of this chapter the focus is on another, perhaps more crucial, feature of the opportunity space—the evolution of aesthetic ideals in the broader cultural realm. This topic sets the stage for the analysis that comes in the fourth chapter in which I show how film was effectively intellectualized as a sophisticated medium of communication. Such intellectual work was initially discouraged by a hostile aesthetic climate that reinforced rigid distinctions between legitimate, highbrow genres on the one hand and low-status, folk or popular genres of culture on the other. The erosion of these distinctions was aided by newly emerging aesthetic ideas and intellectual currents outside the film world. These developments, perhaps most clearly embodied by the Pop Art movement centered in New York, had important consequences for the consecration of Hollywood films.

The boundaries of art, while dependent on many different factors, are particularly susceptible to the influence of artistic experts. The cultural authority of critics and intellectuals is expressed in the pronouncements they make concerning artistic value. When critics and intellectuals in the United States began to find artistic value in film, they made it much more likely that the general public would begin to see film as art for two reasons. First, their cultural authority, which was related to the institutional authority of the organizations and publications with which they were affiliated, made their opinions generally persuasive. Second, the discourse they espoused provided the reading public with analytical tools that the public could itself use to think and communicate critically about film as art. For these reasons, it was important for critics to participate in the development of the art world for film. And yet, prior to the 1960s, intellectuals for the most part shunned the film world. The pool of cultural experts who were promoting film as art in the United States was quite small until the late 1950s (Mast 1981:ch.1). Hollywood was intellectually déclassé. In this view, the cinema was devoid of intellectual value and therefore a waste of time. Although, as will be discussed in depth in chapter 4, later intellectuals were able to find many examples of true art among American films made in the first half of the twentieth century, intellectuals writing before the 1960s were generally quite disparaging of the entire genre.

Why were intellectuals so reticent to take film seriously? Seeing as so many Hollywood classics have since been identified, the answer cannot be that there were no films worthy of their notice. The answer instead is that film was at the wrong end of the cultural hierarchy, the end that included other forms of popular, mass, or folk culture. Kammen (1996:89) notes that "many intellectuals in the Progressive era—ranging from Woodrow Wilson to Jane Addams—did not care for popular culture because it looked to be at odds with their reform agenda: it seemed socially degrading rather than morally uplifting, and for the older Progressives, especially, moral uplift remained the key to progress." One need not have been a Progressive to look down on popular culture, of course. Peterson (1997:86) notes that "[c]onservative humanist intellectuals writing in the 1940s and 1950s . . . reaffirmed a belief in the redeeming qualities of fine art and vilified low culture."

In the first half of the twentieth century, it was taken for granted that the differences between high and low art were real and enduring. Any attempts (and there were attempts) to intellectualize film were suppressed by the prevailing perception of popular or mass culture as inherently inferior to high art. Criticism of mass culture was in part fueled by the technological nature of film, still photography, and recorded music. These new media did not conform to the conventions of serious art. However, even those critics who were intellectually open to the goals and methods of these new cultural forms could be emphatic detractors of mass culture. The criticism was founded on a profound disappointment with the products of the entertainment industry. Perhaps the most influential text in this vein is Max Horkheimer and Theodor Adorno's *Dialectic of Enlightenment* (1972 [1944]). Horkheimer and Adorno, originally writing in the 1940s, argued that the culture industry that manufactured formulaic mass entertainment failed utterly to function as art. The culture industry served to generate profits and had no concern for the promotion of spiritual or intellectual needs among audiences. Rather than capitalizing on the artistic potential of the new technologies to uplift and enrich audiences, mass culture was stupefying them, and Hollywood studio production embodied the worst of mass cultural production.[24]

At approximately the midcentury mark, new thinking about art and aesthetics was gaining ground in the United States. One strain of thought that helped to weaken the critique of mass culture was postmodernism. A postmodernist viewpoint naturally applies to more than aesthetics; however, one of its implications was a new perception of the role and value of art, including the contestation of the traditional cultural hierarchy and the championing of the aesthetics and culture of the everyday life of the average individual.[25]

The postmodern challenge was sufficiently serious to warrant a defense on the part of those who wanted to guard the sanctity of high culture. Bernard Rosenberg (1971 [1968]:6) was one of those guardians, and his arguments were representative of one side of the "mass culture" debate.

> To reject "mass-cult" and "mid-cult" is to espouse high culture—and to do that is to be put down in certain circles as a snob. Very well, there are worse epithets. Shakespeare really does seem to me to be a better playwright than Arthur Miller and a better writer than Mickey Spillane. That they—and Homer and Faith Baldwin—are all popular is as incontrovertible as it is irrelevant. Such enormous qualitative differences separate them that no common frame of reference is broad enough to encompass their works. If to hold such a view is proof of snobbery, so be it. . . .
>
> If, as Jeremy Bentham insisted, pushpin (that is, pinball) brings greater happiness to a greater number of people than does poetry, and if there is no other way to compare poetry and pushpin, it follows that the slaves of the Nielsen ratings are home free. Then by any objective standard *The Beverly Hillbillies* are as good as—in fact demonstrably better than—Mr. Leinsdorf and the Boston Symphony. To prefer Shakespeare to Spillane becomes mere eccentricity, and to publish *Valley of the Dolls* in contravention of one's own better taste becomes a sort of philanthropy—a little self-interested, perhaps, but plainly benign.
>
> If, on the other hand, *Othello* is absolutely better than *Bonanza*, then the Nielsen ratings are not so much a justification as an indictment, and

it makes no difference how many people at any given moment think otherwise. In that case there have to be persuasive arguments for describing *The Beverly Hillbillies*—without apology—as cultural garbage and the people who present the *Hillbillies* as cultural garbagemen.

Such a view of mass culture clings to a narrow evaluative framework, one that judges popular culture according to the standards invented to appraise high culture. Allan Bloom's (1987) *The Closing of the American Mind* still has resonance for many intellectuals today, indicating the continued significance of critiques of popular culture and the contemporary relevance of cultural hierarchy. Despite such defenses, however, critiques of cultural hierarchy have been enormously influential in intellectual circles since the 1960s. Just as with all forms of popular culture, Hollywood films became legitimate candidates for valorization.

In addition to the elevation of popular culture, a different, yet complementary, transformation of cultural standards gradually took place in the United States in the decades surrounding the middle of the twentieth century. This aesthetic revolution is illuminated by Lopes (2002:270), whose history of jazz documents not only the process by which jazz was consecrated, but also the changing historical context in which that consecration took place: "Jazz music, for example, was not simply moving up the hierarchy from low to high. Rather the jazz art world and jazz music threatened to dissolve the very boundaries of low, middle, and highbrow culture." That is to say, during approximately the middle of the twentieth century, as jazz was becoming established as an art form, that very change had the effect of weakening the existing boundaries between high and low culture. As Lopes (ibid.) notes, other authors have examined the changing U.S. social conditions for art, including journalist Russell Lynes's description of borrowings across the lines of highbrow, middlebrow, and lowbrow, and historian Michael Kammen's argument that American culture had democratized at the middle of the twentieth century. This democratization entailed not only borrowings across levels of culture but also a waning in the significance of the formerly powerful distinctions.[26] This is not to say that cultural hierarchy has eroded away to insignificance, of course. Rather, the distinctions between higher and lower cultural forms are not as sharp or immutable as they were once widely believed to be. This partial erosion of the boundaries occurred alongside—probably with some mutual causal influence—the reshuffling of the cultural hierarchy.

Perhaps the best known and most influential aesthetic manifestation of postmodernity was the Pop Art movement, which emerged primarily in New York in the late 1950s. Pop Art is most clearly associated with painting, sculpture, and photography, and the artists most often cited as central to the movement include Andy Warhol, Robert Rauschenberg, Jasper

Johns, James Rosenquist, and Claes Oldenburg. Though Pop Art itself was not primarily a cinematic innovation, this movement nevertheless had important consequences for the critical reception of film, as it had for all artistic genres.

Perhaps the most salient characteristic of the Pop Art movement was its incorporation of elements of folk art, popular culture, and everyday, material goods.

> Pop Art can be considered broadly as that art of the sixties which represents or interprets mass-produced common objects and subjects culled from commercial art—that is, the signs of things and people. . . . Pop Art can also be considered narrowly, as art that represents images selected from commercial art—signs of objects and signs of signs—and, equally important and more radical, art that utilizes the mechanical, and thus impersonal, techniques of commercial art . . . (Sandler 1988:144–45)[27]

Because the rationale grounding Pop Art was the identification of art in objects of everyday life and the extension of artistic methods to "mechanical" techniques, film, especially film of the Hollywood tradition with its populist legacy, was ideally positioned to benefit from these new ideological currents. As Crane (1987:71) notes, Pop Art "attempted to redefine the relationship between high culture and popular culture by revising conventions concerning subject matter and technique that had served to maintain the distinctions between them" and "undermined the prestige of the aesthetic tradition through its veneration of popular culture." The change in the intellectual climate extended beyond the art worlds themselves as traditional boundaries in academic traditions weakened (Heiss 1973:86–98; Rudolph 1977:248). As will be discussed in chapter 3, developments in academia played an important role in legitimating film as art through the institutionalization of film courses and programs.

Yet another tenet of Pop Art facilitated the intellectualization of films— a broadening of the ideology of authenticity. While Marcel Duchamp's famous *Fountain* had already stretched the boundaries of art many decades earlier through the use of ready-made sculpture, Pop Art expanded the boundaries still further. A common technique of Pop Artists was to assemble or recombine existing images, so, like Duchamp, they were not always the creators of all the elements of their works. Such borrowing helped to redefine authenticity in art (Genocchio 2003). Such a view of artists made it easier to accept directors, who likewise were not the sole creators of the final works, as artists as well.

Pop Art facilitated the art world for film, then, by helping to soften, or even reverse, the stigmas of industrial production and commercialization.

Hollywood films in particular benefited from Pop Art's success in a second way as well. While the traditional cultural hierarchy had been founded on a sense of Europhilia, Pop Art was a quintessentially American movement, and it was a celebration of American culture. Edwards (2001:89), citing art critic John Coplans, argues that Pop Art was "a move in art practice from Europe to America" whose devices derived "their force in good measure from the fact that they have virtually no association with a European tradition." "In short," contends Edwards, "it is the 'Americanness' of Pop Art that sets it apart." While film as a whole was further legitimated as art through the premises of Pop Art, the latter's focus on American culture in particular benefited the art world for Hollywood films by freeing U.S. intellectuals to look for art away from European productions and toward domestic films.

Pop Art changed critical notions about the definition of art in precisely a way that facilitated a view of Hollywood films as art. As an art world movement, those who were most importantly affected by the movement were critics and others central to the art world for film. As will be discussed in greater depth in chapter 4, through the dissemination of a legitimating discourse, this group can have a great influence on audience perceptions concerning artistic boundaries. With an ideological foothold provided by the dictates of the Pop Art movement, film criticism was able to flourish as a respectable intellectual endeavor. This development of a group of cultural experts devoted to film, then, was one step toward film's recognition as art among the wider public.

At the same time, we must be careful not to overstate the case—although the hierarchical nature of culture in the United States is not as rigid as it once was, the prestige ordering has not disappeared entirely. Indeed, such a total disappearance would negate our purpose here, which is to explain how Hollywood films achieved the status of art. The distinction between art and non-art is still with us, and it is still a powerful distinction. We have become more catholic in our ideas of what constitutes art, but we have not lost our sense of the potency and authority of art.

SUMMARY

The opportunity space for the growth of an art world for Hollywood films has been analyzed in two phases. In earlier decades the American social context was less conducive to the creation of an art world for film compared to the European contexts. World War I influenced these countries in countless ways, of course, ways much more important and long-lasting than the perception of film as art. But that war and the demographic, geographic, and economic characteristics of early twentieth century urban America facilitated divergent art world tendencies. A reconciliation of that divergence was then assisted by changes in American society following World War II. The size and nature of U.S. film audiences responded to broader social forces that in turn caused film production and consumption to occur in a manner more consistent with expectations about the nature of art. At the same time, aesthetic transformations outside the film world revolutionized ideas about the nature of art in ways that reversed norms concerning the artistic viability of Hollywood productions.

Although we are far from having answered the question of why an art world for Hollywood films developed, we have a good idea of how context mattered. Much of the previous work has focused on how art worlds are created from within or on how cultural hierarchy is influenced by cultural entrepreneurs in support of various high art forms. But an explanation of a causally complex case study needs to be as comprehensive as reasonably possible. And while there are probably other elements of the opportunity space for Hollywood films as art, I would argue that all the elements for which a strong causal argument can be made are included here. We can now move on to examine how change was created from within. Chapter 3 explores the evolving structure and logic of Hollywood production and exhibition over the first seven decades of the twentieth century as well as the focused efforts of film-world participants to endorse and advance film as art.

CHAPTER 3

Change from Within:
New Production and Consumption Practices

AS THE PREVIOUS CHAPTER has argued, timing matters. The changing social environment can influence the chances for successful recognition as art. The focus in this chapter, however, takes us away from the broader context and toward the film world itself. Such a focus makes intuitive sense. We need to look at what is going on inside an art world to understand how that world is successfully constructed. Within that world, there are two major categories of developments.

The first category, as suggested by Becker, consists of those events and activities that can be identified as undertaken primarily in order to further the goal of promoting film as art. Within this category are (1) the creation of film festivals, (2) the *academic study* of film, and (3) film directors' *self-promotion as artists*. This narrower focus is informed by Becker's (1982) persuasive argument that art worlds are the result of focused, instrumental labor by many dedicated participants. In almost all cases, there needs to be a network of actors cooperating in various capacities—the production, exhibition, evaluation, and preservation of art are more work than artists alone can undertake. In a similar vein, DiMaggio (1992) has made a strong case for the importance of studying institutional change. To explain how dramatic theater, opera, and modern dance were legitimated as art he points to the emergence of "institutions with the power to establish authoritatively the value of different forms of culture" and argues that these institutions solidified "boundaries among forms of cultural practice," meaning how the art was created and consumed (1992:21). Just as with other social phenomena (e.g., social movements), the institutionalization of resources is a key to achieving group goals.

In the second category are those developments within the film world that occurred primarily for economic or legal reasons but that nonetheless facilitated the growth of an art world for Hollywood films. Within this category are (1) the changing *mode of film production*, (2) the economic push toward *art houses*, (3) the economics of "*prestige productions*," (4) changing *censorship practices*, and (5) substantive changes in 1960s films. Some of these developments exist within the realm of film production and others in that of film consumption. Taken together, they constitute the major factors from within the film world that helped to create an art world for film. It is also necessary to note that although these factors are discussed in turn, their analytical separation here is not meant to imply that these various developments are unrelated to one another in historical fact. The history of the U.S. film industry reveals an organic evolution in which a complicated set of events are causally related. This interaction will be noted throughout and more fully discussed in the concluding chapter.

FILM FESTIVALS

Film festivals come in many varieties and serve a wide range of purposes. Today there are thousands of film festivals across the globe, allowing a high degree of specialization. Within the United States alone, film festivals exist to showcase, for example, films from certain countries, films made by women, films made by members of ethnic groups, films with specific themes, films of particular genres, and there are even festivals dedicated to the films of certain directors or of certain actors. Some festivals are one-time events, while others, the most famous ones, are held annually. Yet another distinction exists between those that seek to provide a venue for films and those that offer a competition for which various prizes are available.

For most legitimate art forms, awards exist as an integral part of the art world. In literature, an example of a highly developed art world with widely recognized legitimacy, there are many awards available to authors. Perhaps the most prestigious of all of them is the Nobel Prize in Literature. In the United Kingdom, the most prestigious award for literature is the Booker Prize, in Canada the Governor General's Award, and in the United States, there are the National Book Award and the Pulitzer Prize. The prizes are decided by experts in the field, and they are a reliable signal of artistic merit. For real art—that is, how we really know if something is good—the experts deem it so. That is because for real art the other most common measure, popularity, is thought to be a poor indicator of quality (or, for some, perhaps an excellent indicator of the lack of quality).

And so it is with films. Competitive film festivals are effective in demonstrating the artistic worth of particular films. Because they are competitive, and because prizes are awarded by juries who have some claim to expert status in their field, festivals have authority in bestowing artistic merit. Winning the Palme d'Or from Cannes or the Jury Prize at Sundance, for example, is a marker of quality that most audience members would recognize as legitimate. Film festivals can also contribute to the artistic validation of certain films just through inclusion. Festival organizers most often screen submitted films and exhibit only those that they find worthy. In this way, being screened at a well-regarded festival can act as a type of award.

Given their role in creating recognition of artistic merit, the history of film festivals in the United States is of particular relevance to the maturation of the art world for Hollywood films. The Venice International Film Festival bills itself as the world's oldest film festival, first held in 1932. Of course, as a European festival, its influence on perceptions of film as art in the United States was attenuated, and there were no film festivals in the United States in 1932. There were, however, awards to be won—the Academy Awards. Perhaps the most concerted and effective studio effort to manipulate public perceptions of the film industry was the creation of the Academy of Motion Picture Arts and Sciences. In 1927 members of the film industry created the Academy, with its awards following a year later. This happened at a much earlier point in time than the public acceptance of Hollywood films as art in the 1960s. This more than thirty-year discrepancy can be explained by noting the striking difference between the original purpose of the Academy Awards and the 1960s function of film festivals. Far from promoting Hollywood films as high culture comparable to opera or serious theater, the Academy Awards were invented to promote the industry as ethical and seemly. Shale quotes from the Academy's 1929 *Annual Report* concerning the impetus behind the new organization: "But more than this and of greater importance as some of us viewed it, the screen and all its people were under a great and alarming cloud of public censure and contempt. . . . Some constructive action seemed imperative to halt the attacks and establish the industry in the public mind as a respectable, legitimate institution, and its people as reputable individuals" (1993:2). Part of the reason that such steps were necessary was that the industry's reputation had suffered from a number of well-publicized sex and drug scandals in the early 1920s. These included the trial of the very popular Roscoe "Fatty" Arbuckle, who had been implicated in the death of a woman in his hotel room; the murder of director William Desmond Taylor and revelations of a lifestyle centered on drugs and sex; the death of actor Wallace Reid from drug complications; and the hasty divorce of Mary Pickford and her unseemly rapid remarriage to Douglas Fairbanks (Black 1994:30–31). All this happened while the industry was under constant criticism for producing films that contained too much violence and sex, that glamorized unethical behaviors, and that were possibly turning children into delinquents and misfits.[1] The Academy Awards, then, did not carry the same connotations that they do today. The high culture aura that is sometimes attached to the major awards, such as best director and best picture, is in fact as much a result of the development of an art world for Hollywood films as it is a cause of that art world. During their early decades, the awards served to make the industry seem decent and then glamorous, not high art. But as the art world for Hollywood films developed, the Academy Awards found a natural place there and began to fulfill the function of signaling artistic quality.

The Academy Awards notwithstanding, the growing art world for Hollywood films had a pressing need for extracommercial assessments, a way for true believers in the artistry of the films to express their preferences and to canonize the best works. This need was met through film festivals, and an examination of when the festivals were founded suggests that they were integral to the development of an art world for Hollywood films.

It must first be said, however, that it is a difficult task to provide a complete history of American film festivals. There is no single source that has cataloged film festivals on a yearly basis, so it is necessary to piece together the historical evidence from various sources. At the same time, because some festivals last only one or a few years, and others are quite modest in scope, they might leave little or no mark on the historical record.

Despite these limitations, it is nonetheless possible to create a reasonable picture of the growth over time in U.S. film festivals. Figure 3.1 provides information from two types of sources: (1) a combination of post-1985 industry directories and (2) a comprehensive festival directory published in 1970.[2]

The obvious difficulty with using current lists is that festivals that no longer occur are excluded. The 1970 data go partway in correcting for this problem, and the marked similarity in the overall patterns in the 1970 and the post-1985 data boost our confidence in their validity.

According to post-1985 sources, a few festivals were on the leading edge in being founded in the 1950s, the earliest, in these sources, the Columbus International Film and Video Festival, held for the fifty-third time in 2005 and founded in 1952.[3] According to these sources, the vast majority of film festivals in the United States were founded post-1960. The San Francisco International Film Festival was founded in 1958, the New York Film Festival in 1963, the Chicago International Film Festival in 1965, the Seattle International Film Festival in 1974, and the Boston Film Festival in 1985. Only 3 of the 276 current festivals in the sources predate the 1960s, and none of them was founded earlier than the 1950s.

The fact that film festivals in major cities were all founded no earlier than the 1950s is significant. Being cultural centers, it is unlikely that cities such as New York, Chicago, and San Francisco, some of the earliest festivals in the dataset, would have lagged behind other parts of the country in organizing film festivals. From these data we can date the emergence of a formally organized effort to celebrate the artistic potential of film in a very public manner.

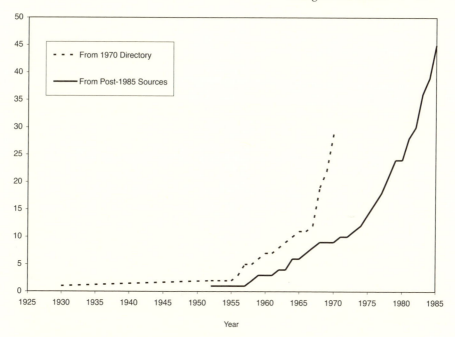

Figure 3.1. Number of U.S. Film Festivals

In contrast to the post-1985 sources, the 1970 directory lists a festival dating back to 1930[4]—the Photographic Society of America/Motion Picture Division International Amateurs Film Festival—which is now known by the name American International Film and Video Festival. It began as and continues to be a festival for amateur filmmakers, considering only those films that are noncommercial. A second early film festival not included in the post-1985 sources is the Ten Best of the West festival, established in 1956 and also exclusively for exhibiting amateur (as separate from "independent") films. It should be noted, however, that the stated purpose of each festival, at least as it was reported in 1970, lacks any reference to art. Whereas a good number of other festivals explicitly state that their purpose is to encourage appreciation of filmmaking as an art form, the 1930 festival's purpose was "To recognize the best of non-professional films" (Zwerdling 1970:22), and the 1956 festival's purpose, "To encourage quality and expert craftsmanship in filmmaking by the amateur filmer."

The major difference between the information from the 1970 directory and the post-1985 sources is that the number of film festivals is reported to have begun to grow in the late 1950s and, at a faster rate, over the 1960s. The major similarity between the two data sources is that, aside from a single marginal festival, film festivals began in the late 1950s and grew during the 1960s, supporting the argument that film festivals were an integral component of the growth of a 1960s art world for film.[5]

In addition to considering their numbers, it is informative to also take into account the nature of these film festivals. It should be noted that the festivals in the dataset are diverse in character and function. Some of the newer festivals are more about entertainment than art, like New York's Asian Film Festival, which described itself in 2003 in this way:

> New York's BEST contemporary Asian film festival brings 22 of the latest and greatest from Korea, Hong Kong, Japan, India, Thailand and Taiwan to the Anthology Film Archives for 12 days of unrelenting entertainment. Whereas most film festivals show sleepy arthouse snoozers that couldn't get a theatrical release if their lives depended on it, ASIAN FILMS ARE GO!!! brings the blockbusters, the newsmakers, the trendsetters, and the scandalous releases from thousands of miles away, right to New York, just to entertain you. (*http://www.subwaycinema.com/frames/archives/nyaff03/nyaff03home.htm*) (accessed December 19, 2006)

Other festivals are quite political in nature:

> In recognition of the power of film to educate and galvanize a broad constituency of concerned citizens, Human Rights Watch decided to create the Human Rights Watch International Film Festival. Human Rights Watch's International Film Festival has become a leading venue for distinguished fiction, documentary and animated films and videos with a distinctive human rights theme. Through the eyes of committed and courageous filmmakers, we showcase the heroic stories of activists and survivors from all over the world. The works we feature help to put a human face on threats to individual freedom and dignity, and celebrate the power of the human spirit and intellect to prevail. We seek to empower everyone with the knowledge that personal commitment can make a very real difference. (*http://hrw.org/iff/2006/about.html*) (accessed December 19, 2006)

And still other festivals are for film purists who would consider only independent productions worthy of exhibition and define Hollywood outside the art world for film:

> Since 1981, the annual Black Maria Film and Video Festival, an international juried competition and award tour, has been fulfilling its mission to advocate, exhibit and reward cutting edge works from independent film and videomakers. . . . Today the works exhibited by the

Black Maria Film and Video Festival explore the human condition as well as the creative potential of the medium. They offer a mosaic of artistically conceived film and video forms (documentary, experimental, animation and narrative) but with an emphasis on cutting edge sensibility. The Festival Tour exhibits the winning works in various thematic and artistic configurations tailored to diverse audiences at venues which are conducive to the genuine appreciation of the work. (*http://www.blackmariafilmfestival.org*) (accessed December 19, 2006)

There exist, nonetheless, festivals that seek to find the art in Hollywood. Consider the following historical facts about the Chicago International Film Festival:

Founded in 1964 by award winning filmmaker and graphic designer Michael Kutza, the Festival's goals were the same then as they are now: to discover and present new filmmakers to Chicago, and to acknowledge and award these filmmakers for their artistry. The first Festival opened in 1965 at the Carnegie Theater, where directors King Vidor, Stanley Kramer, and actress Bette Davis were honored for their contributions to American cinema. Since then, the Festival has grown to become a world-renowned annual event. (*http://www.chicagofilmfestival.org/cgi-bin/WebObjects/CIFFSite.woa/wa/31pages/History*) (accessed December 19, 2006)

King Vidor, Stanley Kramer, and Bette Davis were anything but Hollywood outsiders in need of discovery. The New York Film Festival was similarly friendly to Hollywood productions from its beginning, as was the San Francisco International Film Festival. Today the major festivals such as Cannes and Toronto exhibit many Hollywood films. Major festivals such as these have done more than benefit individual films or the careers of individual actors and directors. Through the news and publicity that they have generated, they have also created an atmosphere in which film as a medium could enjoy increased prestige.

SELF-PROMOTION OF DIRECTORS

In his history of "New Hollywood"—Hollywood following large-scale reorganization of production practices (the abandonment of the studio system) from approximately the late 1960s—Peter Biskind (1998:15) claims that radical changes in ideology and production procedures transformed Hollywood in the late 1960s. Biskind points to many factors in Hollywood's transformation, but he names directors, as a group, as leaders of the revolution. According to Biskind (1998:15), directors wielded increased power and prestige, and unlike their studio-era predecessors who viewed themselves as skilled craftsmen and mere storytellers, this new generation of directors were eager to promote their films as personal expressions and to "assume the mantle of the artist."

This contrast fits well with what we expect to find in the development of an art world for Hollywood film in the 1960s. Directors, as the new center of attention, had an active role in changing popular perceptions about the artistic status of film by promoting themselves as artists. Before accepting this characterization at face value, however, we should verify it with the available historical evidence.

Film scholarship touches on this issue primarily through interviews with directors or through film analyses that attempt to link conclusions about specific films to the publicly or privately stated expectations and goals of the films' directors. The selection of directors to review for this section was driven by two criteria: (1) Was the director significant as determined by the winning of an Academy Award or by having directed a movie that appears on the American Film Institute's list of one hundred best American films? (2) Can evidence about this director's self-promotion as an artist or lack thereof be located?[6] The questions I pose are, How have directors characterized themselves? Have the same directors characterized themselves differently over time? Have directors who have worked more recently characterized themselves differently from those who worked in earlier decades?

A broad overview of the evidence supports the view that self-promotion by Academy Award–winning best directors in the 1960s strengthened perceptions of Hollywood films as art. Directors of the late 1960s and the 1970s embraced the discourse of film as art. In contrast, Academy Award–winning and other of the best-known directors of earlier decades for the most part eschewed that discourse in favor of self-promotion as craftsmen or entertainers.

Consider, for example, Biskind's claim that John Ford and Howard Hawks, directors who made films in the studio era, regarded themselves as technical workers more than as artists. There is, in fact, good support for this characterization. Davis (1995:4) writes of Ford (who won Oscars in 1935 for *The Informer*, 1940 for *The Grapes of Wrath*, 1941 for *How Green Was My Valley*, and 1952 for *The Quiet Man*), "The director liked to pose as a folksy anti-intellectual who merely did 'a job of work' and saw no need to analyze how it was accomplished. Difficult to interview, Ford proved consistently evasive about his craft, which he refused to call art, and safeguarded himself behind sarcasm, lies, and even a guise of illiteracy." He goes on to quote Ford: "'It is wrong to liken a director to an author,' he argued. 'He is more like an architect.' If the director is creative, he puts 'a predesigned composition on film' " (1995:6). With regard to the genre for which Ford is most renowned, "When someone called him the greatest poet of the Western saga, he replied, 'I am not a poet, and I don't know what a Western Saga is, I would say that is horseshit' " (1995:12). Anderson (1981:85) reports a similar quote from Ford: " 'I hate pictures. . . . Well, I like *making* them of course. . . . But it's no use asking me to talk about art.' " Ford built his career during a time when there was little institutional support for portraying himself as an artist, and when the discourse to represent himself in that way was uncommon in Hollywood.

Just like Ford, Howard Hawks was a successful studio-system director. Unlike Ford, though, Hawks never won a best director Oscar. Still, he directed classics such as *Bringing Up Baby* (1938), *Scarface* (1932), and *His Girl Friday* (1940), and he was awarded an honorary Oscar in 1975. Hawks began directing in the 1920s, and throughout his active career, he presented himself as a craftsman and entertainer rather than an artist, as one would expect of a pre–auteur theory director. Nevertheless, his cause was taken up in the pages of *Cahiers du cinema* in the 1950s, where his oeuvre was assessed as a collection of masterpieces. The principles of auteurism proved too foreign for Hawks, however, and he showed himself to be set in his pre-auteur ways even during the boom times of the art world for Hollywood films. In a 1970 discussion at the Chicago International Film Festival the following exchange took place:

> Q: You say that you are an entertainer, but the French critics in the last few years have been treating you as something more than that. Do you think they're right?
>
> A: Oh, I listen to them, and I get open-mouthed and wonder where they find some of the stuff that they say about me. All I'm doing is telling a story. I've very glad that they like it, and I'm very glad that a lot of them are copying what I do, but they find things. . . . I work on the fact that if I like somebody and think they're attractive, I can make them attractive. If I think a thing's funny, then people laugh at it. They give me credit for an awful lot of things that I don't pay any attention to. (quoted in McBride 1972:24)

Ford's and Hawks's resistance to self-promotion in the 1960s and 1970s surely indicates that they were not cultivating the image of themselves as artists in earlier decades.

The Third Man (1949) is probably the film of Carol Reed's most admired by critics. Reed began making films in the 1930s, though he won the 1968 Oscar for *Oliver!* In 1950 Reed gave a distinctly pre-auteur account of his role and the role of films generally, as described by Wapshott (1990:305–306):

> In a *New York Times* interview in 1950 he commented: "I don't believe the cinema is a place for little lectures on how everybody should live. I don't think audiences want them either, unless they are very original and striking. Personally I dislike the infusion of amateur politics into films. Certainly that is not the director's job." He did not much like politics in anything. . . . He had little notion of "art" and considered his trade something done as a business. A great film-maker was above all one who pleased his audience. . . . He once summed up his attitude to film-making and to films: "The most important purpose of the commercial film-maker is to produce entertainment which will draw the largest possible number of the paying public into the cinema, and (this is a most important condition) keep them there."

By and large, directors of the studio era reflected the prevailing perceptions of themselves and of film as existing outside the realm of art. William Wyler was a prolific director of dozens of successful films and won the best director Oscar in 1942 for *Mrs. Miniver*, in 1946 for *The Best Years of Our Lives*, and in 1959 for *Ben-Hur*. Wyler has his critics among film scholars, but his films have also inspired high praise from some leading scholars such as André Bazin (Stein 2002). Yet Wyler himself "never claimed to be an 'auteur' " (Herman 1995:212). Instead, Wyler characterized himself as at the service of writers, saying "It's like the music world; I am not the composer, but the conductor" (Anderegg 1979:preface).

Billy Wilder, best director in 1945 for *The Lost Weekend* and in 1960 for *The Apartment*, was even more emphatic in rejecting an intellectual conception of the artist for himself. In a 1960 interview, when asked about his art, he replied

> Look here, my friend. I don't want to talk about Art. I am an artist but I am a man who makes motion pictures for a mass audience, I am making pictures on all levels. To be a mechanic working in a back-alley garage, tinkering away for years and coming out with the one little automobile, that is one thing, but to work on an assembly line and come out with a Cadillac—that is something else. That is what I am trying to do here. (Horton 2001:32)

Wilder, then, could go along with the idea that he made art—well-crafted and smart film work—but not the kind of art that film critics were mostly writing about: highbrow, theoretically informed, and ideologically permeated cinema. In a 1970 interview Wilder again expressed his resistance to being portrayed as that type of artist: "To begin with, I don't want you to think that I am imbued with my own importance. That I am a very high-browed, *auteur-de-cinema* type. I am a craftsman, I try to do it as well as I simply can" (Horton 2001:64). It is interesting to see that in 1970 Wilder was familiar with auteur theory but unwilling to adopt it. This opposition probably reflects the fact that Wilder had worked in Hollywood for more than thirty years prior to the U.S. adoption of auteur theory, by which time his ideas about himself and his work were well formed.

That seems also to have been the case with George Cukor, director of *Adam's Rib* (1949), *The Philadelphia Story* (1940), and *My Fair Lady* (1964). Cukor was clearly reluctant to accept the *auteur* label. When asked in a 1972 interview if there had been anything specific he had wanted to say in his films, he replied,

> Oh *no*! If you do your work, you do everything. You express yourself, you get paid, you do everything. All this attitudinizing is peripheral. And I defy you to do a good job and not get money for it. (Of course some shrewd people make a hell of a lot more money than the rest, and I don't despise that.) But when they talk about freedom to express your own ideas, to follow your inspiration untrammelled by commercial considerations, and so on, I think they're talking about a fantasy. (Long 2001:75)

Such self-characterizations by some of the most renowned and respected directors now seem oddly self-deprecating and strangely to belittle their chosen medium. But these directors likely did not intend to be demeaning. Instead they were simply using the discourse of the film world that was familiar to them.

Furthermore, for those early directors who did not shy away from the word "art," the context of their comments shows that they were still not quite conversant in or embracing of the fully theorized high-art account of film. One such director was Michael Curtiz, who directed his first Hollywood film in 1926 and later directed *The Adventures of Robin Hood* (1938) and *Casablanca* (1942). Rosenzweig (1982:11) reports that Curtiz once said, "I put all the art into my pictures I think the audience can stand." Rosenzweig (1982:173) also notes that Curtiz could be a strong proponent of the artistic potential of film: "[M]otion pictures are not a pure art. They are the composite of all five arts: literature, painting, architecture, music and sculpturing." This belief in film as art, however, did not manage to translate into self-promotion as an artist. Kinnard and Vitone (1986:7) provide an account Curtiz gave of his goals as a director: "To make the best pictures I can that will give audiences their money's worth; to please myself as much as I can without forgetting that the pleasure of my audiences comes first. Thus only do I think I can make any substantial contribution to the art of motion pictures." So although Curtiz could accept film as art (perhaps a reflection of his European origins), he nonetheless presented himself as working to please an audience, something that true artists do not do. Art for art's sake precludes commercial considerations.

The contrast with Hollywood directors who began to work shortly before or after 1960, while not absolute (studio-era Academy Award–winners Frank Capra and Elia Kazan frequently referred to themselves as artists), is conspicuous. Consider John Schlesinger, best director winner for *Midnight Cowboy* (1969), whose comment on his work accurately reflects the major premise of auteur theory: "It is inevitable that a director's own attitudes will subconsciously creep into his films . . . despite the fact that movie-making involves collaboration with so many other artists" (Phillips 1981:179).

Likewise, Tony Richardson, best director for *Tom Jones* (1963), keenly supported the auteur theory's elevation of the director as the unifying artistic source in the cinema. Welsh and Tibbets (1999:88) characterize Richardson in the following way: "Part of the irresistible allure of the cinema to him was the possibility of being the primary creative force and having complete control over the work. In an article that he wrote for *Granta* in 1962, he argues forcefully that 'the impress of the director's personality upon his material constitutes his style.' " In a 1965 interview, Richardson reiterated this view, saying "I feel I just want to go on working in the cinema always. The director in the cinema is a real creative force, while in the theater he's just an interpreter of the text" (Welsh and Tibbets 1999:89).

New Hollywood directors were clear about the director's privilege to self-expression in movies. Martin Scorcese said, "What matters to me is that I get to make the pictures—that I get to express myself personally somehow" (Pye and Myles 1979:194). Hollywood directors in the late 1960s and in the 1970s routinely articulated auteurist principles in connection with themselves and their work. Conveying their message became a central motivation to work at all. In the studio era, producers had clearly been in command, so it was with authority that Harry Warner of Warner Bros. could say, "We'll make the pictures; let Western Union deliver the messages" (Zierold 1991:246). But the power to send messages had become the directors', and they were not afraid to say so, as Terry Gilliam has done : "I don't send my messages via Western Union; I send them by cinema. *Twelve Monkeys* is kind of a warning shot across the bow of humanity. It's the ever-presence of nature and nature taking its revenge" (Emery 2000:322).

These directors' self-promotional efforts, however self-aggrandizing, were warmly received and even encouraged by the mass media. For example, a 1968 interviewer for *Playboy* asked Stanley Kubrick:

Much of the controversy surrounding *2001* deals with the meaning of the metaphysical symbols that abound in the film—the polished black monoliths, the orbital conjunction of Earth, Moon and Sun at each stage of the monoliths' intervention in human destiny, the stunning final kaleidoscopic maelstrom of time and space that engulfs the surviving astronaut and sets the stage for his rebirth as a "star child" drifting toward Earth in a translucent placenta. One critic even called *2001* "the first Nietzschean film," contending that its essential theme is Nietzsche's concept of man's evolution from ape to human to superman. What was the metaphysical message of *2001*? (reprinted in Phillips 2001:47)

Kubrick can hardly be faulted for responding at an equally intellectual level of analysis:

It's not a message that I ever intend to convey in words. *2001* is a nonverbal experience; out of two hours and nineteen minutes of film, there are only a little less than forty minutes of dialog. I tried to create a *visual* experience, one that bypasses verbalized pigeonholing and directly penetrates the subconscious with an emotional and philosophic content. To convolute McLuhan, in *2001* the message is the medium. I intended the film to be an intensely subjective experience that reaches the viewer at an inner level of consciousness, just as music does; to "explain" a Beethoven symphony would be to emasculate it by erecting an artificial barrier between conception and appreciation. (reprinted in Phillips 2001:47)

On the one hand, directors' self-promotion as artists might be partially explained as a natural response to a definition that was imposed on them by the rest of the developing art world. On the other hand, a self-comparison to Beethoven can only be seen as a willingness to fully exploit this definition. So although directors were not simply fabricating the idea that they were artists, their enthusiasm to play that role contributed to the further development of an art world for Hollywood film.

Particularly well documented are Alfred Hitchcock's efforts at self-promotion.[7] Kapsis's study of the building of Hitchcock's reputation as a film master documents an array of art world forces,[8] and Hitchcock's own efforts were not the least of them (1992: see especially pp. 73–93). These efforts occurred primarily in the 1960s, and one such effort was the coaching of studio executives to issue press releases that played up the high art angle. Kapsis (1992:93) quotes from the official press kit for *Marnie* that mentioned that the Museum of Modern Art had exhibited a selection of Hitchcock's films, labeled Hitchcock a "creative genius" and a "Master of Cinematic Art," and alluded to the reverence that French audiences had for Hitchcock's art.

In the main, the evidence shows that directors in the 1960s and later actively engaged in constructing artistic status for themselves by participating in art world activities and by publicly characterizing themselves as artists in conversations and interviews that were made public. It is possible that some of these American directors took their cues from European directors (to name a few, Bernardo Bertolucci, Ingmar Bergman, Luis Buñuel, and, of course, the *nouvelle vague* directors such as Eric Rohmer, Claude Chabrol, François Truffaut, Alain Resnais) who readily participated in the construction of their own reputations as Artists.[9]

As King (2002: 88) and others have noted, another way of understanding the different behavior of directors in New Hollywood (King uses the label "brats") is to point to the different training that the directors received—namely, that they studied film in an academic setting. In contrast, the typical career path of earlier directors had begun with on-the-job training through apprenticeships, mostly within the studio system, though for those whose careers began in the 1950s, some got their start in television.[10]

The evidence, then, supports Biskind's (1998) assertion that earlier directors downplayed their reputations as serious artists while New Hollywood directors capitalized on auteur theory to promote themselves, a theory they often learned in academic programs. The training of directors is just one way in which universities helped in the creation of an art world for Hollywood films. As the next section explores, the growth of film studies figures prominently in the U.S. art world for film.

Ties to Academia

To varying degrees, universities have institutional legitimacy. What this means is that if an intellectual subject gets taken seriously by the academic community, it will likely get taken seriously by the rest of the public, particularly those who have postsecondary degrees, as well. The increasing academic involvement with film had important consequences for the status of film as art. Previous authors have argued that ties to academia, through publications and inclusion in curricula, have helped to legitimate opera, dramatic theater, and dancing as high art (DiMaggio 1992), as well as symphonic music and the plays of Shakespeare (Levine 1988), jazz (Peterson 1972), and Impressionist painting (White and White 1965). Film has benefited similarly.

University Curricula

As anyone who has had anything to do with designing a curriculum knows, the process of deciding what is included and excluded is highly political. There is never consensus about what is most worthy of being taught to young minds. This is true in the sciences, as we have seen with evolutionary theory, as well as in the arts, as we have seen with the evolution in the literary canon toward greater gender and ethnic inclusivity. The result of curriculum decisions can be interpreted as the outcome of a struggle for institutional recognition.

In this way art benefits from a connection with universities and colleges. Just as with film festivals, academic study bestows artistic worth on its object. The founding of film studies departments began in the 1960s and has continued to grow. The *College Blue Book* series, beginning in 1923, provides listings of all institutions of higher education and details the programs they offer. From this source it is possible to discern that the number of degree programs that are in some way connected to the study of film has steadily increased since the late 1960s. Prior to that time no degree programs related to the study of film could be found.[11]

There is agreement within the literature on the history of film studies that the vast majority of film departments were founded after the post– World War II growth in higher education. Allen and Gomery (1985:iii) claim in their work on film history that university courses on film were rare and came only from those few "brave academics whose love for the movies prompted them to write and teach film 'on the side,' while today [1985] such courses are prevalent in universities."

In film departments founded prior to 1960 (e.g., the University of Southern California and Columbia University), the purpose of the programs offered was to teach filmmaking.[12] It was only in the 1960s and 1970s that film departments began to focus on the study of film history and theory.

It is useful to examine the founding dates of some of the most renowned departments (as rated by *U.S. News & World Report*).[13] Carroll (1998:1) writes that the program at New York University (number 1 on *U.S. News & World Report*'s list) was one of the first academic departments of film history and theory in the United States. It was still in the process of being formed in 1970, not having progressed as far as having its Ph.D. program accredited. The American Film Institute's graduate program (number 4 on the list) was founded in 1967, while the program at the California Institute of the Arts (number 5) was created in 1971. Columbia University (number 6), although it had earlier established a film department, first offered a master of fine arts in film, radio, and television in 1966. Florida State's program (number 9) began only in 1989, and the cinema department at San Francisco State University (number 15) "was founded amid the political activism and artistic experimentation of the 1960's." Syracuse University (number 17) began to offer its master of fine arts in film studies in 1976.[14] In sum, there appear to have been few or perhaps no academic departments offering degrees in the critical study of film theory and history prior to the 1960s. Rather, a wave of new departments of film studies began in the 1960s, and the number of departments has continued to grow.

Morrison, in a research study sponsored by the Carnegie Commission on Higher Education, arrives at a similar picture of the academic history of film in the United States (1973:15–21). Among Morrison's main findings is that the first major in film studies was offered by the University of California in 1932. However, the "first full-fledged scholarly film program with a Ph.D. was established by New York University in 1970" (1973:15). The number of courses strongly concerned with film in any academic context stood at 86 in 1946, 113 in 1949, 161 in 1953, 275 in 1957, and 305 in 1959. Despite the presence of film-related courses in the 1940s, Morrison asserts that the "major growth in film, however, occurred in the sixties; film in the university is basically a product of this decade" (1973:16). While only 10 undergraduate major programs existed in 1959, in 1971 there were 47; while there were 850 courses offered in 1964, there were 2,400 in 1971. Morrison's findings are solidly in agreement with the information available elsewhere concerning the incorporation of film into university curricula.[15]

There are several arguments to make regarding the importance of film programs in the development of an art world for film in the United States. Much of the discourse on film as art was developed in academic settings (the contributions of this discourse are the focus of chapter 4). In addition, film programs have trained a number of Hollywood directors, who were then able to bring an academic perspective to their work (discussed below in this chapter) and self-presentation. Perhaps most important of all has been the institutional legitimacy that universities have extended to the film world.

In addition to a general affirmation of films as worthy of study, universities also play a role in canon formation. In every art world, there are certain works that are widely accepted as the best of the genre and certain artists worthy of revisiting and teaching to successive generations. Painting has its canonized figures such as Picasso, Goya, Kandinsky, and Rembrandt. These and other painters are part of the canon in large part because they have been the focus of academic study. This attention within universities is the means by which claims are made and substantiated for the artistic worth of only a small portion of the artists and artworks in a genre. The existence of a canon is important for maintaining the coherence and legitimacy of a genre because canonical works serve as exemplars for defining and defending artistic value. Every art world needs and has a canon.

DiMaggio (1992) argues that the institutional legitimacy of universities played a role in establishing canons in dramatic theater, opera, and dance. Corse and Griffin (1997) make a more detailed argument for the role that universities play in canon construction. Through hiring faculty members and creating fellowships that target specific genres or works, universities selectively focus attention and influence the amount of scholarship that is produced. By making these positions available, universities likewise provide the basis for the *networks* of scholarship that are necessary to make an impact. University libraries and presses also directly influence the physical availability of materials for future study.

Film studies programs, then, worked not only to legitimate film as a medium, but also to canonize particular cinematic works. Those films and directors that regularly appear on course syllabi and in textbooks represent great works and great artists, with the most regularly taught films being closer to the core of the canon. An examination of five popular introductory textbooks reveals a long list of films and directors that appear to have canonical status. Among the directors most frequently appearing in the tables of contents of these books are a group of the usual suspects: Buster Keaton, Alfred Hitchcock, D. W. Griffith, Satyajit Ray, Louis Buñuel, Ernst Lubitsch, F. W. Murnau, Orson Welles, Leni Reifenstahl, Ingmar Bergman, Federico Fellini, Robert Bresson, and Michelangelo Antonioni.[16] A wider survey of textbooks would, of course, fill out this list with many other directors whose films are the subject of academic attention.

Publishing

Another measure of the increase in academic attention given to film is the number of texts published in the field of film criticism and the aesthetics of film. An ideal data source for a measure of the number of books published on these subjects in a given year is WorldCat, which is the online catalog of the world's largest library consortium.[17] Figure 3.2 displays the results from a search for books dealing with the analysis of films. First, there is a sharp increase in the number of books on film aesthetics or criticism beginning in approximately 1966, and this increase continues to the end of the time period examined, 1990. Second, before 1965, the number of books on film aesthetics or criticism was extremely small. There were on average 2 books published and theses written per year between 1925 and 1964 under subject headings containing the words (motion pictures) and (aesthetics or criticism). Figure 3.2 strongly supports the argument that the 1960s were a decisive period in the creation of an art world for film, and is consistent with the assertion by Allen and Gomery (1985:26) that "[t]he vast majority of books and scholarly arti-

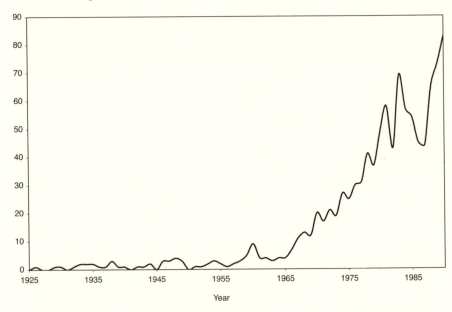

Figure 3.2. Number of English-Language Books on Film in WorldCat Catalog, 1925–1985. Note: From subject keywords (motion pictures)—(aesthetics or criticism).

cles on American film history have been written since 1960." From these data, it appears that the production of academic work on the subject of the cinema in the 1960s altered perceptions about the worthiness of film as a topic for serious discussion and analysis.

We might ask whether these results are an artifact of the way the WorldCat library works or of how the cataloging was done. To answer this question I performed a search with the same limits within the catalog of the Library of Congress. From that catalog a similar pattern emerges, especially concerning the timing of the increase. To further test the possibility that the WorldCat catalog is idiosyncratic, I performed a search for books on aesthetics or criticism of literature and compared the outcome to the same search of the Library of Congress catalog. Again, the patterns were the same. It is therefore unlikely that the trend for books on film analysis is merely a result of how the cataloging was done.

In order to fully understand what these publishing data represent, however, it is necessary to understand the historical context for publishing in general over the time period of interest. How do the results for books on film analysis compare to other kinds of books? The *Statistical Abstract of the United States* provides data on the number of all new books published each year from 1950. Data prior to 1950 are available in a resource

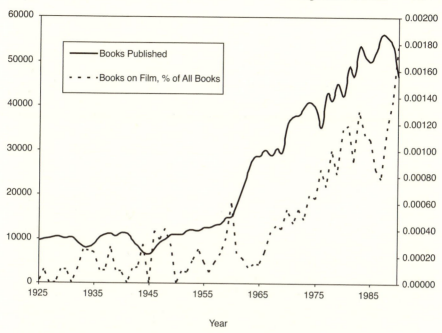

Figure 3.3. Number of All Books Published versus Books on Film as a Percentage of All Books

created by the United States Department of Commerce and the Bureau of the Census (1989).[18] Together these confirm that book publishing expanded in the 1960s (see figure 3.3). Between 1925 and 1990 there was an increase in the number of books published in the United States, from 9,574 to 46,738. While the overall number of books has greatly increased, the timing of the increase is of particular interest. There was a very small and gradual increase in the number of books published until the end of the 1950s; following 1960 there were much greater year-to-year increases. This depiction of the history of publishing in the United States is explained by Coser et alia as influenced by increases in literacy and college graduation rates, the expansion of the higher education system, global increases in knowledge production, and growth in the popular culture industries (1982:25).

Tebbel (1987:440) paints a similar picture of the history of publishing, attributing major changes in publishing to "the unprecedented expansion of education, propelled at the upper level by the millions of servicemen who were enabled to go to college by the GI bill, and at the lower level a little later by the baby boom." In addition, Tebbel cites progress in information technology as also having contributed to the increase in publishing.[19]

Because there were more of all books being published, a question arises concerning how to understand the observed increase in English-language books on film criticism or aesthetics after 1965. Is the increase in film books, then, merely a consequence of this overall expansion in publishing rather than a measure of a real increase in academic attention to film? Several ways of examining the data indicate that the increase in film books is a real increase in academic attention to film. First, the increase in the number of books on film outpaces the more general increase in publishing. As Figure 3.3 shows, when the number of books on film is divided by the number of all books, the upward trend beginning in the late 1960s remains. Even when controlling for the overall increase in publishing, the publication of film books increased. Second, the timing of the increase for film books is slightly after the general increase. The increase in film books appears to occur approximately six years after the increase for all books. The lag for film books supports the notion that there are other factors involved and that books on film may have increased for reasons other than the general expansion in publishing. Comparisons of the beginning of the increase for film books with the beginnings for literature and math support this interpretation (see figure 3.4). For each field, the increase occurs closer in time to the general expansion in publishing, and in each case the increase appears to predate the increase in film books.

A third angle for viewing the data provides support for the assertion that the diffusion of the perception of film as art was tied to the growth in the production of academic work on film studies. A comparison of not relative differences but rather absolute differences between film and the related art form of theater (or drama) highlights the fact that an extremely small number of books on film aesthetics or criticism was published prior to the 1960s.[20] Books on drama or theater aesthetics or criticism were plentiful; the average yearly output between 1925 and 1965 was just over 100 new books or new editions. This figure contrasts with 2 books per year for film analysis over the same period. For further comparison, on average over 409 books on literary aesthetics or criticism were published each year between 1925 and 1965. These differences are consistent with the idea that both literature and theater or drama have been established as art forms since at least the beginning of the dataset—1925 (cf. DiMaggio 1992; Leary 1976:ch.1; Levine 1988).

The increase in the 1960s in books on film, then, should be interpreted as having a different significance than the increases for other fields. Unlike in literature or theater, publications on film aesthetics or criticism were almost nonexistent prior to the 1950s and quite scarce until the mid-1960s. The implications for the creation of artistic status are different in a case where there is an increase from some established level to an even greater level, than in a case where there is an increase from nearly zero to

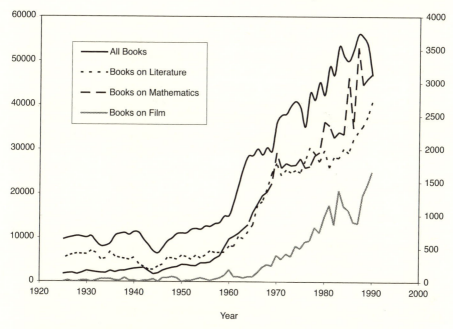

Figure 3.4. All Books versus Books from Three Fields. Note: Data on film books have been scaled to fit on second y-axis.

a moderate level. Prior to the 1960s there was no real body of academic work on film criticism or aesthetics. In contrast, thousands of books on the aesthetics or criticism or literature and the aesthetics or criticism of theater or drama had been published. The increase in film books, therefore, although mirrored by increases elsewhere, was significant for the diffusion of the idea of film as art.

The figures on publications pertain to the art world for film generally, rather than for Hollywood films per se. While some of the publications were specifically about Hollywood, many were not. In the same way, academic courses and programs on film covered film both inside and outside Hollywood. The evidence about the link to academia is still relevant, however, because in the United States the growth of an art world for Hollywood films closely followed the growing awareness of any film as art. In the United States, interest in film as art got a kick-start from an artistic interest in European films, but the broadening of that interest led quite quickly to acceptance of the art in Hollywood. This link between acceptance of the European films as art and acceptance of Hollywood films was facilitated by the fact that French theorists had already made the case for Hollywood films as art.

In addition to the increases in film study programs and in books on film aesthetics or criticism, film scholars claim that the legitimacy of film studies within the academy has steadily grown (Blades 1976; Bywater and Sobchak 1989; Easton 1997). The academic study of film has become not only more prevalent in recent decades, but also more highly respected. Such respect is both representative of and contributes to the acceptance of film as a valid form of art. As centers of cultural authority, universities were an important part of the new field of film insofar as they provided legitimacy for the intellectualization of a form of entertainment.

The American Film Institute (AFI)

The long-term success of art worlds requires the institutionalization of resources to preserve, disseminate, instruct, and advance art forms. Such institutionalization can come in various forms. For instance, art museums often perform these functions for painting and sculpture. Nonprofit opera companies provide the organizational support required to put on expensive opera productions. Dance studios must be established in order to train dancers in the techniques of modern dance. In the same way, Hollywood films required institutional support. While film scholarship and training had begun to occur in universities, the art world for Hollywood films benefited from the creation of organizations devoted specifically to advancing the art of American film.

The most important effort outside a university context to institutionalize resources devoted to the intellectual study of American film has been the American Film Institute. There is some historical debate regarding the credit due to some of the figures involved, but plans for the AFI were announced by Lyndon Johnson when he signed the National Arts and Humanities Act on September 29, 1965.

That Act also established the National Endowment for the Arts (NEA), which provided most of the funding for the AFI as an independent, nonprofit nongovernmental organization. As Johnson signed the legislation that enacted the NEA, he said, "We will create an American Film Institute, bringing together leading artists of the film industry, outstanding educators, and young men and women who wish to pursue this twentieth-century art form as their life's work" (quoted in Yoffe 1983:16). According to McBride (1983:1), the stated goals of the AFI were to "advance the understanding and recognition of the moving image as an art form, to help preserve film and video for future generations, and to develop new talent."

As with most young institutions, the AFI had difficult beginnings, and as with most young institutions, the difficulties had to do with funding. While the AFI served to reinforce the needs of an art world for Hollywood films, its very existence first required a baseline level of faith in an art world for Hollywood films. Funding for arts, as now, was spotty enough for the most established of them; for film it was still worse. Nevertheless, there was enough faith to get the AFI running, and its first director was George Stevens Jr.

Although the AFI, like other arts institutes, drew funds from agencies such as the National Council of the Arts, the Ford Foundation, and the National Endowment for the Arts, it was fortunate to have industry sources to rely on, such as the Motion Picture Association of America. Additional funding has come from individual members of the film community as well as the major studios.

A primary justification for the AFI was film preservation. Because all films shot before 1950 used nitrate film stock, the original negatives of American films were at risk of being lost forever due to disintegration. In addition, without a central repository for films, many were lost due to mismanagement or lack of interest. In fact, there was little interest in film preservation from the industry itself during the first several decades of commercial cinema. During that period, prior to television or home video, the only revenue to be gained from films was through their initial theatrical release (King 2002). The archives of many major studios are far from complete, and the original negatives of many of Hollywood's most famous and well-loved productions are lost (King 2002). The AFI, then, facilitates the archiving and cataloging of films in conjunction with other organizations such as the Library of Congress, and it has been instrumental in the preservation of thousands of historic films.

The training of film artists was another justification for the AFI. After the dissolution of the studio system, there were far fewer opportunities for directors, particularly, to apprentice and to learn on the job. Although it had not been clear at the outset what form the educational arm of the AFI would take, the AFI in 1969 established the Center for Advanced Film Studies, which McBride (1983) reports was intended as a graduate school. The educational mission of the AFI ostensibly sought to foster the talent and vision of young film artists, but realistically it also needed to teach the practical skills the industry required as well as to initiate useful industry contracts. Today the program is called the AFI Conservatory and it offers master of fine arts degrees in six disciplines: cinematography, directing, editing, producing, production design, and screenwriting.

The tension between the artistic and commercial goals of the AFI were also evident in the Institute's other major goal, that of film scholarship. As Callenbach (1971) notes, there has been controversy since the beginning surrounding the degree to which the AFI should focus on scholarly research and publication. The industry funding on which the AFI came to rely was rarely dedicated to serious intellectual work as defined by the standards of art history or cultural studies scholarship. But in the early years of the AFI, there were many serious and well-publicized efforts to promote film as art. For example, seminar series in which directors participated to discuss their films as art were high profile. Also, film screenings helped to raise awareness of film classics and to contribute to the development of the American film canon.

It is not an easy task to promote the art of Hollywood in an environment so clearly focused on returning profits on multimillion dollar investments. As will be discussed in chapter 5, the tension between disinterested art and commerce has always been an important limitation in the degree to which Hollywood productions can be consecrated as high art. All the same, the AFI has had a hand in helping win broad acceptance of the idea that Hollywood films can be art.

UNITED STATES, ENGLAND, GERMANY, ITALY, AND FRANCE: CHANGES IN THE INDUSTRIAL AND SOCIAL HISTORY OF FILM

The creation of film festivals and ties to academia, and the self-promotion of directors are film world developments that were intended to advance the legitimacy of Hollywood films as art. Just as with any art form, it takes many participants serving in various capacities to first of all produce the art (and film is one of the most collective of art forms to produce) and then to exhibit and evaluate the art in ways that are appropriate for art. It takes true believers in the merit of film as art to do the work that is necessary for the wider public to understand how and why film is art.

In addition to these focused activities, there were other changes within the film world that were not designed to advance film as art, but nevertheless contributed to that effort. The following sections of this chapter examine several major changes in the film world and discuss how they influenced perceptions of the artistic nature of filmmaking. The current section compares the historical conditions of film production in the United States and those countries that initially led European production—England, Germany, Italy, and France. This comparison is analytically useful because it allows us to judge how production practices varied with acceptance of film as art. The historical record shows that instead of fitting two discrete categories, it appears that there was a continuum in the degree to which production conditions encouraged the acceptance of film as art among the countries. While conditions within the film world in the United States strongly militated against film as art, conditions in England were somewhat less of an obstacle, and those in Germany, Italy, and especially France were more encouraging.

Pre–World War II Production Conditions

In both Europe and the United States, the definition of what art is depends partly on an opposition between creative and commercial activities. Ideally, artists are uniquely talented individuals motivated to create art by a need to express themselves (Becker 1982:ch.1). Profit seeking is thought to detract from the nobility inherent in the artistic process. As Bourdieu (1993:ch.3) argues, only the pursuit of nonmaterial success is considered "legitimate" in the field of artistic production.[21] Commercial activities are, on the surface, incongruent with the aims of an art world and more in line with entertainment and amusement.[22] These norms surrounding cultural production have important implications for the status of film as art and can help to explain why film achieved that status earlier in Europe than in the United States.

Although during the first decade of the twentieth century the film industries in France and Italy had been larger than the industry in the United States, World War I altered the situation substantially. "After 1914 those countries directly engaged in the war drastically curtailed their film production: celluloid and high explosives are made from the same ingredients. The Italian, French, and English studios suffered a subsequent decline that was to last a generation or more" (Knight 1957:51). There is some debate about whether Germany's studios declined, as Sklar (1994:46) reports, or whether "the German film industry expanded during the war" (Elsaesser 1996:139), but there is nonetheless agreement that after several years, the German film industry was in a stronger position than the industries in the other European countries (Saunders 1994:5). Despite this strength within Europe, the industry was economically weak in comparison with Hollywood. Armes (1985:71) compares Hollywood and German production: "What is particularly striking is the contrast in tactics adopted by the two giants: the one seeking supremacy through the sheer quantity of films produced for immediate local production while the other sought successfully to create a prestige product that could be marketed worldwide." A small number of prestige productions could never be as profitable as a large number of productions for mass consumption. It was clear by the end of World War I that the American film industry dominated the world market (Knight 1957:107) and "was said to produce some 85 percent of the films shown throughout the world and 98 percent of those shown in America" (Sklar 1994:47). American production consistently far outstripped that of France (Crisp 1993:11), England (Hartog 1983:59), Germany (Saunders 1994:10), and Italy (Buss 1989:2). Thompson and Bordwell (1994:85) provide the following figures:

> Throughout the silent era, industry experts believed that French production was in a crisis. In 1929, for instance, France made 68 features,

while Germany produced 220 and the United States 562. Even in 1926, the worst pre-Depression year for European production, Germany had managed 202 films to France's 55, while Hollywood outstripped both with about 725. In 1928, one of the best years for the Europeans, France made 94 films, compared with 221 for Germany and 641 for the United States.

By the 1920s, then, Hollywood had become a global capital for film-making. The city itself came to represent an emergent industry that was perceived to epitomize both wealth and glamour. Filmmaking in the United States was a lucrative mass culture industry. In contrast, the film industry in European countries was characterized by financial difficulties and varying degrees of government stewardship and subsidization. No-well-Smith et alia claim that "Italian film production between 1905 and 1931 can hardly be described as an *industry*" (1996:1, italics in original). In prewar decades when the number of films produced rose steadily, this expansion "was driven by motives other than profit," and filmmaking "was often associated with traditional systems of artistic patronage (numerous Italian aristocrats subsidised early films)" (Nowell-Smith et al. 1996:1). In addition, the "Italian industry did not have enough of a home audience to support either a comprehensive star system or a studio system founded on mammoth production for the popular market" (Buss 1989:7). Consequently, the domestic film-production industry collapsed. Usai (1996:123) provides some sobering numbers about Italian film production: "In 1912 an average of three films a day were released (1,127 in total, admittedly many of them short); in 1931 only two feature films in the entire year."

Similar predicaments faced the industries of Germany, England, and France. Although output increased in Germany following World War I, "the industry never rested on a firm financial basis" (Ott 1986:26). During the time of the Weimar Republic, much of the output from producers "was experimental" (discussed further below) "and lacked solid commercial underpinnings" (Saunders 1994:12). English production was likewise hobbled; "there was no concentration of production to rival Hollywood, the industry as a whole was under-capitalized. . . . [T]alent was not richly rewarded in the way that it was in Hollywood. . . . as a result there was a steady stream of British acting talent across the Atlantic to Hollywood" (Armes 1979:32). In France, too, the native industry suffered from a small native market, as well as poor organization that caused widespread financial hardship (Bardeche and Brassilach 1938:226).

France, however, was the only European film-producing country where the government did not provide assistance to the industry before the 1930s (Knight 1957:93). The creation of the largest and most productive film studio in Germany, Universum Film A.G., was achieved through co-operation between the government and private firms. The industry bene-fited from the extension of loans and subsidies to various firms in Ger-many during the 1920s (Monaco 1996:31), and government sponsor-ship and frequent direction of the industry increased in the 1930s under the Nazi regime. The Italian industry was shaped to a still greater extent through national public, economic, and cultural policy accompa-nying the rise to power of Fascism in 1922 (Nowell-Smith et al. 1996:3). At that time the state "set up an infrastructure for the Italian cinema industry that was to provide a solid basis for its post-war development by creating the Istituto LUCE, the Ente Nazionale Industrie Cinemato-grafiche, ENAIPE (the state body for importing films), film clubs, Cine-citta and the Venice Festival" (in 1932) (Buss 1989:12). Government as-sistance in Britain came in the form of legislation restricting the number of American imports (Armes 1979:73). Various forms of restrictions were eventually legislated in Germany, France, and Italy as well to bolster do-mestic production.

In sum, the European film industries produced fewer films for fewer people, often requiring government assistance to do so. And as we saw in chapter 2, while film was sometimes a mass entertainment in Europe, it was also frequently enjoyed by intellectuals and higher SES audiences. In contrast it was mainly populist in the United States. The end result was that in Europe there was a weaker link between domestic film-making on the one hand and the creation of wealth and the operation of an oligarchical system of studios on the other. In America, however, this link was strong and salient in the public mind thanks to the glamorous image of Hollywood.

Because filmmaking in the United States was a large scale and profitable business run by a few large studios, it was also, under these conditions, similar to assembly-line production. Staiger (1985) describes the histori-cal evolution of modes of production in the American film industry. Be-tween 1896 and 1907, films were made according to the "cameraman" system of production, the defining quality of which was the location of both conception and execution of the film from start to finish in one per-son. Between 1907 and 1909, the predominant mode of production was the "director" system, in which "one individual staged the action and another person photographed it" (117). At this point the terms "pro-ducer" and "director" were used synonymously, as there was very little division of labor in the filmmaking process. The director was responsible for managing virtually all aspects of the film.

From 1909 to 1914, as demand for films greatly increased, the predomi-nant mode of production became the "director-unit" system. To meet the increased demand, production was systematized so that "all the compo-

nents to produce a film resided within a predictable set of employees"
(Staiger 1985:121) whose work was now separated and subdivided "into
departmentalized specialities with a structural hierarchy" (124). Profit
maximization goals, with an emphasis on efficiency and "scientific management," encouraged a shift to a "central producer" system in 1914,
which "centralized the control of production under the management of
a producer" (128) whose job was "planning the work and estimating
production costs, through a detailed script" (135). The work of the producer and the director was now split, and a great deal of control over
how films were made rested with the producer.

A shift to the "producer-unit" system in 1931 meant that producers
would give more specialized attention to only a few films at any one time,
necessitating an increase in the number of producers working for a studio.
Producers could then more closely observe and control day-to-day opera-
tions and costs for the movies under their jurisdiction. The "producer-
unit" system stayed in place until approximately the mid-1950s. As will
be discussed in greater depth, this mode of production contrasts with the
mode common in European industries as well as to the one that was to
follow in the American industry, which was to be more conducive to perceiving the production of film as an artistic process.

Among the major European studios, the mode of production in British
studios was most similar to the American, and the French mode the least
so. The studio system, where approximately five to eight major studios
produced the vast majority of films, not only in the country but also in
the world, was unique to the United States. Beginning in the late 1920s,
the English industry came to more closely resemble the American industry
insofar as a relatively high percentage of the films produced (although
there were far fewer in total) came from a small number of producing
companies (Ryall 1997:28). Hawkridge (1996:136) notes that "By the
end of the 1920s the British film industry was transformed. The shift to
vertical integration established a stronger industrial base, and . . . the pro-
tective legislation introduced in 1927 did also lead to an expansion of
the industry."

The German film industry was more decentralized than the British. In
Germany, although the number of films produced declined from 646 in
1921 to 228 in 1925, the number of producing companies rose from 131
in 1918 to 230 in 1920, 360 in 1922, and to 424 in 1929 (Ott 1986:29).
Many companies produced only one or two films in a year, and some
fewer than that.

Before the 1920s, Italian production was also highly decentralized.
However, the number of studios declined dramatically after World War I,
from a height of approximately five hundred (Nowell-Smith et al.
1996:1). This can be accounted for by the decline in film production,

which dropped to fewer than fifteen films nationally per year (Buss 1989:8). Likewise in France, "instead of a half dozen or so large studios grinding out a year's supply of pictures for their affiliated theaters, most of the studios were small, their facilities rented by production firms often set up specifically to make a single picture" (Knight 1957:93). Thompson and Bordwell (1994:86) provide a detailed explanation for the decentralized structure of the French film industry in the 1920s, pointing to "domestic business traditions" wherein French industry in general was dominated by smaller companies rather than larger corporations formed through mergers. They also point out that the vast majority of theaters and production firms were privately owned by individuals. Thompson and Bordwell argue that the tendency toward small production companies was self-perpetuating: as an inherently risky business endeavor, production companies had often struggled, and this history of high risk discouraged the large investments out of which large companies could be created. They note that in the late 1920s the budget of the average French film was one-tenth the budget of the average Hollywood film.

Crisp (1993:37) notes that the French industry was highly disorganized well into the 1930s and lacked "the legislative framework or any strong internal professional regulation" that could have developed the industry beyond its "patchwork" nature. There are many ways to make a film. As a complex product of a complex production process, films involve an enormous amount of decision-making and collaborative input. The nature of that cooperative effort, however, is shaped by the organizational and industrial conditions of production. In Hollywood's studio system, the director's opinion was subordinate to the producer's, and the producer was responsible for hiring the director and managing his, and everyone else's, work (Staiger 1985:136). As a consequence, in the 1920s directors were virtually unknown to the public and were simply assigned by studios to work on pictures (Knight 1957:130).

In contrast, the French mode of production "allowed for a high degree of directorial control over the production process" (Crisp 1993:307) such that "the least regarded director in France enjoyed the degree of control and decision making enjoyed by the most favored 10–15% of directors in Hollywood" (Crisp 1993:309). What is more, unlike in the United States, an "overwhelming percentage of the directors had fine arts or university training" (Crisp1993:159).[23]

In Germany and Italy, as well, the role of the director was more substantial than it was in Hollywood, while in England a large amount of control and responsibility in film production rested with the producer (Armes 1979:Ch.5), a situation more similar to the American mode of production.

The very different production conditions and backgrounds of directors can be cited as leading to the strikingly different paths taken by European and Hollywood directors. German Expressionism, French Impressionist film, and the Italian neorealist cinema that was to come in the 1940s represent trends in filmmaking that were avant-garde, more experimental, and less commercial than the various Hollywood traditions (Rees 1996:96).

In sum, the pre–World War II American film industry was the most out of line with expectations concerning the nature of artistic production. The mode and scale of production in England was somewhat less so, and those in Germany and Italy conformed rather well with expectations concerning artistic production. It was conditions in France that most closely resembled those of established art worlds, as indicated by its relatively low levels of capitalization, corporatization, and centralization, and its high level of orientation toward directorial control over production.

The Transition from the Studio System to Director-Centered Production

Until the 1950s, Hollywood films were made according to the studio system whereby directors (as well as actors) were signed to a contract with a studio that obliged them to make the films that the studios, which retained a great deal of creative control, were interested in having made (Tuska 1991:Introduction). The studio system began to dissolve following the 1948 Supreme Court ruling that the incorporation of production and exhibition facilities was monopolistic (Mordden 1988:367). The studios were forced to divest themselves of their theater holdings. "With no guarantee of exhibition, fewer movies could be made" (Mordden 1988:368). Faced with legal troubles of vertical control, shrinking potential profits, and uncertain of which films to make, the studios changed their production method by leasing studio space to independent directors to make their own films (Phillips 1990:16).

The significance of this change in the way films were made is tied to notions about the nature of art and artists. The new method of production allowed directors to foster an image of independence.[24] As mentioned, in earlier decades directors were largely unknown and perceived as technical workers in the process of film production. As a result, the major studios based their marketing efforts on the actors and attached no importance to the publicity potential of directors (Knight 1957:130).

In the years following the abandonment of the studio system, a new school of thought regarding film was imported to the United States from France. Film criticism in Europe, particularly in France in the *Cahiers du cinéma*, had developed along different lines. In the mid- to late 1950s the

French *nouvelle vague* elaborated an approach to the appreciation of film that by the 1960s had stimulated a new form of American film criticism (Sarris 1968). As mentioned, this approach was auteurism, which posits that it is the director who is the driving artistic force in filmmaking, and that to understand a film correctly requires paying close attention to effects of the director's creative choices on a film's content. The director is responsible for integrating "the contributions of cast and crew into a unified whole" (Phillips 1990:11). Moreover, the theory notes that auteurs are recognizable for their ability to shape films according to their personal visions within the economic and organizational confines of production.

The importation of auteurism was set in motion by a 1962 seminal essay by Andrew Sarris, "Notes on the Auteur Theory." By the late 1960s there existed "a critical mass of influential journalistic reviewers who in the years to come would prove to be staunch supporters of the auteur perspective" (Kapsis 1992:101). Auteurism eventually enjoyed general, though not complete, acceptance among journalistic writers on film and also had many supporters among academic critics.[25] An important implication of the adoption of auteurism is that film criticism was provided a powerful tool for connecting with existing beliefs about the nature of art and artists (Zolberg 1990:7). By emphasizing the autonomy and individuality of the director, auteurism conforms to Romanticist notions about art and to the "'charisma' ideology which is the ultimate basis of belief in the value of a work of art" (Bourdieu 1980:263). True art requires the input of a unique genius. Bywater and Sobchak (1989:53) write, "One of the aims, then, of *auteurism*, is to justify an intellectual interest in an area that had previously been considered simply mass culture, the products of which, like paperback romances and detective fiction, were formerly beneath intellectual scrutiny. Where there's an artist, there must be an art."

White and White (1965), in their study of the transition from the academic to the dealer-critic system of the production of paintings in nineteenth-century France, argue that just such an ideology moved the recognition of genius from a quality of the painting to a quality of the painter. Critics, who were interested in establishing their reputations as influential intellectuals, were successful in promulgating this theory in part because it was in harmony with other themes concerning the role of painters and other artists. When film reviewers focused on the film as a whole, there was little familiar ground for grouping film with the other arts. If no true genius could be specifically located (the actor? cameraman? editor? producer?), then it was difficult to maintain that a film could be a work of art.[26] It was a large-scale collaboration produced by specialized workers, as with an automobile.

What is more, film's technological nature and its organization as an industry worked against it, particularly when influential Frankfurt School thinkers were highly critical of "mass culture" on both political and aesthetic grounds (see chapter 2). Auteurism, however, provided a rationale for film as art that both countered mass culture objections and corresponded to popular notions of the relationship between an artist/ genius and the work of art. Films were now safe to appreciate because they were perceived to be the creation of artists rather than the products of an industry.

The importation of auteurism to the United States in the 1960s closely followed major changes in the structuring of the motion picture industry. This restructuring provided directors working in Hollywood with new-found independence. Europe had its auteurs (e.g., Jean Renoir, Sergei Eisenstein, Rene Clair, G. W. Pabst) as early as the 1920s and 1930s. Of course, the film industry in Europe had never been fully oriented toward commercial interests, and filmmakers had never been constrained by a studio system. Yet they were available as a model for how directors should be perceived. Auteur theory, with its claims for artistic status for directors and their work, became a viable perspective to apply to films, both new and old.

How Conditions of Artistic Production Influence Perceptions of Artistic Legitimacy

The U. S. film industry was the world leader in film production following World War I while also receiving no government subsidies. The size of the American audience supported a film market of several hundred productions per year, which in turn encouraged the evolution of a studio system. In this system it was difficult to hold up examples of autonomous, freely creative artists. There was, therefore, a disjuncture between how films were made and the need for public recognition of artists in order to view their products as art.

To varying degrees, production conditions differed in European countries. There were the most similarities between the American and British film industries and in the social conditions under which they operated. There were far fewer similarities between American production and the German and Italian industries. The French film industry was least similar to the American, and can be seen to represent a set of conditions that was relatively conducive to the promotion and diffusion of the idea that film was a properly artistic medium. With the major legal and economic changes that turned the industry on its head in the postwar period, the production practices of American studios changed drastically. Director-centered production brought the American industry much closer to European modes of production and more consistent with public expectations concerning artistic production.[27]

Within the sociology of culture, the most detailed and systematic analysis of the underlying mechanisms of artistic legitimacy is Bourdieu's (1993) work on fields of cultural production. This work provides a useful set of terms and concepts to articulate the causal links between changing production conditions for film and its increasing artistic legitimacy.

As discussed in chapter 1, Bourdieu's concept of a "field" of cultural production focuses on the relations between cultural producers and consumers. Through the concept of field, Bourdieu has examined cultural production in an effort to explain, among other things, the dynamics of cultural consecration and the process whereby certain cultural products and practices legitimately gain and retain high status. A field is "a separate social universe having its own laws of functioning independent of those of politics and the economy . . . and which is constituted as it establishes its autonomy" (Bourdieu 1993:163). The concept of field is especially useful for analyzing intellectual endeavors, and one can speak of a large number of fields—literary, philosophical, educational, juridical, medical, and so forth.

Fields, then, are separate, with autonomy and their own laws, and they are functionally differentiated. How are such characteristics manifested? Perhaps the best way to conceptualize a cultural field is to imagine ourselves in the shoes of an artist. Let us take the case of a film director in the 1960s, one who is sincere about making films in order to express personal messages, create beauty, and experiment with aesthetic conventions. If an artist is well integrated into a field, he or she will be aware of a complex system of evaluation for art works in that field; the way films are evaluated, for instance, will be different from the way theater is evaluated.

The first difference is in the substance of the art. There are certain canonic film works whose characteristics can act as touchstones from which experimentation should take place. In this way, there is a film vocabulary and grammar. *Birth of a Nation* (1915), in which D. W. Griffith invented many of the standards for narrative storytelling in film, is one such touchstone. *Citizen Kane* (1941) is another. A film artist needs to be conversant in the conventions of film for successful experimentation to take place.

A second difference is in the sources of recognition. In addition to knowing the language of film conventions, a film artist will be familiar with the field's specialized system for recognizing excellence. Artistic merit will be bestowed by winning the right awards at the right film festivals; by being of interest to and approved by the right film scholars;

by being well reviewed by the right critics; and by recognition from other highly regarded film artists. A film artist will seek this symbolic capital. To the extent that sources for obtaining this symbolic capital exist, the field is independent. But independent of what? The answer is that the field is more independent from the ruling logic of the rest of society: the marketplace. In consumer society, economic capital is the ultimate goal. Through our production activities, our labor, we seek the capital that is available in the field of economic production—money. The economic field is the larger field or the context within which other, more specific ones operate.

This is what makes cultural production special. Legitimate art is created within fields of production whose logic strays from that of the marketplace. Artists seek not economic capital, but symbolic capital, which moreover, is field specific. Winning the Booker Prize is not meaningful to a film director; it is an inappropriate currency in the field of film. The field of film has its own awards. So the seeking of these awards, and symbolic capital from other sources within the field, is what film artists do.

Now that we see how fields of cultural production in general operate, we can move on to a more subtle distinction between different kinds of fields of cultural production. In Bourdieu's (1993:ch.3) analysis, a natural division exists within fields of cultural production between large-scale and restricted production. In fields of restricted production, cultural goods are produced for an audience whose members are primarily cultural producers themselves. This is a relatively small audience with a great deal of cultural capital available for appreciating art. In contrast, fields of large-scale production are organized to create cultural goods that will appeal to nonproducers of cultural goods and as large a market as possible. These two categories represent ends of a continuum along which all cultural production can be classified. Symbolist poetry is a good example of a field of restricted production. The audience for Symbolist poetry is small (even smaller than the audience for poetry in general), and the audience members are quite often poets or authors themselves. Rock music is a good example of a field of large-scale production. A major goal of the producers of rock music is to appeal to as many people as possible, the vast majority of whom are not musicians and who require little cultural capital to appreciate the music.

Bourdieu argues that there is a fundamental opposition between the logic of restricted fields and the logic of large-scale fields. In the most restricted fields, there is an unwavering focus on the enhancement of a cultural product's symbolic value. Critical success trumps economic success or popular success. For works that consistently find audiences for decades—"classics" that were never blockbuster successes—there is some added value in the long-time accumulation of economic capital because "standing the test of time" is one of the most prestigious criteria for awarding symbolic capital. In this way, economic capital still has a place in restricted fields of production. Contrarily, the generation of capital in fields of large-scale production is focused on quick returns on investments, just as in other, noncultural, fields of production that follow economic principles more directly. Adherence to these principles makes large-scale fields, in an analytical as well as in a real sense, dependent on the economic field. Restricted fields enjoy much more autonomy because they develop their own criteria for the production, consumption, and evaluation of their products. All cultural fields of production can be located on a continuum with restricted production at one end and large-scale production at the other.

The purpose of describing here Bourdieu's analysis of fields of cultural production is to understand how changing modes of film production are related to the increased legitimacy of Hollywood films as art. It is important to recognize, then, that those fields of cultural production that function in a manner closer to the restricted end of the continuum (e.g., painting, sculpture, poetry, opera) produce goods that are more readily acceptable as art. This acceptance reveals a cultural bias that is derived from Romanticist norms concerning the role of artists and what art properly is. True art is inspired by genius and by innate talent. In fields of large-scale production the explicit focus on profits is incompatible with these Romanticist notions. The cultural products of large-scale production are therefore suspect as art (e.g., popular music, television shows, romance novels).[28]

Hollywood filmmaking has never and will never occur on the restricted scale on which poetry occurs. Nevertheless, it is important to recognize the variation in the kind of production that was taking place both in the film world in general and within Hollywood. Many European productions of earlier decades (although not currently) could be characterized as operating within a field of restricted production. Take, for example, the Impressionist films of 1920s French directors such as Jean Epstein and Germaine Dulac. These directors made films with tiny budgets and sought to experiment with film as art, even if they did not explicitly disavow profit potential. Some of their films veered toward the mainstream of French cinema enough to see some profit, in contrast to the Surrealist school, whose films "could never reconcile popular and intellectual audiences" (Lanzoni 2002:49). Nevertheless, their expressed purpose was artistic success and recognition from other artists and knowledgeable audience members. This was not the blockbuster formula.

Hollywood films have always been profit oriented. But one of the most significant changes in Hollywood following the studio era is the perception that some directors were working under conditions similar to re-

stricted production. When the old formulas had begun to fail, when director-centered production became the norm, when TV became the default
drama for the masses, studios did not know what to do.[29]

And so they gave directors freedom to seek their own artistic vision,
and these directors discussed their freedom to make the films they wanted
to make like it was an inalienable right. They played down the industry
expectations that the freedom was meant to translate into good box office,
and instead played up their own expectations that the freedom would
translate into artistic success. They were not making films in order to pack
theaters on opening weekend. They wanted recognition from their peers
and from the critics (the ones who were fair-minded, anyway). Directors
put forth a fantasy image of filmmaking as a field of restricted production,
an image that film reviewers and the press participated in constructing,
not because any of these groups wanted to deceive, but rather because
they all wanted it to be true. In reality, the economics of film production
had not changed so drastically. Profits were still paramount to the ability
of filmmakers to continue to find work, and film was still a field of mass
production. But this reality was downplayed in order to project an alternate image that better matched emerging values and preferences.

Purification through Venue:
From Nickelodeons to Art Houses

Intimately tied to the changing economic conditions of the industry was
the mode of exhibition for films. As Levine (1988) and DiMaggio (1982;
1992) have argued, the nature of the physical space for artistic exhibition
has implications for the status imputations that audience members will
make. Decisions concerning where to exhibit a cultural product can influence both the composition of the audience and the kind or genre of
culture that is included—and by extension the culture that is excluded—
for exhibition. In the cases discussed by Levine and DiMaggio, the desig-
nation of separate theaters for legitimate drama, of museums for painting
and sculpture, of opera houses separate from venues for other forms of
musical theater, and of symphony halls separate from other venues for
popular music, all contributed to the legitimation of these cultural products as art. Similarly, Peterson argues that the performance of jazz in "concert halls, academic workshops, and recording studios" contributed to
the creation of a fine art element in jazz (1972:146).

Between the turn of the century and the late 1960s, the exhibition of
American cinema experienced a similar transition. While the initial mode
of exhibition contributed to impressions of film as disreputable and unsa-

vory, developments in the 1950s and 1960s helped to more clearly isolate a high art element in film from which the status of the medium of film as a whole benefited.

The beginnings of exhibition in nickelodeons have been detailed in chapter 2. Thereafter, the industry more aggressively sought to widen its audience. The primary strategy for achieving this goal was not to change the nature of the films being shown, but instead to change the nature of film exhibition. By the 1920s the largest studios had begun to buy and construct theaters for showing their films as part of a business plan that sought to vertically integrate the companies, giving them full control over production, distribution, and exhibition. Many of the new theaters were palatial (Stones 1993:35). They were often enormous, seating several thousand people, and they commonly had exotic décor (e.g., The Egyptian, The Oriental). The new theaters were constructed with exacting attention to detail and luxuriously outfitted.

The strategy worked. As Sklar describes, "working-class people appreciated amenities as much as anyone else: the larger and more pretentious the theaters, the greater numbers they drew" (1994:45). And yet, the new theaters also managed to "expunge the working-class neighborhood character from the movie going experience to make it more respectable in the eyes of the middle class" (quoted in Baxter 1993:25). The "movie palaces" of the 1920s both broadened the socioeconomic base for the film audience and helped to increase the total size of that audience.

Many theaters were still small and not luxurious, especially in rural areas. However, the majority of filmgoers were going to downtown theaters in large cities, and these tended to be the newly constructed "movie palaces." Such palaces were step one in a chain of transformations in film exhibition. The first step did not achieve the goal of making Hollywood films believable as art. Rather, it made them more respectable. In the case of film, the journey toward art followed the path of increasing respectability. DiMaggio (1992) and Levine (1988) trace similar historical paths for the legitimation of the arts they study.

The next major change in the nature of film exhibition came in the 1930s. As described by Gomery, the subsequent strategy employed by film exhibitors to increase their market was the installation of air-conditioning. "Movie theaters were one of the few public institutions in which the middle-class and poor citizens of the United States could indulge in cool, dehumidified comfort until well into the 1950s. . . . The comparative advantage of air conditioning to movie exhibition in the United States during the 1930s and 1940s cannot be overestimated" (1992:76).

Like the previous strategy, this one successfully increased the total size of the audience. But it also further entrenched the practice of exhibiting films of every genre within the same theaters. It created more integration and worked against audience segregation by class.

The next major change in the way audiences viewed films was the post–World War II proliferation of drive-in theaters. In 1946 there were 102 drive-ins in the United States, approximately 1,000 in 1949, more than 3,000 in 1954, and 4,000 in 1958 (Stones1993:186). This trend was clearly related to suburbanization. Following World War II, theaters moved along with a portion of the population to the suburbs. Drive-ins were popular partly because they were novel and partly because of the conveniences they offered. Parking was, obviously, not difficult, unlike with most urban theaters; there was no need to dress up, as was common for a trip to the cinema; staying in the car made taking children and infants easier; and for many audience members, the outdoor theaters were closer and easier to get to (Stones 1993:183–94). The popularity of drive-ins did not represent an increase in the popularity of filmgoing, but rather a shift in where audiences saw films. There was a sharp decrease in filmgoing during the 1950s. However, this decrease might well have been more dramatic in the absence of drive-ins. Moreoever, the national statistics might obscure significant regional variations—it could be the case that filmgoing decreased less in warmer regions where drive-ins would have been more feasible year-round. Overall, this change in the mode of exhibition did not affect the composition of the audience; it merely reflected changing residential patterns.

The next major development in film exhibition was most influential on the status of film as art. Changing economic realities again altered the way that audiences were to view films. This was the art house movement, which began slowly in the 1950s and accelerated in the 1960s. Stones states that "in its purest definition, an 'art house' is a theater that caters to a specialized audience of film lovers, those who embrace movies as a serious art form akin to dance or literature" (1993:199). While art houses can be *defined* in terms of the audiences who patronize them and the types of films they show, the art house movement must be *explained* in reference to the economic conditions of the American film industry.

While art houses, specializing in showing foreign language (almost exclusively European) films, have existed since the 1920s, they were few in number and generally unsuccessful. Gomery argues that the many art house failures clearly demonstrate that audiences would not respond to a film-as-art policy and that "case after case" shows that art houses could not remain in business for long (1992:174). The only exceptions were theaters located in ethnic neighborhoods showing films from the native countries of the local residents. This situation changed drastically following the divorce of the major studios from their theater chains. The 1948 ruling against them by the Supreme Court, known as the *Paramount* case,[30] found that they had fixed admission prices and forced smaller exhibitors to take all of their output in order to get the "A" material, and by 1954 they had sold off all their theaters (Puttnam 1997:171). This decision was monumental, and the literature on the history of the film industry commonly remarks that it drastically altered the business models of both the studios and the theater owners. These newly independent theaters still needed to exhibit films. It was precisely during the 1950s, however, that the decline in cinema attendance and rising production costs forced the major American studios to curtail the number of films they made.

With more freedom now to choose where their films came from, and a shortage of domestic supply, many theaters looked to Europe for films to exhibit. Smaller theaters, in particular, were less able to afford the high rental cost of first-run major studio productions, and so were more likely to exhibit foreign films. Rather than responding to a preexisting strong demand for European films, theater owners were merely enacting a business strategy of putting *something* on the screen. They became venues for European films to avoid going out of business even though they "rarely espoused film as art" (Gomery 1992:181).

By 1956 the number of art cinemas had reached two hundred; ten years later it was five hundred; by the late 1960s (including film societies presenting the best of the European art cinema) the total exceeded one thousand (Gomery 1992:181).[31]

The art house served both the manifest function of exhibiting non-Hollywood films and the latent function of putting forth an example for U.S. audiences of how film could be art (Twomey 1956). Until this time, recognition of any film as art was limited mainly to intellectuals who valued the better European productions. Art house practices enhanced the status of film through the creation of a cinema experience that was much different from the traditional experience.[32]

The art house, both in name and in function, embodied the idea of film as art in its purest form. By showing only non-Hollywood productions, art houses allowed audiences to have a clear perspective of exactly what constituted cinematic art. By being able to refer to a body of work as artistic, the idea that film could be art was more convincing. By catering to primarily well-to-do and educated audiences who were also likely to attend other artistic performances (Gomery 1992:189), film as a genre could benefit by association from symbolic enhancement (Lieberson 2000:126–30).

Over time art houses began to exhibit controversial Hollywood films as well. In the 1960s the line between foreign films and Hollywood films was blurred rather than maintained by art houses. But art houses had served the useful function of increasing and broadening recognition of an art world for European film. From there it was a short step to doing the same for Hollywood films.

The economics of the industry had an important yet indirect impact first on the status of film as a genre and second on the status of Hollywood films, mediated through the mode of exhibition. Without the thought of manipulating definitions of film as art, studios and exhibitors did just that. In the early decades of the century, their efforts, if anything, discouraged a redefinition of film as art. Exhibition needs resulted in lumping audiences and genres together. After the Paramount decision brought an end to vertical integration and to the studio-owned chains, combined with shrinking audiences and a revived European industry, economic realities resulted in a mode of exhibition that encouraged a redefinition of film as art through the separation of audiences and genres.

PRESTIGE PRODUCTIONS

The actions of the American film industry's most important players, the major film studios, have contributed in various ways to the changing status of film. Earlier in this chapter I examined the influence of the changing mode of production at the major studios. While production methods are influential, they do not represent an attempt on the part of studios to alter perceptions concerning the status of film as art. They represent an effort to maximize profits, and the resulting change in artistic status was quite unintentional and indirect.

However, during the first several decades of commercial film, the studios needed to counteract damaging stereotypes and widespread disapproval of the film industry. Under such conditions, the studios were compelled to produce films that could help to cleanse the genre of its reputation as a medium of poor quality, as cheap, sensationalistic spectacle. Any given film is produced with the express purpose of creating a profit, not to elevate the status of an industry in which a studio's competitors are also operating. However, the recurring need to appeal, through more reputable products, to a segment of the population that was repelled or displeased by the predominant industry image, eventually had an influence on the overall nature and perception of the industry. Such efforts continued for approximately thirty years and facilitated the success of later efforts by studios to make film not only respectable but also prestigious. Although there is little evidence that studios were concerned with public perceptions of whether film was popularly defined as "art" per se, studios were interested in making a certain proportion of their films of higher technical quality, with respectable themes, and often linked to well-known works in other genres. The studios' efforts at making prestigious films, although motivated by a search for higher profits, then facilitated the acceptance of the claims of film as art being made by others in the film world.

As detailed earlier, the film industry had an inauspicious beginning in the United States. In response to these problems with respectability, in the first decade of the twentieth century the film studios imported film adaptations of classic novels and stage plays, starring established stage actors, such as those made by the French production company Film D'Art (Mast 1981:43). The showing of *Queen Elizabeth*, starring the famous stage actress Sarah Bernhardt, "handed the movies a tremendous up-market boost. Hitherto regarded as a pastime for the ignorant masses, the motion picture became socially respectable" (Eames 1985:8).

It is perhaps an overstatement to say that the importation of the Film D'Art films altered perceptions of the film genre single-handedly. Uricchio and Pearson (1993) recount the troubles the industry had during the first two decades of the century with its image as junk entertainment. To change this image, the film industry in the first two decades of the twentieth century tried to align itself with more esteemed entertainments and cultural institutions. To do so, the industry as a whole produced films dealing with literary, historical, and biblical subjects in order to "reposition itself in American society as a mass entertainment acceptable to all social formations rather than a cheap amusement" (1993:41).[33] Paramount Pictures went far to raise the status of some of its productions by creating a label for a production wing, Famous Players in Famous Plays, which would focus on "Class A" pictures (Mast 1981:98). Just as the label suggests, these films would feature well-known stage actors in well-known plays, linking these films to the respect accorded to legitimate theater (Eames 1985:8).

Universal studios employed a similar tactic. During the 1920s it produced expensive adaptations of *The Hunchback of Notre Dame* and of *The Phantom of the Opera*. For each, the method of exhibition was roadshowing, in which the film was shown at only one large theater and traveled to different cities, and the price of admission was higher than average (Hirschhorn 1983:14). Similar to Paramount, Universal created a separate label, Super-Jewel Productions, for its prestige pictures (Hirschhorn 1983:15).

In terms of their production values, studios continued to strive to gain respect for themselves and the films they put out. Warner Brothers's prestige films of the 1930s were meant to establish the studio as a competent production house and to make an example of itself as a "respectable" and "culturally proper" Hollywood studio (Roddick 1983:233–34). The movies were adapted from well-regarded literary and theatrical works, were expensively made, had long running times, and had a glossy, polished look. Warner Brothers was not unlike other studios in making some of its films according to these specifications. At Columbia Pictures in the 1940s the segmentation of production was institutionalized with the "quality" film at the apex and the "series" film at the base (Dick 1992:10).

An excellent example of a studio's efforts to generate prestige for a film is the case of Walt Disney's *Fantasia*. Luckett (1994:218) describes the studio's tactics, which included a great deal of publicity concerning the film's incorporation of classical music[34] and an endorsement from Igor Stravinsky, whose *The Rite of Spring* was featured in the film. Luckett (1994:219) notes that the aim of the publicity was not to sell the film as a work of art:

> Advance publicity of this kind clearly attempted to rework the cultural position of Disney, but rather than placing Disney in the position of disseminating high art in the guise of mass culture, this publicity seemed to position *Fantasia* as a product worthy of the elite. Efforts to build Disney's cultural capital indicated that *Fantasia* would be of interest to an audience new to Disney (who needed to be informed about the film).

The creation of prestige productions was essentially concerned with broadening the audience for film and therefore bringing in a larger proportion of the potential market. Ironically, another important tactic employed by Disney in the case of *Fantasia* was to restrict access to the film. Shown only in a few large cities at any one time, it was more difficult for audiences to see the film, "helping to construct its exhibition as a special event" (1994:228). To avoid missing out on profits, the exhibition runs were extended while "last-chance-to see-it" advertisements urged audiences to see the film months before the run was planned to end.

By the late 1940s audiences had come to expect the professionalism and craftsmanship of prestige productions in all films. "B" quality entertainment could be had for free on television. As Hirschhorn expresses it, "Mindless escapism was all very well but at 40 cents a throw it had to have a look of quality about it" (1983:156).

Although quality was a concern, "art" per se was not. Prestige productions were primarily designed to increase the size of the audience. Although some individual filmmakers may have been motivated by artistic impulses in working on these productions, the aim of the studios was clearly to generate profit. Redmonds and Mimura describe the situation at Paramount: "Under [Barney] Balaban, Paramount had been almost entirely free of any concept beyond pure entertainment. With the exception of *Lost Weekend* in 1944, the company had found that films with social significance did not pay off at the box office" (1980:243). Studio decisions were inevitably based on a calculation of what would sell tickets. In a 1950 interview with *Time* magazine, Darryl Zanuck, vice president in charge of production at Twentieth Century-Fox, said, "People will accept enlightenment if it is skillfully served to them. They will not go to the theater for enlightenment alone" (1950, June 12:72). In other words, because intellectual subject matter does not appeal to large audiences, it must be presented in an entertaining manner. Creative decisions, then, are not made with only artistic concerns in mind, lest the resulting production not bring in large audiences.

During the 1950s and 1960s, studios remained interested in capturing more highly educated audience members through enhancing the prestige of their films. This interest was amplified by the economic reality that the size of the film audience was declining rapidly while the audience makeup shifted. The composition of the audience changed (see chapter 2) as more working-class audience members stayed home to watch television and more highly educated patrons began or continued to go out to see films. Perceiving this new audience as more sophisticated, studios marketed their films appropriately. Roadshowing, as a method of exhibition, increased in the 1950s and 1960s. Roadshowing became especially appealing to studios following the divestiture of their theater chains, when "the emphasis shifted to the marketing of individual film titles . . . [t]he most prestigious films were the 'roadshows,' those high-profile, star-filled pictures that played exclusively in one theater in each major market" (Stones 1993:140). Twentieth Century-Fox in particular would release "important" films to certain theaters that became prestige houses and ran only roadshows on a reserved-seat basis (Solomon 1988:135). This practice aligned filmgoing with attendance at live theater, and was conceived both to set off certain films as high quality and to make a trip to the cinema a special event worth choosing over television.

Because the audience for films was shrinking during the 1950s and 1960s while production costs were simultaneously increasing, the function of film promotion changed. Balio describes the necessary shift studios made to heavy marketing of specific films to market niches (1987:197–201). Using documents from the archives of United Artists, Balio demonstrates how advertising campaigns "had the goal of delineating and controlling how the picture should be perceived and interpreted. By developing appropriate language and image, United Artists hoped that the media would 'read' the picture in a predetermined way" (1987:201). Prestige productions were marketed as important and exciting events to appeal to potential patrons of higher socioeconomic status. However, Balio is clear on the studio's intent, quoting a United Artists executive in Europe:

> It is clear to the mind of distributors who the audience is for their pictures. They do not have any intellectual pretentions [*sic*] about film as art. They are selling film as entertainment to a mass audience. They

hype the action, the sensational elements, the elements of the pictures that will grab an audience from the ages of from about 16 to around 30. (1987:219)

The film studios' prestige productions, and the production of prestige, progressed over time from a general effort to ameliorate the image of the industry or the entire studio's work to focused manipulation of perceptions concerning the quality of particular films. In doing so, the studios were responding to changing needs defined by evolving cultural, social, and economic contexts. When the integrity and respect of the industry were in doubt, prestige productions were useful to ward off accusations that films were debased and a threat to legitimate culture. The first line of defense for the studios was to link their products to other established art forms by adapting well-known novels and stage productions. The other primary means by which certain productions were designated as prestigious was through devoting a great deal of additional expense in order to ensure that those films appeared well crafted. The sound needed to be clear, the lighting correctly illuminating, the editing smooth, and the sets and costumes visually appealing. Of course, such changes can partly be explained by the advancement of technology. However, even the best technology can be improperly employed without due effort and attention to detail.

It is fitting that the studios were not intending to convince the public, through added expense and enhancing the glossiness of production values, that certain films were art. In fact, expense and glossiness accentuated the extent to which film was a collaborative venture and a big-business venture. As discussed previously, perceptions of what art properly is are at odds with the role of commerce in cultural production. It is precisely those films that do not appear to be studios' most expensive and fussed over products, films that are more directly the expression of an individual artist, that resonate as art for audiences.[35] Although these expensive productions did *not* redefine film as art, they *were* a precursor to such a redefinition. As Solomon notes, the studios advertised with the phrase "millions in the making" in an effort to equate cost with quality (1988:107). "Quality" cultural products can be termed middlebrow, and middlebrow status moved film one step away from lowbrow and one step toward highbrow. By raising the status of film to a reputable cultural realm, rather than shoddy junk entertainment, these productions made the later leap to film as art easier to accept for the general public.[36]

By the 1950s and 1960s, the film industry in general had established its value. The development of prestige products focused on marketing particular films to a broader audience, to draw in audience members of higher socioeconomic status. The most important way in which certain films were packaged as prestigious was through an exclusive mode of exhibition. Roadshowing, although in use for prestige productions since the 1920s, became a common way of setting off cinema attendance as a cultural event. In these three ways—linkage to established arts, expensive production, and exclusive exhibition—studios generated prestige for their products. Although the studios were not aiming to position their products as art, and did not do so through these means, these actions can be seen as having contributed to the eventual redefinition of film as an artistic genre.

THE EBB OF CENSORSHIP AND THE COMING OF ART

One of the most important developments in the film world that facilitated a redefinition of film as art was the relaxation of censorship. Before the 1950s, the American film industry was subject to stringent regulations, mostly self-imposed, concerning the content of the films produced. Although censorship of films existed in Europe, that censorship varied depending on changing political regimes and, unlike in the United States, was not based on the characterization of film as degenerate and dangerous. Following legal decisions that won constitutional protection for film under the First Amendment in the 1950s, censorship both from within and without the industry abated in the United States.

The consequences of this evolution in the nature of censorship are twofold. First, the legal decisions served to reinforce and institutionalize characterizations of the nature of film. Second, the resulting relaxation of censorship permitted an evolution in the content of American film production that in turn brought films more in line with prevailing norms concerning the role and thematic concerns of art.

Censorship in the United States and Europe, 1900–1952

The history of censorship in the American film industry is almost as old as the industry itself. As early as 1907, the city of Chicago enacted a law to censor inappropriate film themes (Couvares 1996:2). May reports that on Christmas Day 1908, all of the approximately 550 theaters and nickelodeons in New York City were forced to close. The city's mayor, McClellan, ordered the closures in response to "the call of every Protestant denomination in the city" to protect the minds of children from corruption (1980:43). Theater owners, virtually all of whom were recent immigrants, protested. "The controversy smacked of an older cultural war between native Protestants and ethnic Americans" (May 1980:44). In 1909 New York exhibitors encouraged the creation of a Board of Censorship to prescreen all films shown in the city in order to avert having their theater licenses revoked for exhibiting indecent or objectionable material. By 1914 the Board had evolved into the National Board of Censorship of Motion Pictures. Nearly all film producers, most of whom were based in New York, voluntarily submitted to the Board's authority to avoid negative publicity and political opposition (Czitrom 1996:34–35).[37] By this time, in many cities across the nation local authorities instituted censorship committees to prevent the exhibition of immoral and indecent motion pictures (Black 1994:11–12).

It was in this cultural climate that the U. S. Supreme Court decided in 1915 that films did not merit protection under the First Amendment. In the case of *Mutual Film Corporation v. Industrial Commission of Ohio*, the Court upheld the right of states to enact statutes providing for the censorship of films prior to their exhibition. As Jowett argues, this decision "would affect the course of the motion picture industry in the United States for the next 35 years, and have a profound effect on the nature of the content which this new medium would be allowed to explore" (1989:59).[38] The reasoning of the court is telling regarding the dominant perspective on the film industry at the time:

> It cannot be put out of view that the exhibition of moving pictures is a business pure and simple, originated and conducted for profit, like other spectacles, not to be regarded by the Ohio constitution, we think, as part of the press of the country or as organs of public opinion. They are mere representations of events, of ideas and sentiments published and known, vivid, useful and entertaining no doubt, but, as we have said, capable of evil, having power for it, the greater because of the attractiveness and manner of exhibition. (quoted in Jowett 1989:68)

It is important to note that this ruling did not set film apart from other forms of art in terms of whether censorship was constitutional. Literature was also subject to censorship. The legal status of film in 1915, therefore, is not evidence that film was "shortchanged" as an art form relative to other art forms. (Evidence of the valuation [or devaluation] of film as art can be found instead in critical writings [see chapter 4]). The legal position outlined above is more telling of the predominant views of the validity of censorship in 1915. The ruling belies a conception of free speech that is greatly dissimilar to current ideas concerning freedom of expression. Because they were viewed as just another commercial activity, films were denied the status of speech and hence were denied the freedom granted to the press (de Grazia and Newman 1982:5). While film did not differ from other media in legal principle, the need for censorship of films was felt to be more pressing. This public perception was based on film's immense popularity and on the recognition that film's visual nature made it an exceptionally influential medium. Unlike literature, films were subject to prescreening by licensing boards, depending on the location, at either the municipal or state level or both (Randall 1968). For other media, censorship could only be enacted after a product had been successfully brought to market.[39]

Lacking any legal protection against censorship, the industry could see that there was a significant risk of strict government oversight of the content of their products. They much preferred self-censorship, over which they would have some degree of control, to government censorship. Moreover, catering to the objections of all the various regionally based censorship boards was harmful to profits (Smith 2001:275). While the National Board of Review was already in place to censor films, it was organized by the industry itself, and its influence declined as the New York studios who had orchestrated it disappeared and new Hollywood studios appeared. However, its legacy was the establishment of the "basic terms" of a voluntary censorship that would be taken up shortly by the new major players in the film industry (Czitrom 1996:37).

In 1922 the major Hollywood studios created the Motion Pictures Producers and Distributors Association in order to fight off national censorship and to create a policy of self-censorship (Knight 1957:112). Will H. Hays resigned as postmaster general to head the Association, and his name came to represent the Association, which was known as the Hays Office (Sklar 1994:83). The introduction of the Hays Code (see Bardeche and Brasillach 1938:208–209 for a summary of the Code) drastically reduced the number of themes, story lines, and actions that films could depict. Not only did the code explicitly forbid specific controversial topics such as adultery and criticism of religion, but it also used vague language to preclude the inclusion of "vulgarity" and "obscenity." Films that questioned prevailing moral and political views were not to be made.

The Hays Code of 1922 was superceded by the Hays Production Code of 1930, which updated the Code to apply to talking films (see Black 1994:302–308 for a draft of the Production Code), and it was more strictly applied following strenuous demand from Catholic and other groups in 1934.[40] The effect of such interdictions was "to prohibit a vast range of human expression and experience. . . . It is unnecessary to belabor the obvious point that the code cut the movies off from many of the most important moral and social themes of the contemporary world" (Sklar 1994:174).[41]

A couple of examples demonstrate how the Code could strictly limit the possibilities for artistic expression. In the realm of government and justice: "The courts of the land should not be presented as unjust. This does not mean that a single court may not be represented as unjust, much less that a single court official must not be presented this way. But the court system of the country must not suffer as a result of this presentation" (quoted in Black 1994:305). In the realm of sexuality:

> Dancing in general is recognized as an Art and as a beautiful form of expressing human emotions. But dances which suggest or represent sexual actions, whether performed solo or with two or more, dances intended to excite the emotional reaction of an audience, dances with movement of the breasts, excessive body movements while the feet are stationary, violate decency and are wrong. (quoted in Black 1994:308)

Such was the pre-WWII situation in the United States concerning the limits of what the cinema was able to do. Comparisons with the degree of censorship in European countries, where notions of film as art were in place earlier, show that films there were far less restricted in the material available to them.

Censorship in England was the responsibility of the British Board of Film Censors, which was voluntarily created by producers in 1912. The censors were guided by a set of rules that banned treatment of immoral topics (e.g., prostitution, extramarital sex, white slavery, seduction, etc.) as well as the treatment of politically sensitive subjects (e.g., criticism of the monarchy, the police, or religion, etc.). Compared to Germany, Italy, and France, censorship in England was quite similar to that in the United States, though perhaps slightly less restrictive due to the opposition of a vocal left-wing intelligentsia (Richards 1997:167–71). Moreover, Corrigan reports that the censors were never greatly concerned with morality, focusing only on politically sensitive films (1983:29).

Both German and Italian cinema had been freer yet from censorship that sought to ban any and all suggestions of immorality in films. There were no analogous industry-led boards or associations to prevent films dealing with sexual themes or other unconventional or more risqué topics. State censorship for such purposes did exist in Germany (Ott 1986:26). However, until the end of the 1920s, only one per cent of all films reviewed by the German state censors failed to gain approval (Abrams 1996:650). Censorship for political reasons was on the rise in Italy beginning in the late 1920s due to the concerns of the Fascist government there (Buss 1989:12). Similarly, censorship of political themes and issues pertinent to Nazi-party interests increased in Germany in the 1930s.

Censorship influenced film production the least in France. Crisp reports that the few French advocates of a moral code were "ineffectual" and that the "industry had clearly not seen itself as under serious pressure from this moral discourse to modify the nature of its product" (1993:258). As a result, "[i]t was precisely in France, where cultural traditions and institutions resisted the moral strictures of a censorship system, that sexuality and deviance could be freely explored." (1993:xii).

TABLE 3.1.
The Catholic Church's Evaluation of French and American Films: 1930–1935

	A (general exhibit)	B (adults only)	C (to be avoided)
U.S.	50%	40%	10%
French	20%	25%	55%

Source: Crisp (1993:259).

A good measure of the different effect of censorship in America and France on the content of their films can be found in film ratings by the Centrale Catholique du Cinéma (Catholic Cinema Center), organized by the Catholic Church in France to direct audiences to acceptable films. Table 3.1 shows that among the films reviewed by the Center between 1930 and 1935, 50 percent of American films were suitable for general exhibition, 40 percent were suitable for adults only, and 10 percent were to be avoided. Among French films, however, only 20 percent were suitable for general exhibition, 25 percent were suitable for adults, while 55 percent were to be avoided. To a greater extent than American films, French films appear to have explored a range of topics considered by the Catholic Church to have been controversial or inherently immoral.[42]

Altogether, censorship in England, Germany, Italy, and France existed to a lesser degree than in the United States. In the same way that the mode and scale of production differed from the American case, lax European censorship more easily facilitated the acceptance there of film as art.[43]

Censorship in the United States: After the Miracle Decision

Following WWII the situation in the United States slowly began to change and to more closely resemble the looser restrictions in Europe. The first major post-WWII development in the U. S. concerning film censorship was the United States Supreme Court decision in the *Burstyn v. Wilson* case in 1952.[44] This was the first case concerning film censorship that the Supreme Court had agreed to hear since the 1915 *Mutual* case. The specific case before the Court was an appeal by a New York film distributor, Joseph Burstyn, of the decision made by the New York State censors (Wilson was the commissioner of education and a member of the censorship board) to revoke the license for exhibition of the Italian film *The Miracle*. In what has come to be known as the *Miracle* decision, the Supreme Court declared that state laws allowing for censorship of "sacrilegious" films were unconstitutional because they abridged free speech and free press. It stated that

> It cannot be doubted that motion pictures are a significant medium for the communication of ideas. They may affect public attitudes and behavior in a variety of ways, ranging from direct espousal of a political or social doctrine to the subtle shaping of thought which characterizes all artistic expression. (quoted in Jowett 1996:265)

While the Court did not provide absolute protection from censorship, starting with this case and continuing over the next several years, it determined that censorship of "sacrilegious," "harmful," or "immoral" films was unconstitutional.

In *Roth v. United States* (1957), although the case dealt with print materials, the Supreme Court advanced legal thinking about the nature of obscenity (Riley 2000). The Court determined that obscene material did not deserve constitutional protection and could therefore still be censored by state laws. But the Court also adopted a narrower view of what could be deemed obscene; that "sex and obscenity are not synonymous," that "portrayal of sex, e.g., in art, literature and scientific works, is not itself sufficient reason to deny material the constitutional protection of freedom of speech," and that only material that appeals to the prurient interest, without "even the slightest redeeming social importance" and going beyond "contemporary community standards" can be considered obscene (*http://caselaw.lp.findlaw.com/scripts/getcase.pl?court=us&vol=354& invol=476*, accessed December 19, 2006).

The consequence of *Roth v. United States* for the film industry, then, was support for the inclusion of treatments of sex and nudity in films that were tempered by concern for community standards and a redeeming context. This narrowing of obscenity gave filmmakers increased legal protection for making films that treated sex, as well as other controversial topics that might have been labeled obscene such as abortion and adultery. And because the cultural revolution of the 1960s provided the incentive to make such films, Hollywood studios moved in this direction.

The struggle to reduce censorship was not over, though, and continued throughout the 1960s. The power of communities to censor films prior to their release was upheld in the 1961 case of *Times Film Corp. v. Chicago*, under the argument that the prevention of the utterance of obscene speech was constitutionally warranted. In allowing local censorship, the Court did not explain why films should be treated differently from any other medium. In reaction, Bosley Crowther, film critic for the *New York Times*, wrote, "The effect is to continue the ancient stigma of motion pictures as a second-class, subordinate art" (quoted in Jowett 1996:270). That effect, however, was not to last. Despite the *Times Film Corp. v. Chicago* ruling, within the next several years censorship at the state and city levels quickly disappeared. In part this was because further rulings required licensing boards to reform their decision-making processes to be quicker and to involve judicial participation. But in part it is also likely that a diminution of public pressure for censorship contributed to the decline.

These developments in the legal sphere are important not only for the statements they made concerning the role of film in American society. They also sparked change in the film industry's own methods for managing censorship issues. In terms of the effect on the content of films, change in the industry was more important because the bulk of censorship in the film industry was self-censorship. The Production Code, established in 1930, was in effect until 1966, despite the dismantling of legal foundations for censorship in the 1950s. The incentive for maintaining the Code, to avoid negative publicity, remained, and it was the well-founded fear of protests, often from Catholic organizations that would target offending studios and theaters with precision, that forced the studios to mostly abide by the Code.

However, the reasons for discarding the Code were becoming increasingly salient, and although the Code was in effect, by the 1960s the studios were following the letter of its law but not the spirit. As far back as 1949, Darryl Zanuck at Twentieth Century-Fox expressed in a company memo that there was clearly a segment of the audience that would pay to see more sex in their films. However, there was no way to meet this demand in the face of the Production Code (Solomon 1988:78).[45]

In the 1960s the studios developed a method for both complying with the Production Code and circumventing it. The method was to acquire a subsidiary distributing company, particularly one specializing in importing European films. Balio (1987) describes how Columbia Pictures acquired art-film distributor Kingsley-International in order to distribute a film starring Brigitte Bardot, *And God Created Woman*. Columbia knew that the film would have been denied a Production Code seal, and its agreement with the Motion Picture Association of America forbade it from distributing a film without a seal of approval. The agreement, however, did not specify what a subsidiary might have done, and so Columbia could benefit from distributing controversial films without having to accept any negative consequences.

Balio (1987:226–27) argues that the same motivation compelled United Artists to acquire Lopert Films. The importation of these foreign-made films was encouraged by the changing economics of domestic film production. First, production costs were rising rapidly. After the guarantee of exhibition was taken away, the studios made far fewer films, cutting the "B" production and concentrating on "A" production, while at the same time salaries were "skyrocketing" to secure the best talent (Solomon 1988:146). In addition, "there was no guarantee of first-run play dates until after the picture had been completed and previewed, and no idea of total bookings until after the first-run returns" (Sklar 1994:287).

This meant that it became much more difficult to know which films would have large audiences. It became more common to experience huge losses on expensively produced films while reaping enormous profits on less expensively made films. The purchasing of rights to and distribution of finished productions was one way the studios learned to help deal with this uncertainty. These were always less expensive than making their own films at a time when production costs were rising and could provide higher percentage returns on their investments. The purchasing of European productions in particular was encouraged by the growth in "a narrower, more sophisticated, and more particular audience" (Solomon 1988:148) (see also chapter 2), a market the studios were unable to fully exploit with their own productions, hampered as they were by the Production Code.

The historical scholarship on the film industry is consistent with Hirsch's (1972) characterization of culture-producing organizations and the strategies they employ to manage their high-risk environment. Hirsch (1972:654) argues that culture-producing organizations (1) deploy contact men to organizational boundaries, (2) overproduce and differentially promote new items, and (3) co-opt mass media gatekeepers. In particular, Hirsch's finding that such organizations deploy contact men to organizational boundaries, as links to artistic communities where they locate new cultural items, is reflected in the studios' connections to independent and European distributors. The overproduction and differential promotion of cultural items describes the method that the studios adopted when they began to invest more heavily in certain films in the hope that they would become blockbuster hits. Because the "star system" and popularity of films in general generated publicity, mass-media gatekeeper co-optation was never as important an issue for the film industry as for book publishing or record producing. Nonetheless, as a response to declining attendance, film studios began to advertise more extensively in the 1960s (see chapter 4).

During the course of the 1960s the standards concerning what was permissible in films changed dramatically (Randall 1968:230). By the mid1960s, rather than trying to circumvent the Code, the studios began to confront and defy it. They had gained a legal foothold for challenging the Code after the 1952 *Miracle* decision, and because they were catering to a narrower and better-educated audience, there was more to gain from challenge than compliance. What is more, the rising profile of foreign, especially European, filmmaking heightened the Hollywood studios' awareness that their inability to take on controversial issues was a competitive disadvantage (Jowett 1990:22).

As a result of changing values and standards, and the example of foreign films, during the 1960s, Hollywood studios advocated for a large number of changes to the Code in order to gain seals of approval for the films. In part these actions were necessary to differentiate their products from the entertainment available on television. A 1967 article in *Time* magazine noted that "[b]y now, television has all but taken over Hollywood's former function of providing placebo entertainment" (December 8:67). In 1966 the Code was dramatically liberalized, which further encouraged the treatment of controversial themes. The Code was superseded in 1968 by an age classification system devised and applied by the industry itself. While the specific labels for classifying films have changed somewhat, this system is still in place today.

The change in censorship both reflected and contributed to changing ideas about the role of film in American society. The contradiction in the Supreme Court rulings between 1915 and 1952 represents primarily a move toward intolerance of censorship in society. In each case, the rulings were applicable to artistic media other than film, and so cannot be taken as indicators of changing perceptions of film. However, the rulings are significant insofar as each played a different role in determining the boundaries of the content of films exhibited in the United States, and they therefore helped shape the nature of films that were made in Hollywood. This influence is particularly important because there is an overlap between those characteristics that are of interest to censors and those commonly associated with art. After the 1952 ruling, Hollywood films gradually began to incorporate more controversial material and to address these topics in a variety of ways that did not merely reiterate the clearly defined moral dictates of the Production Code. In so doing, the body of work produced by the film industry could more closely conform to existing definitions of art.

Of course, relaxation of censorship likewise allowed Hollywood to produce its share of junk, films that exploited themes of sex and violence in degrading and mindless ways. Then as now, audiences needed to differentiate the good from the bad. But film scholars have identified and made the case for a large number of films that capitalized in a positive way on the increased permissiveness regarding content in the 1960s. Films such as *Bonnie and Clyde* (1967), *Midnight Cowboy* (1969), *The Wild Bunch* (1969), and *Psycho* (1960) were controversial when first released. But they are examples of the kinds of films that have been upheld as Hollywood's artistic output, and they would never have been released without the relaxation of censorship restrictions.

THE CRISIS OF THE 1960s FORCED HOLLYWOOD DOWN NEW PATHS

The contraction of the American film industry detailed in chapter 2 created a set of responses at the level of film content. These responses were aimed at restoring profits under conditions of great uncertainty. As it happens, some of these responses also facilitated the growth of the art world for film, profit orientation notwithstanding.

I will briefly outline three kinds of responses to financial uncertainty that shaped the new direction of Hollywood's output—experimentalism, differentiation, and playing to audience segmentation. All three responses reinforced one another and worked harmoniously as separate rationales for achieving similar results—productions that pushed aesthetic and normative boundaries.

Like any other industry, the Hollywood film industry was alarmed by the financial crisis brought on by the defection of audiences to other forms of recreation. Among the many strategies open to the industry, experimentalism was one course of action that some film producers chose. By experimentalism I am referring to the rejection of the best known and most reliable film conventions in favor of adopting untried characteristics. The motivation is simple to understand: the existing formulas do not work, so something new must be tried. As a complex, multifaceted cultural production, there were many film elements with which to experiment, such as characterization, camera techniques, editing techniques, acting conventions, subject matter, and the like. Some of this experimentation was technical in nature, to capitalize on the visual and audio advantages of the theater experience over television. But Hollywood also experimented with the aesthetics and subject matter of films. Playing with established conventions and pushing aesthetic and moral boundaries is an expected characteristic of art. Such experimentation was virtually absent during earlier periods when filmgoing was the default recreational activity of the majority of the population and the industry was financially healthy. From the perspective of studio executives, pushing boundaries had been unnecessarily risky.

Experimentation is further encouraged by the complexity and difficulty of cultural production. Having complete knowledge about what does not work implies nothing about what does work. As studies of culture-producing organizations have shown, creating cultural products to effectively meet the tastes of audiences is tremendously difficult. The production methods employed by such organizations reveal that even the best producers have a highly imperfect grasp of how best to meet the changing tastes of audiences. As a result, culture-producing organizations engage in various strategies to maximize profits under conditions of high uncertainty (Bielby and Bielby 1994; Hirsch 1972). Imitation, in particular, is a natural and common way for organizations to replicate past successes when they don't fully understand the mechanisms for success. Hollywood had relied heavily on imitation in previous decades. However, when imitation and reliance on established methods resulted in dramatic losses in the 1950s, Hollywood was open to more radical departures from established traditions. At that point, not only could the studios not understand what audiences wanted, but film production was (and still is) also so unpredictable and difficult a process that they could not reliably produce the kinds and quality of films they were aiming for. Experimentation, then, is encouraged not only because producers are not sure of what audiences want but also because, even if audience desires are known, the highly complex production process is sufficiently uncontrollable that experimentation increases the odds that at least some of the final products will satisfy those desires. Some of the more memorable Hollywood films to have successfully experimented with conventions were *2001: A Space Odyssey* (1968), *Bonnie and Clyde* (1967), and *Easy Rider* (1969).[46]

The second thrust of the response to financial crisis was to differentiate the product from the biggest competitor. Prior to the invention of television, the closest competitor for film audiences was radio. In fact, the two media were sufficiently different that the competition was not clearly direct. Just as it can be today, listening to music could be a way to spend time that supplanted a trip to the movies, but it could not substitute for the act of watching something. Similarly, there was neither an effective way to respond to the competition posed by radio, nor an effective need. By offering a visual dimension to entertainment, films essentially filled a different recreational niche. Television, however, occupied the same niche for visual, dramatic entertainment. When faced with such close competition, Hollywood needed to provide audiences with a rationale for choosing their product over television. Films needed to be sufficiently different so that audiences had a reason for going out to theaters instead of what became the default option, staying in to watch television.

The television market was understood as the new mass market—make the product bland so as not to alienate anyone. With films, the strategy turned to differentiation from television and blandness. This drive to differentiate dovetailed with the impetus to experiment. Television was rapidly expanding—there was good reason for television production not to experiment but rather to maintain the status quo and imitate successful productions. Hollywood needed to quickly and decisively show how it was not only different from but also better than television.

The third response to shrinking audiences was a new conception of who the audience members were and thoughts about how to better attract and retain potential audience members. Again, this strategy complemented the others. By playing to audience segmentation, Hollywood recognized that the varying interests and expectations of different demographic groups, some of whom wanted a change from the traditional Hollywood fare their parents had consumed so heavily. Maltby (2003:168) explains that this recognition was already under way during the 1950s so that "Hollywood's willingness to combine serious social subjects with varying degrees of sensation appeal in 'adult' dramas" was "one sign that Hollywood was gradually recognizing that the mass audience had fragmented." With television providing the standard option, Hollywood needed to target various groups, particularly young adults. The way that Hollywood targeted young adults was to include film content that appealed to their engagements and interest in the social changes of the 1960s: the sexual revolution, the antiwar movement and other political protests, and race relations (Schatz 2003:22).

Experimentation, differentiation, and targeting of audience segments were three methods for achieving the one goal of making new and different films that would win back audiences. These changes in studio mentality were necessary. The industry was unprofitable, and so it needed to radically change direction. The result was that it started to produce content that was more in tune with accepted notions of what art should be and what art should do. Hollywood no longer slavishly followed the dictum that popular films needed to be as inoffensive as possible. Maximizing profits meant that efforts needed to be made to push aesthetic and moral limits. Certainly many films in the 1960s, such as *The Sound of Music* (1965), were conceived along the old lines of thinking and were still meant to be for Middle America. But only in the 1960s, when the industry was desperate, did the industry also follow a different production logic that veered, at times, closer to art.

Summary

This chapter has presented evidence for the relationship between changes in a large number of institutional arrangements and practices of production and consumption on the one hand, and the legitimation of Hollywood film as art on the other. A major lesson to be learned from studying U.S. film history is that the causal path that led to an art world for Hollywood films was largely indirect and unpredictable. While seeking profits, many of the principal actors working within the film world found their way to art. The unintentional effect of contributing to an art world was serendipitous.

Yet other developments in U.S. film history were directly and predictably focused on nurturing the art world for Hollywood films. The groups and individuals behind these developments are the art world participants described by Becker (1982). They are the peripheral members of that world who perform the necessary acts of explanation, preservation, and exhibition that are expected of real art.

The historical comparisons with several European film industries provide a good deal of analytical leverage to explain how American production and consumption practices initially constrained a Hollywood art world, and then later assisted it. At the same time, evidence about European cinema reveals that art world development there provided a pathway for legitimating Hollywood film. More evidence about this link, and the necessary sequence of Europe first and Hollywood second, will be explored in the following chapter.

Although the growth of an art world for Hollywood films occurred in the 1960s and 1970s, it is worth noting how more recent developments in the U.S. film world—namely, the growth of independent cinema—have been shaped by that setting. The perception of Hollywood as a viable home for filmmakers to make meaningful films was most widely and strongly held in the 1970s. However, during the 1980s, as the blockbuster formula dictated more and more of the decision-making of the studios, that perception began to wane. The blockbuster strategy, after all, meant the routinization of the production process in order to maximize studios' profits, and it required decisions that put risk reduction and marketing and licensing opportunities ahead of all else.

During the 1980s, then, there were shrinking opportunities in Hollywood to make films that continued in the tradition of the 1970s. There was no shortage of interested filmmakers, however. There have always been independent film producers in the United States, independent meaning not affiliated with one of the major Hollywood studios, but their output has been minor in the quantitative sense. In the 1980s a number of new independent distributors and producers grew who distributed and/or made films that were more innovative, more avant-garde, or more commercially risky than what the Hollywood studios were typically willing to invest in. These were companies such as Vestron, Island, Cinecom, and Miramax (Perren 2001).

The 1980s, then, could be characterized as a time when although there were still occasional works of art perceived to be coming from Hollywood studios, the general perception was that the art world for film in the United States had shifted to independent productions. The questioning of the aesthetic possibilities of film had long passed; the premise that films could be art was taken for granted. But Hollywood was perceived to have largely forsaken its golden age. In the 1990s, however, the industry saw a blurring of the boundaries between the major studios and independent distributors/producers. Either through acquisition (such as Disney's purchase of Miramax in 1993) or through the creation of affiliated studios (such as Sony Pictures Classics) the major studios co-opted the independent film movement in the United States (Epstein 2005:20). Although the studios' actions were economically motivated—if anyone was going to be profiting from these films, they would be the ones—this blurring has helped to sustain the idea that Hollywood films can be art.

While chapter 2 explored the significance of events and developments outside the film world, this chapter presented evidence of actions taken by art world members, some of whom worked closer to the core of that world, and others of whom were more peripheral. As argued in chapter 2, the same actions taken at two different points in time can have very different effects and meanings. Therefore, we can only understand how the historical evidence presented in this chapter bears a causal relationship to Hollywood art world growth in light of the larger context in which it occurred. The positive changes toward art world growth from within the film world coincided in the 1960s with the creation of a much more favorable opportunity space outside the film world. Coincidence might not be the best concept to describe that time, as the changes from outside and within were surely mutually reinforcing. These linkages will be discussed further in chapter 5.

In the United States in the 1960s, the time was right for the changes in the film world to take hold and to change perceptions. But the full story of the diffusion of a perception of film as art requires reference to yet another factor. The diffusion of the *theory* behind why film is art is the subject of chapter 4.

CHAPTER 4

The Intellectualization of Film

IN THE PREVIOUS CHAPTER we saw how an array of events and actions within the film world helped to generate a widespread definition of Hollywood films as art. This chapter is a continuation of that analysis. Here we examine yet another development within the film world, but one of a special nature that warrants a separate investigation. This development is the creation and dissemination of *a discourse of film as art*. We can see examples of this discourse in many places, such as in books on films, like the British Film Institute Modern Classics series. Here are excerpts from the back covers of two of the volumes in the series:

> With its pairing of a perverse, invasive anti-hero and a questing, self-searching heroine, *The Silence of the Lambs* is a narrative of pursuit at several levels. In this study Yvonne Tasker explores the way the film weaves together gothic, horror and thriller conventions to generate both a distinctive variation on the cinematic portrayal of insanity and crime, and a fascinating intervention in the sexual politics of genre.

> *Jaws* exerts an extraordinary power over audiences. Apparently simplistic and manipulative, it is a film that has divided critics into two broad camps: those who dismiss it as infantile and sensational—and those who see the shark as freighted with complex political and psychosexual meaning. Antonia Quirke, in an impressionistic response, argues that both interpretations obscure the film's success simply as a work of art. In *Jaws* Spielberg's ability to blend genres combined with his precocious technical skill to create a genuine masterpiece, which is underrated by many, including its director.

How did we get to the point where the analysis of the shark is perhaps more frightening than the shark itself? More important, what is the significance of *how we talk about films* for understanding changes in perceptions of film as art?

We can begin by acknowledging that accepting Hollywood films as art was a struggle. Because art is a special category of culture, one that bestows honor and prestige, it is limited. There is some risk associated with labeling culture as art if there is no consensus on the appropriateness of that labeling. That risk is the revealing of a lack of cultural knowledge. We are therefore reluctant to apply the label except conservatively. The difficulty for Hollywood films, then, was in explaining why this crowd-pleasing, stimulating, and fun cultural production should be so honored. Such a claim needed to be rendered legitimate.

The New Shorter Oxford English Dictionary defines legitimacy as "Conformity to law, rule, or principle; lawfulness; conformity to sound reasoning, logicality." This definition makes it clear that central to the notion of legitimacy is *justification* through conformity to a rationale. In order to qualify as legitimate, that which is being evaluated must be in accordance with an appropriate standard for differentiating between legitimate and illegitimate. The legitimacy of Hollywood films as art, therefore, was dependent on conformity to a set of genre-specific conventions for defining and evaluating art.

And how are we supposed to know what these are? These conventions are provided by the discourse of art experts, whose job it is to create and engage in discourse about art. That's simply what they do.

Becker's (1982) analysis of how art worlds function relies heavily on the institutionalization of resources. But Becker also views the growth of critical commentary as a crucial step in the creation of any art world. Subsequent to the creation of a network of cooperative groups and individuals, "all that is left to do to create an art world is to convince the rest of the world that what is being done is art, and deserves the rights and privileges associated with that status. . . . Work that aspires to be accepted as art usually must display a developed aesthetic apparatus and media through which critical discussions can take place" (339). As with the rest of his argument, Becker's analysis applies to Hollywood films.

The next step for us, then, is to find the writings of film experts. The obvious place to look is in film reviews. Film reviews, of course, are not the same as a record of audience members' interpretations and impressions of films. They do not provide us with the definitive readings and understandings of films. A vast body of work in cultural studies makes clear that meanings are never so easily determined (During 1999). Nevertheless, the claim for the power of film experts being made here is not that they provide meanings for audiences. Rather, I argue that film experts inform people that there are meanings to be found, and provide a set of tools for interrogating films. Film critics teach audiences how to think about films (Poe 2001:93) and provide the discursive elements that people are supposed to use to talk about films (Jankovich 2001:37).[1]

In this chapter I first review in anecdotal fashion the history of U.S. film discourse. Early examples show how standards of film discourse assumed a common definition of film as junk culture. Although the idea of film as having artistic merit enjoyed some circulation, U.S. writers most often derided this view, a fact that was acknowledged by supporters of film as art. The second task of this chapter is to provide reliable, empirical evidence concerning the role of discourse in creating an art world for Hollywood films. This is accomplished through an analysis of a sample of film reviews from large-circulation, middlebrow publications. The content analysis of film reviews provides an integral piece of the explanatory puzzle regarding Hollywood film as art, and it also redresses an important gap in the sociology of art more generally. Empirical evidence for the development of a critical discourse is almost entirely absent in the literature on cultural hierarchy. Though many authors stress the importance of the development of a legitimating ideology, no previous study empirically documents change over time in the constitutive elements—the vocabulary and critical techniques—of such an ideology. I aim to do so here.

This chapter then addresses the issue of *the link between cultural experts and the general public*. The ultimate explanation of this book concerns the acceptance of Hollywood films as art among a large segment of the public, particularly (though not exclusively) those with postsecondary education. In order to make a strong case for the importance of discourse in explaining that acceptance, it is necessary to provide evidence of a link between the creation of that discourse and reception of that discourse by the public. This link is found in the analysis of film *advertisements*. Because advertisements must appeal to the public, changes in the nature of advertisements can be taken to correspond to changes in what people find appealing. The appearance in film advertisements of critical discourse about films shows when this discourse began to matter to at least a considerable portion of the public.

Finally, this chapter examines the relationship between the critical appreciation of foreign-language and English-language films. The evidence from reviews shows that *the perception of foreign films as art acted as a pathway for the legitimation of the art world for Hollywood films*.

Early U.S. Film Discourse

At the turn of the century, when moving pictures were not much more than flashes of jolting images or jaunty vignettes, the discourse about film was simply descriptive. In general, Americans talked about film as a curiosity and as an amusement. There was no need to have reviews of such films, which were worth seeing for their novelty. As films grew in length and adopted the narrative format, it became possible to discuss the stories that were told and the acting as well.

By the second decade of the twentieth century, film reviews began to comment on the quality of the film as a whole as well as its various components. The most basic assessment began with the technical competencies that could be expected of a good film, though film technology was still rather rudimentary. In addition, because there were several hundred films released every year, there was a substantial body of work with which a film could be compared. The use of the film medium for dramatic entertainment had become the norm. Everyone knew that that's what a film was supposed to be. The acting, the story, the production values, and the originality could all be evaluated relative to other films.

Although nickelodeons became widely popular in the last few years of the nineteenth century, there was a lag of several years before newspapers and magazines began to regularly publish film reviews. The *New York Times*, for instance, published its first film review in 1913. (*Variety* began to publish film reviews as early as 1907, but that publication is written for the entertainment industry itself, rather than for a general audience.)

While the conventions of films themselves stabilized, so did the conventions of film reviews. Early film reviews in the *New York Times* were humorlessly descriptive and had a plodding and distanced tone. This style was either shared or imitated by other early reviewers for other newspapers. The most important aspect of these reviews for the question at hand is the approach they took toward understanding films: that of film as entertainment.

This dominant perspective of film, however, was already being challenged in the second decade of the twentieth century. The idea of film as art, while growing and gaining wide currency in Europe, was taken up by some avant-garde or aesthetically adventurous American intellectuals. One of the earliest American efforts to legitimate Hollywood films as art is found in the work of Gilbert Seldes, whose 1924 book *The Seven Lively Arts* was an impassioned plea for recognition of the genius of the best of popular culture in an array of media. Seldes explicitly advocated a perception of film—the best films, not all of them—as art, and he supported this view with film analyses. Seldes was well positioned and respected among public intellectuals in the 1920s and 1930s, and so his book influenced the thinking of some intellectuals and a portion of the reading public. Nevertheless, Seldes did not alter wider attitudes about film as entertainment. Buhle (1987) characterizes the long-term reception of the book: "for more than thirty years, critic Gilbert Seldes's *The Seven Lively Arts* (1924) stood alone as a sympathetic treatment of popular culture, recognized but not taken particularly seriously" (quoted in Kammen 1996:117).

It is not quite accurate to characterize *The Seven Lively Arts* as having stood alone in its treatment of popular culture. In fact, the perception of film as art was shared by enough cultural commentators that they represented a position that could be attacked by mainstream writers. A good example of the tension that existed between the positions can be found in the following 1931 *New Yorker* film review of *City Lights*. (Directed by Charlie Chaplin, *City Lights* is currently considered a "classic" of great artistic value.)

> Occasionally, you know, strange and unfortunate things occur to persons of such acclaimed place when they settle back for a while to enjoy their triumphs. There is the constant headiness, anyhow, of the great public's applause, and also so many excited little articles appear in various select journals spiced richly with such terms as "genius" and "artist" that the reading of them may cast a sad spell over the subject. To be sure such journals have a small circulation as a rule, yet I suspect that the persons so dealt with usually contrive to unearth them and ponder on their arguments. The results may be disastrous. There grows an inclination to be more dramatically an artist, one with a mission, a significant message, an interpretation, and that aspiration has killed many a delightful talent. . . . I might wax eloquent about the meaning of his clowning, its relation to the roots of human instincts, had I at all the official vocabulary for that kind of thing, and did I not suspect that it tired many people the way it does me. (February 21:52)

The reviewer's comments confirm that the idea of film as art existed in 1931, but that this idea was mainly confined to avant-garde journals, with a "small circulation" waiting for filmmakers to "unearth" them. The more mainstream opinion, as represented by this *New Yorker* reviewer, is one of opposition to the notions that Charlie Chaplin could be an "artist," that words such as "artist" and "genius" could be applied to a filmmaker, and that films should attempt to convey a message or allow for interpretation. Films, the reviewer is saying, do not serve that purpose, and are better for it.

We can usefully contrast this near embarrassment of confusing Chaplin's films with art with the predominant intellectual bent of French and German writers of the 1920s. Hake (1990:88–89) documents the "love affair between Chaplin and an entire generation of German left-liberal intellectuals" that began in the 1920s and describes Chaplin's initial reception by French critics:

> After years of political turmoil, in the midst of great social change and at the outset of a veritable revolution in the cultural sphere, German intellectuals first learned about Chaplin through Ivan Goll's cinema-peom, *Die Chapliniade* (1920). Goll had fallen under Chaplin's spell during the late teens when his films were first shown in Paris and when the "little tramp" emerged as the new hero of the literary avant-garde, leaving traces on the work of such diverse writers as Louis Dellus, Blaise Cendrars, Louis Aragon, and Jean Cocteau. What they perceived in Charlot, as he was affectionately called, was the utopian vision of a

cinema free of the constraints of filmic realism and devoted solely to exploring the aesthetic qualities of the new medium. . . . [M]ost French critics praised Chaplin for the expressive beauty of his gestures and movements, rather than for the portrayal of human struggle and social injustice in his stories.

The incongruity between mainstream American perceptions of Chaplin, as represented in the *New Yorker*, and mainstream European perceptions of Chaplin is clear. In an extensive study of Chaplin's career, Maland's (1989:155–56) description of U.S. critics in the 1930s helps to clarify the boundaries of the opposing schools of thought alluded to in the *New Yorker* review. Maland sees a growing rift in 1930s views on Chaplin. On one hand are reviewers such as Kate Cameron whose "review in the *New York Daily News* typified the first group: 'It had been hinted that Chaplin had gone serious on us and that he had a message of serious social import to deliver to the world in Modern Times. No such thing has happened, thank goodness. . . . There is nothing of real significance in Chaplin's work except his earnest desire, and his great ability, to entertain.' " Maland argues that this first group was politically and aesthetically conservative. On the other hand are the "modern liberal and social radical critics" who wrote for publications such as *New Masses*, *New Theater*, and *Partisan Review* (though a very few also could be found in large-circulation, mainstream publications), and who not only praised Chaplin's leftist politics but also hailed him as a "creative genius."

While there was some debate about the right way to appreciate Chaplin, those who saw Chaplin as an artist were small in number and less likely to be writing for mainstream publications, and, more important, they were often quite reluctant to extend this critical disposition to the rest of American cinema. Chaplin was exceptional.[2] That is to say, even among those who would call Chaplin an artist, the idea that Hollywood films were art was specious because Chaplin's work was set apart from the rest of Hollywood production.

Chaplin's reception by American film commentators, then, is most useful as an illustration of the extreme polarization in early film discourse. The vast majority of film writing, though, was firmly anti-art, and frequently anti-intellectual.

Time magazine is one mainstream publication that exhibited these tendencies in its film reviewing. The following two excerpts come from separate reviews published in 1940 that are fascinating because they not only take a narrow view of films as entertainment, but also openly deride the perception of Hollywood films as art. The first is from a review of *Balalaika*, a film about a family living through the Russian Revolution. The second is from a review of *My Son, My Son!* about an English novelist and his son who dies in World War I.

Unfortunately, Hollywood has now got the idea that "social significance" has something to do with the amusement business. (January 1:29)

Class picture is a trade term for films with a better than average cast, a resolutely esthetic director, and uplift. They are aimed at people who want ideas with their entertainment. Often they are made from second-rate novels with a purpose. Usually they are bores, frequently they are flops. (April 1:70)

The staunch opposition to the inclusion of "social significance" or "ideas" in Hollywood films that is seen in *Time* in 1940 looks bizarre to our eyes. That is because in the meantime our standard understanding of Hollywood films evolved to make social significance and ideas hallmarks of good filmmaking. In fact, the following appeared in a 1980 film review in *Time* of *The Stuntman*: "The movie delights in the play of ideas and in its own unsuspected ability to play fast, loose and funny with them. It is refreshing to see a movie that sends ideas instead of autos crashing head-on" (Sept 1:58).

In short, early U.S. film discourse is different from more recent U.S. film discourse. This is not to say that the whole idea of Hollywood films as art is a recent invention. That is not the case. Instead, the success of this idea, as measured by its wider acceptance among a segment of the public, is the recent invention. It was only after wider acceptance that writers did not have to apologize for their extreme, fanciful perception of films, as Raymond Chandler did in a 1948 article he wrote for the *Atlantic Monthly* in which he argued that despite all the flaws with Hollywood, it often turned out genuine works of art. Still, he could not make this claim without acknowledging that it made him vulnerable to derision. While explaining his position that Hollywood films can be art, he averred, "I say this with a very small voice. It is an inconsiderable statement and has a hard time not sounding a little ludicrous" (1948, March, p. 24).

Just when, then, did the change in U.S. film discourse occur, so that it no longer sounded ludicrous to write about the best Hollywood films as art? What does the timing of that change imply for the influence of discourse on perceptions of film as art? And what are the specific elements of U.S. film discourse?

THE INTELLECTUALIZATION OF FILM REVIEWS: 1925–1985

There is an obvious source of information about the details of film discourse: film reviews provide accessible, long-term evidence for the evolution of an intellectualizing discourse in the film world that was readily available to the general public in popular periodicals.[3]

In this section we will explore the results of a content analysis of film reviews in order to identify the important elements of an ideology of film as art and to locate the period when film discourse began to support and legitimate film as art. The results show that a substantial change in film discourse occurred in the late 1960s.

The film-review sample consists of reviews beginning in 1925 and ending in 1985. The year 1925 is an appropriate starting date because at approximately that time films began to resemble their current form. Film technology allowed filmmakers to make films that were long enough to maintain a narrative structure and that had sufficiently good picture quality for reviewers to focus on interpreting the films as art rather than as merely technical works. The year 1985 is a suitable ending date because it allows ample time for following the alteration of the opportunity space (see chapter 2) for critics to develop a new film aesthetic.

The first film reviewed from each month for every fifth year in the period, starting with 1925, from three different popular periodicals (the *New York Times,* the *New Yorker,* and *Time*) was selected. These periodicals were selected for several reasons: they are three of a very small number that published film reviews continuously during the time period under study; they are mass-circulation periodicals widely available to a large public; and they are considered influential trendsetters, and hence other reviewers are likely to adopt the practices of the critics for these publications. In addition, the second reviews published each month for the years 1950 to 1975 were also selected and analyzed. The rationale for these was to get a clearer picture of the kinds of changes that were occurring during and surrounding the period of most interest according to the historical evidence from the previous chapters. This method generated 13 time periods, with 36 reviews in 1925 to 1945 and 1980 and 1985, and 64 reviews in 1950 to 1975. The total number of reviews is 684.

While there is an enormous amount of information that can be gleaned from film reviews, the content analysis hones in on two variables in order to measure when and how film discourse evolved. First, specific terms associated with artistic criticism in other highbrow artistic genres are counted, and second, the use of critical devices and concepts that facilitate an analytical, interpretive approach to film, rather than a facile, entertainment-minded approach are enumerated. More description of these variables is given below.[4]

Changing Language

One of the perils of doing historical work is that it is difficult to step outside the present-day frame of mind. There is a risk that we will see historical evidence very differently from how it was seen by contemporaries. When dealing with discourse, the hazard comes from the fact that language is always changing. Applying today's perspective to reviews written in 1925 can create misunderstandings.

For this reason, generating a list of "art discourse" terms to measure the degree to which critics discussed film as art requires first sampling reviews from the *New York Times*, the *New Yorker*, and *Time* of classical music performances and recordings and of painting exhibitions from the year 1925. Using both the first music review and the first painting review from each month, a primary list was compiled for each publication (only the first six months were available for music reviews for the *New York Times*, which did not pose a significant problem since music reviews were, on average, twice as long as in *Time*). Each primary list consisted of any term that was considered characteristic of highbrow art criticism from its respective publication. A secondary list of terms was created by including any term that was on at least two primary lists, that is, which appeared in at least two publications' reviews of painting and/or music in 1925. This list was then pared down to include those words thought to have the strongest "art discourse" connotations.[5]

Without a safeguard against a modernday bias in the reading of reviews, the selection of terms that resonate with a contemporary knowledge of critical terminology would have led to finding more "art discourse" terms in later periods independent of any change or lack of change in the nature of film reviews. By confining the terms to those found in 1925 reviews, any bias would work *against* finding these terms in later periods. In addition to the terms found in this way, three more terms pertaining to the interpretive analysis of a narrative structure were added: "genre," "irony," "metaphor." Two other terms were also counted: a proper name followed by the suffix "ian" (e.g., Hitchcockian) or by the suffix "esque" (e.g., Felliniesque), as an indication of an academic tone.

The terms were then counted by their appearance in the film review sample. Accurate counts were achieved by scanning the reviews into Microsoft Word through the use of optical-character-recognition software and then using the "find" function. Each review was corrected for spelling errors that occurred in the scanning process.[6] All variants on a term were also counted. For instance, "art," "artist," "artistry," "artistic," and "artistically" would each qualify to be counted as "art." A term was counted only if it was used in a sense that relates to art commentary. If a film as a whole or some aspect of the film was described as "brilliant," the term "brilliant" was counted. If a bright light, something shiny, or any concrete object was described as brilliant, the term was not counted. The term "work" was counted only if it applied to the film as a production, not if it was being used to denote labor or any other nonartistic sense, and so on. The terms were divided into two groups based on their rhetorical functions.

TABLE 4.1.
Number of "High Art" and "Critical" Terms: 1925–1985

Year	Total Number of "High Art" Terms	Total Number of "Critical" Terms	Total Number of "High Art" and "Critical" Terms
1925	15	4	19
1930	16	2	18
1935	21	0	21
1940	1	4	5
1945	12	9	21
1950	12	2	14
1955	13	7	20
1960	31	12	43
1965	36	15	51
1970	109	47	156
1975	66	41	107
1980	65	38	103
1985	47	31	78

Note: The 1950 to 1975 time periods rely on seventy-two film reviews per year, double that of the other time periods.

The first group is designated as consisting of "high art" terms that imply an erudite assessment and expert judgment in the context of the evaluation of culture. These words are: "art," "brilliant," "genius," "inspired," "intelligent," "master," and "work." The second group is designated as consisting of "critical" terms, words that are used in the analysis of texts. These words are: "composition," "genre," "irony," "metaphor," "satire," "symbol," and "tone."

Table 4.1 presents the count of "high art" terms, "critical" terms, and the total of the two. The counts are not adjusted for the different number of reviews analyzed in the 1950–75 period, when 72 reviews are sampled rather than the 36 in other periods. In order to draw any conclusions about the trends found in the results, we must first account for the greater sampling around the period of interest. Table 4.2 does this by first presenting the information needed to standardize the counts by time period. The second column presents the total number of words written in the reviews. The third column then presents the mean number of words per review by dividing the total words by 36 in 1925–45 and 1980–85, and by 72 in 1950–75.

Table 4.2.
Number of "High Art" and "Critical" Terms Divided by Total Film Review
Words: 1925–1985

Year	Total Number of "High Art" and "Critical" Terms	Total Number of Words in Reviews	Mean Number of Words per Review	Number of Terms Divided by Total Review Words
1925	19	12140	337	0.0016
1930	18	14250	396	0.0013
1935	21	14903	414	0.0014
1940	5	12206	339	0.0004
1945	21	15626	434	0.0013
1950	14	26164	363	0.0005
1955	20	25638	356	0.0008
1960	43	28243	392	0.0015
1965	51	28632	398	0.0018
1970	156	50214	697	0.0031
1975	107	54521	757	0.0020
1980	103	40761	1132	0.0025
1985	78	34215	950	0.0023
Spearman's rho			.74**	.67**

* $p < .05$ ** $p < .01$ *** $p < .001$ (one-tailed tests)

The results of this calculation are interesting because they confirm the expectation that critics who are taking film seriously will write lengthier reviews. Longer reviews allow them to provide in-depth, fully elucidated analyses, as opposed to the more superficial treatments of earlier periods. The fewest words were written in 1925, when a review averaged 337 words. This number remained relatively constant until 1965. After 1965 the mean number of words increased dramatically, peaking in 1980 at 1,132, and then decreasing somewhat in the final time period to 950.

The question that naturally comes to mind is whether the increase in "high art" and "critical" terms is a result of the increase in the length of the reviews. More of these terms might be present because longer reviews provide a greater opportunity for them to appear by chance. To answer this question we need to calculate the ratio of the number of "high art" and "critical" terms appearing in all the reviews of a given year to the total number of words in all reviews. This ratio is presented in the final column and provides evidence that the increase in special terms is not merely a

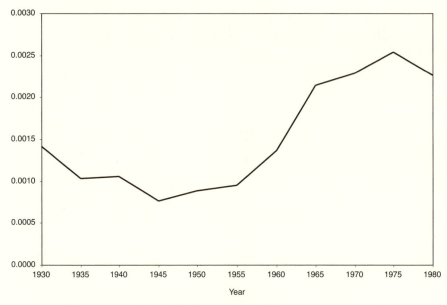

Figure 4.1. Number of Specialized Terms Divided by Total Number of Review Words: 1930–1980 (Moving Average)

reflection of longer reviews. Between 1925 and 1960 the ratio does not exceed .0016. In 1965 the ratio rises to .0018 and in 1970 it is .0031. Proportionally, there is a sharp increase in the density of the specialized vocabulary between 1965 and 1970. There is a break in the data following 1965 that is sustained until the end of the data set.[7] Table 4.2 also includes the results of a statistical test of the strength and direction of the association between the counts of terms and year. The test results strongly support the assertion that the reported increases in the mean number of words per review and in the density of the specialized vocabulary represent real increases and not random variations due to sampling errors.[8]

Moreover, there is a break between the 1965 and 1970 time periods—after 1965 the total count stays higher—that is more easily observed graphically. Figure 4.1 presents the moving average (three periods) of the count of both "high art" and "critical" terms divided by the mean number of words per review. It is a visual depiction of the density of the specialized vocabulary. The moving average smoothes the trend line. For 1930, for instance, the data point reported is the average for 1925, 1930, and 1935, and so on for all the data points. In this way, the figure is less influenced by single time periods and more representative of the general trend. In this case, the trend is up in the 1960s and remains there. The data, therefore, do not support the idea that the increase in the specialized vocabulary is merely a reflection of the increase in the length of reviews. Instead, the data suggest that the increase in the number of "high art" and "critical" terms is the effect of the nascent tendency to treat film as an art form, and that the desire to utilize a specialized vocabulary necessitated contextualization and greater explanations, resulting in lengthier reviews.[9]

There is an alternative explanation—that editors demanded increased output from reviewers, and that reviewers then filled that space with a highbrow artistic vocabulary by chance. It could have been the case that critics changed their reviews merely as an attempt to fill a "news hole" generated by editorial decisions. This competing explanation needs to be addressed.

If there were an increasing concern with cultural coverage in general, which may have been manifested in longer film reviews, then perhaps the change in style of film review is an artifact of this editorial concern, unrelated to ideas about the artistic possibilities of film. There are three possible responses to a larger news hole. Reviewers could write longer reviews, more reviews, or both. There is some evidence to argue that longer reviews are not merely a result of a larger news hole. We may use the years 1935, well before the period of change, and 1975, after the change, as benchmarks. In 1935 the number of film reviews published in the first monthly issue of *Time* and the *New Yorker*, and in the first seven days of each month in the *New York Times*, averaged 5.2. In 1975 the three periodicals published an average of 2.9 film reviews in the first issue/first seven days. This represents a decrease of more than 40 percent in the number of reviews published and is hard to square with an argument that an increasing news hole accounts entirely for the longer reviews. Furthermore, Brown (1995) reports that while there were 766 films released in the United States in 1935, there were 604 domestic releases in 1975, enough for more than 11 film reviews per week and far in excess of the average of 2.9 found in the three periodicals. Clearly, the number of films available for review cannot explain the reduction in the number of reviews published. While it may be true that editors wanted more film reviews in total, perhaps in response to reader demand, it surely is significant that reviewers responded by writing in greater depth about fewer films, rather than simply reviewing a larger number of films. It seems that critics were electing to review films in an entirely different mode—in-depth analysis of a few, rather than a larger number of descriptive reviews.

Changing Techniques and Concepts

The second measure of the change in film review is the use of critical devices and concepts. These devices and concepts are the comparisons and distinctions that critics use and the thought modes that critics employ when reviewing films.[10] This analysis includes data gained through coding of both manifest and latent information (Holsti 1969). Before turning to the data, I will describe the eight techniques that were counted and provide a justification for each.

1. *Positive and negative commentary.* It is characteristically thought that high art is complex and does not lend itself to easy interpretation or appreciation. Rather, it is difficult to understand or to like or dislike categorically. The first technique I count is the appearance of both positive and negative commentary in the same reviews. Reviews that address film as art expected to have a more complex, in-depth approach to film involving evaluation of many aspects on different levels, resulting in more mixed reviews. Such a mixture of commentary exists, for example, when a reviewer praises the actors for their interpretations of their lines but also finds fault with the tone that the director decided to give to the material.

2. *Director named.* The second technique is reference to the director by name. Serious art forms require recognition of the artists by name, and in the case of film, this means the director (Blewitt 1993). Furthermore, this technique in particular is expected to increase in the 1960s, due to the introduction of auteurism, to American film criticism.

3. *Comparison of directors.* The third technique in the content analysis is the comparison of the director to another director. Discussion of high art very often places the work in the context of other works so that the work can be evaluated in a more sophisticated and informed manner (Eitner, 1961).

4. *Comparison of films.* For the same reason, comparison of the film to another film is expected to increase. Making connections between different works can allow critics both to justify their analyses and to display their cinematic erudition.

5. *Film interpreted.* A supposed defining characteristic of "art," as opposed to "entertainment," is that it is thought-provoking and in some way a form of communication through metaphor. Examples include, "It seems reasonably clear that she means her movie to be a wry and sometimes anguished parable of political corruption and betrayal" (*Time*, October 6, 1975, 65) or "she bends this material onto a statement about how women are trapped and self-entrapped in our society" (*New York Times*, November 1, 1975, 17:1). Such statements are not plainly factual; they are subject to debate and require creative inference on the part of the critic. In his book, *Making Meaning*, David Bordwell considers the role of interpretation in film criticism:

> Now more than ever, scholars take the construction of implicit and symptomatic meanings to be central to understanding the arts. . . . This search has shaped the history of film theory and criticism in important

ways. When film study broke away from journalism on the one side and fandom on the other—when, that is, it became academic—it could have become a subdivision of sociology or mass communication studies. It was instead ushered into the academy by humanists, chiefly teachers of literature, drama, and art. As a result, cinema was naturally subsumed within the interpretive frames of reference that rule those disciplines. (1989: 17)

Bordwell asserts that "interpretation-centered" criticism prevails in film studies due to its eventual association with other types of cultural criticism.[11]

6. *Merit in failure*. Viewing the same aspect of a film in opposite ways is indicative of a complex, multifaceted approach that is typical for highbrow art that relies on resolving tensions between beauty and harshness to achieve its effect (Eitner 1961). An example of this evaluation on two levels is, "If Pontecorvo's film is flawed throughout, it is nevertheless an amazing film, intensely controversial even in its failures" (*New Yorker*, November 7, 1970, 159).

7. *Art versus entertainment*. Posing a scheme of art versus entertainment, or serious versus commercial film is the seventh technique. Critics can be expected to develop a canon, and they must justify why some film is good (or serious art) and some film bad (or commercial entertainment). A fault can be expected to appear between "real art" and film that is motivated by profit or obviously and intentionally oriented toward a mass market (Bourdieu 1983; 1980).[12] "There are times when the movie teeters on the edge of commercial cuteness" (*Time*, February 3, 1975, 4) is an example of the drawing of such a distinction. Another can be found in the following closing lines: " 'The Baby Maker' is the first picture James Bridges has directed, and it is customary to be kind on the occasion of a directorial debut, but this debutant has, with his first step, entered the old Hollywood society of commerce. There is not a single one of the carefully planted 'sensitive' nuances in the picture that I felt meant anything to James Bridges or told the truth about any emotion he has ever had" (*New Yorker*, October 10, 1970, 137). Distinguishing between "popular" film and "serious" film allows critics to define a canon that excludes standard Hollywood productions. One of the effects of creating a canon is the delineation of a subgroup of the art form that critics can refer to as representative of their ideas concerning what is good art (DiMaggio 1992). It provides a set of exemplary works to which critics can appeal to defend their ideological ground. The identification of these "serious" works also allows critics to dismiss other films as essentially a different kind of cinema, thereby maintaining the artistic integrity of "real" cinema.

8. *Too easy to enjoy.* A similar distinction can be expected more often in later periods based on a "disgust at the facile" (Bourdieu 1984:486). Real art requires effort to be appreciated and cannot be enjoyed merely on a superficial level (Canaday 1980). Treating film as art encourages disdain for films that are "too immediately accessible and so discredited as 'childish' or 'primitive' " (Bourdieu 1984:486), while finding value in complexity and subtlety. A negative evaluation of "cuteness" is another way that this distinction is drawn, as indicated in the following example from a 1975 review from *Time* of the film *Touch and Go*: "Even more drastic, the film has an insinuating cuteness, like De Broca's much-cherished *King of Hearts*. De Broca works hard at being likable, and makes it, finally, altogether too easy" (June 2, 50).

Two reviews appearing forty-five years apart in the *New Yorker* show how critics at different times differed in how they held films to this standard:

> I don't like movies about people who work, and I don't like movies about people who have things the matter with them. (I work and all my friends work, and we all have things the matter with us. We go to movies to forget.) (April 6, 1935, 77)

> I don't mean it as a compliment when I venture . . . that it will prove to be her most popular picture so far. It is an easy movie to enjoy, which is the whole trouble. (March 3, 1980, 112)

Table 4.3 presents the percent of reviews that include at least one of each of the techniques by year, together with a measure of how steadily the techniques increase over time. Despite differences in the frequency of use and in the magnitude of increase, the big picture that emerges is that these techniques increased in use across the board, and the largest increases occurred roughly between the late 1950s and early 1970s.

While each of these devices can individually contribute to an intellectual, sophisticated approach to film review, the use of multiple techniques changes the nature of reviews to a greater extent. Column 9 presents the percent of reviews in which at least three of the techniques were utilized. Until 1960 only a very small portion of reviews used at least three of the critical devices. At that time the proportion steadily rose, reaching its highest value in 1980 of 81 percent. It is apparent that critics were concentrating the use of these critical concepts and techniques in their reviews beginning in the 1960s.[13] Column 10 shows that, despite writing lengthier reviews, critics were also using these devices at a greater rate on a word-by-word basis in later time periods. Column 10 shows the percentages in column 9 divided by the total number of words in all reviews for a given time period.[14] There is a considerable difference between the pre- and

TABLE 4.3.
Percentage of Reviews Using Specific Critical Techniques: 1925–1985

Year	Technique									
	(1)	(2)	(3)	(4)	(5)	(6)	(7)	(8)	(9)	(10)
1925	36	47	3	8	3	0	11	0	8	0.02
1930	33	33	3	8	3	0	0	0	3	0.01
1935	53	19	0	17	14	0	3	3	6	0.01
1940	33	50	0	6	17	0	3	0	6	0.02
1945	53	36	3	6	25	0	6	0	6	0.01
1950	60	42	0	17	21	3	13	13	15	0.04
1955	46	47	1	10	19	4	13	14	17	0.05
1960	63	72	1	14	33	7	8	17	38	0.10
1965	57	82	1	18	43	7	18	15	49	0.12
1970	61	88	14	36	74	21	22	19	69	0.10
1975	58	86	15	38	68	8	15	19	67	0.09
1980	78	100	11	42	69	25	19	8	81	0.07
1985	53	100	17	28	56	6	22	14	50	0.05
Spearman's rho	.68**	87***	.58*	.81***	.93***	.88***	.85**	.74**	.90***	.74**

Note: 1 = presence of both positive and negative commentary in review; 2 = director is named; 3 = director is compared with another director; 4 = film is compared with another film; 5 = presence of an act of interpretation; 6 = merit is seen in failure; 7 = opposition drawn between serious vs. commercial film or art vs. entertainment; 8 = film is criticized for being "easy," or for lacking subtlety; 9 = percent of reviews in which at least 3 techniques are used; 10 = column 9 divided by mean words per review.
* $p < .05$ ** $p < .01$ *** $p < .001$ (one-tailed tests)

post-1960 time periods, with a large increase occurring in the later period. This now familiar pattern attests to the changes that occurred in the 1960s in the field of film criticism.[15]

The content analysis demonstrates in a structured fashion the subtly changing goals and methods of film review between 1925 and 1985. The most common technique, naming the director, seemingly became a necessity by the 1980s. In fact, *Time* magazine began to include the name of the director under the title of each film being reviewed only in the 1970s. Since the 1930s it had been listing the name of the studio and film's title. The *New York Times* changed its practice in the 1970s as well. From the 1920s to the 1960s each review was prefaced with the title of the film and a list of credits. Although there was some variation in order, before the 1970s the director was never listed first. In reviews from 1925 and 1930, the actors were listed first, usually followed by the author of the story and perhaps the screenwriter, then the director. In reviews from 1935 to 1955, the actors were listed last. Original authors and screenwriters were listed first, usually followed by the director and in turn the producer. However, if the film was a musical, the director could be listed after the songwriter. In reviews from 1970 onward, the director was always listed first. The greater emphasis on the role of the director is consistent with the acceptance of the idea that the director was central in understanding the artistic qualities of film.

Taken together, the critical techniques and specialized vocabulary measured here are an indication of the change in the late 1960s in the intellectual posturing of the reviewers and in the overall tone of the reviews.[16] Although some early reviews do incorporate some of the specialized vocabulary and techniques, these instances are deviations from the general trend.[17]

Is Change in Film Reviews a Reflection of Change in Films?

Now that we are reasonably certain that film reviews have changed in particular ways, we need to think more about what drove the change. I have been advocating the thesis that the changes were part of the development of an art world for film. As cultural experts adopted the idea that films were art, this idea was reflected in their writing.

There is an obvious counterpoint to be made here. This analysis will directly address the main alternative hypothesis concerning changing film reviews and will help to establish whether critics were merely responding to the changing qualities of film. My argument begs the question of whether the relationship between the work of critics and the status of film is a spurious one. Do both result from a shift in the nature of films themselves? If films became more artistic, it may have caused both a shift in the content of reviews and an elevation in the status of film. Unfortunately, I am unable to provide an objective measure of whether films become more artistic over time.[18] However, it is possible to analytically control for the extent to which films are artistic through an examination of reviews from two different time periods for the same set of films.

The first volume of the *Film Review Index* (Hanson and Hanson 1986), a resource for film scholars, provides references for film reviews from a variety of sources for films made before 1950. I collected a sample containing all films for which two reviews from popular periodicals could be located, one from the year the film was released in the United States and the second from no earlier than 1960.[19] Most often, these pre-1950 films earned a second review because they were being shown at a film festival or because it was the anniversary of the film's original release. Other times

TABLE 4.4.
Number of "High Art" and "Critical" Terms in First and Later Film Reviews
of Twenty Films

Period	Total Number of "High Art" and "Critical" Terms	Mean Number of Words per Review	Number of Terms Divided by Mean Words per Review
First review (1915–1950)	20	503	0.0020
Later review (1960–1982)	103	1500	0.0034

Note: Counts allow for variants of the terms, e.g., "masterpiece" "masterful"
"masterwork," etc.

the second review indicated that the film deserved to be discussed because
it had been neglected the first time around. Popular periodicals were defined as high-circulation newspapers and magazines written for general
audiences and not focusing solely on film or art. This method generated
twenty films whose original reviews were published between 1915 and
1950[20] and whose later reviews were published between 1960 and 1982.[21]

Table 4.4 shows how the language of first reviews as a group compares
to that of the later reviews as a group. The former contained 17 "high art"
terms and 3 "critical" terms. The latter contained 84 "high art" terms and
19 "critical" terms. The total number of film-review words in the twenty
original film reviews was 10,064, while the total number in the twenty
later reviews was 29,993 (not in table). For first reviews, the total number
of "high art" and "critical" terms divided by the total number of film
review words is .0020. For later reviews, the figure is .0034. Thus the
pattern found in the larger sample repeats; not only did later reviews contain more of a specialized vocabulary, but critics were also more likely to
utilize this vocabulary on a per-word basis. This finding is important because it demonstrates that the same films were reviewed with a different
vocabulary at different points in time.

Table 4.5 compares the two groups according to the techniques used
in reviewing. Several important similarities and differences from the previous sample are apparent. Just as in the larger sample, comparing the director to another director and comparing the film to another film are strongly
associated with later time periods. Also, explicating implicit meaning in
the films jumps from 30 percent in first reviews to 85 percent in later ones.
Although there was most often no effort to find a message in the films
when they were first reviewed, it became almost standard to treat the films
as a form of communication.

TABLE 4.5.
Percentage of Reviews Using Specific Critical Techniques in First and Later Reviews
of the Same Twenty Films

Technique	Reviews from 1915–1950	Reviews from 1960–1982
(1) Presence of both positive and negative commentary in review	40	55
(2) Director is named	85	90
(3) Director is compared with another director	0	35
(4) Film is compared with another film	0	75
(5) Presence of an act of interpretation	30	85
(6) Merit is seen in failure	0	5
(7) Opposition drawn between serious/art vs. commercial/entertainment film	15	20
(8) Film is criticized for being "easy," or for lacking subtlety	5	0
(9) At least three of the techniques are used	20	75

Usage of some of the other techniques is not, however, as strongly linked to time period. Using mixed commentary and drawing a distinction between serious art and commercial entertainment are only slightly more likely to be part of a later review, as is finding merit in failure, although it appears only once. Finding fault with an easy or obvious film also appeared only once, although, unexpectedly in the earlier time period. Interestingly, seventeen of the twenty film reviews in the early period named the director, while eighteen of the reviews in the later period did so. It is possible that those films made by renowned directors are more likely to survive over time to be re-reviewed.

The two groups of reviews differ greatly in the use of at least three of the enumerated techniques. Whereas only 20 percent of first reviews use at least three techniques, 75 percent of the later ones do so. This finding is important because it illustrates the change in overall style and goal. The same films received a critical treatment much different in nature in the post-1960 era.

To further our understanding of the meaning of these results we can refer to a comparison of the twenty first and later reviews to the larger sample of reviews, broken into two time periods. The early group of twenty reviews of the same films was published between 1915 and 1950; these are compared to all reviews from the years 1925 to 1950. The later

TABLE 4.6.
Comparison of Special Twenty Reviews with Other Reviews
from Two Time Periods

Period	Same Twenty Films		General Sample	
	Terms	Devices	Terms	Devices
Early	0.002	20%	0.0011	7%
Later	0.0034	75%	0.0024	54%

group of twenty reviews of the same films was published between 1960 and 1982; these are compared to all reviews from the years 1960 to 1985.

In table 4.6 we see that the reviews of the twenty early films appear more likely to contain a specialized vocabulary and technique than other reviews of the period. However, the magnitude of the increase in the use of the vocabulary and the techniques between the early and later periods is nearly identical for both the twenty reviews of the same films and for the general reviews. One possible explanation for why the twenty reviews of the same films differ from the general reviews is that there is a high proportion of reviews of foreign-language films among the twenty reviews of the same films. As will be discussed below, reviews of foreign films contained a specialized vocabulary and specialized techniques earlier than did reviews of English-language films.

Overall, the comparison of reviews of the same films lends support to the argument that the observed changes in film review are not merely a reflection of an increase in the artistic nature of films, but instead represent an evolution in critical practices. Critics were acting as influencers rather than as mirrors.[22] This is not to say that reviewers can write anything they wish, but rather that there are options open to reviewers in how they critique culture. In the period following the creation of a more favorable opportunity space, film reviewers chose to treat film as an art form rather than as mere entertainment.

Among the twenty films reviewed twice, the Disney animated film *Snow White and the Seven Dwarfs* provides an excellent example of a film that was approached in a radically different way the second time around. The review from the *New Yorker* after the film's premiere in 1938, although acknowledging the film's appeal for adults, treated the film as a simple cartoon. The entire review is 307 words long, and the conclusion reads:

He has perhaps overdone the wicked stepmother, and just for a moment or two has tinted the film with too lurid a touch. In one other element, too, I think Mr. Disney's judgment has erred. The language of the dwarfs is funny, but it must be called a little tough. It smacks too much of the language of the streets, and in a film like this it should be most literate, punctilious, and polite. No nice dwarf, Mr. Disney, ever says "ain't." (January 15,52)

In contrast, the August 2, 1973, review in the *Village Voice* began with the assumption that the film operates on multiple levels and therefore should be carefully analyzed within the context of Disney's oeuvre:

> Disney is for children as much as Chaplin and Keaton are, by which I mean that children understand the broadest aspects of these artists— the lowest slapstick comedy and, in the case of Disney, the terror— but little else. "Bambi," for example, with its subtle mood studies, its deliberate lack of story-line and identification figures, left the largely children's audience I saw it with restless. . . . On a narrative level this sense of the past and emphasis on family relationships make the films, like fairy tales, fertile ground for Freudian analysis. As in the Grimm original, "SNOW WHITE AND THE SEVEN DWARFS" centers around a sexual jealousy between an overweeningly vain queen and her innocent step-daughter.

This excerpt is just a small portion of the much longer review, but it is typical of the tone, posturing, language, and technique found throughout the review. This same incongruity between time periods can be found in reviews of foreign-language films as well, as they too, like Hollywood films, were initially defined by most U.S. intellectuals as entertainment. How else to explain the *New Yorker* reviewer's refusal to engage Jean Renoir's *The Rules of the Game* as a serious work? *The Rules of the Game* is one of the most acclaimed films of all time. *Sight and Sound*'s (of the British Film Institute) publication of its once-a-decade poll of critics has found the film near the top of the list of best films since 1952. Here is the entire *New Yorker* review (April 22, 1950, 105):

> "The Rules of the Game" is a Jean Renoir picture that was made in France before the war. It is an extremely dull description of a weekend in the country, full of aimless philandering and general slapstick. Lord knows what M. Renoir had in mind when he confected this one, but it certainly reveals none of the skill that went into "Grand Illusion."

Except for a comparison of the film with another film by Renoir, this review neglects to engage with the film according to any of the conventions that were later incorporated into reviewing. By criticizing the film as "dull" without any acknowledgment that the film might have had other artistic goals, the review also implicitly reinforces an approach to films as entertainment. Consider, by way of contrast, the *Village Voice*'s closing lines in a 1961 (January 26, 12) review:

Renoir's formal command of his film is beautiful. During the last part of the picture, the camera moves about almost like another guest. It must be some quality of Renoir's that makes his camera lens seem always a witness and never a voyeur. The witness here communicates a powerful mixture of amusement and disquiet. "Rules of the Game" was made in 1939, after all; it is not only a wonderful piece of filmmaking, not only a great work of humanism and social comedy in a perfect rococo frame, but also an act of historical testimony.

The findings from the analysis of the two sets of reviews of the same films are congruent with Becker's (1982) expectation about what actors in a developing art world will do. He writes, "aspirants [to the status of art] construct histories which tie the work their world produces to already accepted arts, and emphasize those elements of their pasts which are most clearly artistic, while suppressing less desirable ancestors" (339). The act of analyzing and sacralizing older works within an art world has the effect of creating a canon of "classics" and a coherent aesthetic regarding an art form.[23] Importantly, the canonization occurs retrospectively rather than with the introduction of the cultural product.

FILM REVIEWS APPROACH BOOK REVIEWS: A COMPARISON WITH LITERATURE

We now have a good sense of how film reviews changed in the 1960s. But although the trends are fairly clear concerning the changing nature of film review, we need to better understand why these trends are occurring. A comparison with trends in literature can help to answer some questions that arise, such as, are changes in film review a result of changes in artistic review in general? Do these changes really represent a movement toward a "high art" mode of review? Reviews of fiction provide a suitable basis for comparison because literature, especially that which is advertised in the publications examined here, was well established as an artistic medium long before the time period under study (Leary 1976:ch.1). In addition, both art forms generally involve a narrative, and neither involves a live performance in the presence of an audience. The convergence of trends in film review and book review would support the argument that the function of critics in the film world was coming to resemble the function of critics in other established art worlds.

So as to compare film reviews and book reviews in as objective a manner as possible, further content analysis is in order. The book-review sample consists of reviews of fiction from the same three periodicals from which the film-review sample was drawn (the *New York Times*, the *New*

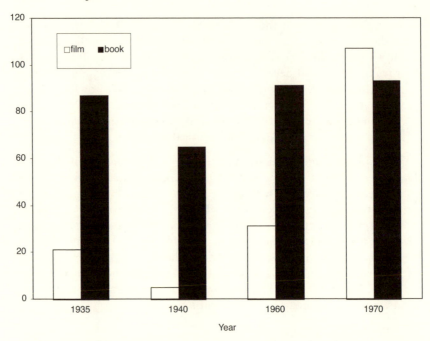

Figure 4.2. "High Art" and "Critical" Terms in Film and Book Reviews: 1930, 1940, 1960, 1970

Yorker, and *Time).* In order to economize on labor, four time periods were chosen to illustrate how the two sets of reviews compare initially (1935 and 1940), just prior to the major changes in the film world (1960), and immediately following the major changes in the film world (1970). The first available review from each month from the three periodicals provided thirty-six reviews for each of the four selected years (N = 144). The content analysis here replicates the analysis of film reviews, first counting the use of specific terms,[24] and then counting the use of critical devices.[25]

Figure 4.2 illustrates how the total counts of "high art" and "critical" terms found in the book reviews compare to the counts in the film reviews. The totals of all terms for each time period in the book reviews are fairly stable. The total in 1970 of 93 terms is quite close to the total of 87 in 1935. This contrasts with the total terms for film reviews, which lag far behind in 1935 and 1940, increase moderately in 1960, and then increase dramatically in the final time period. This count of "high art" and "critical" terms demonstrates a convergence in the specialized vocabulary of film and book review.

Figure 4.3 then shows that the same trends obtain after taking into account the length of the book and film reviews. This figure represents

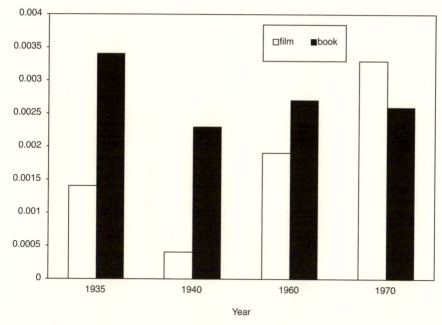

Figure 4.3. Number of Specialized Terms Divided by Total Words in Film and Book Reviews: 1930, 1940, 1960, 1970

the number of specialized terms divided by total review words. What is not directly represented in the figure is the fact that the number of words used to compose the average book review increased from 717 to 1,012, an increase of 41 percent over the initial period. However, despite this lengthening, film reviews were much more similar to book reviews in 1970 than in any of the earlier time periods. With the average film review having 414 words in 1935, film reviews were 73 percent shorter than book reviews. The difference between them shrank to 13 percent in 1970. Dividing the "high art" and "critical" terms by the total review words gives us the density of the specialized vocabulary. Although the density of the vocabulary for book reviews changes only slightly over time, for film reviews it follows the same pattern as the number of words overall, converging with book reviews in that last period.[26]

The overall picture that emerges, as represented in figures 4.2 and 4.3, is one where book reviews provide a fairly stable standard for the vocabulary of artistic discourse, and the vocabulary of film review approaches this standard, particularly post-1960, after initial deficits.

Figure 4.4 provides further evidence of the convergence in book and film reviews. This figure shows that the percent of film and book reviews using three or more of the specified techniques follows the same pattern.[27]

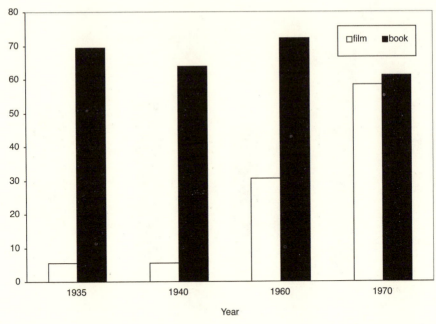

Figure 4.4. Percentage of Film and Book Reviews with Three or More Specified Techniques: 1930, 1940, 1960, 1970

Again, book reviews exhibit stability while film reviews initially lag and then catch up in the final time period.

Although it is not presented, one of the most salient findings is the consistency with which authors are mentioned in book reviews—100 percent in each time period. This is not a surprising result; it is natural to discuss the author when reviewing literature. However, literature contrasts with film insofar as the credit for the final work of art is focused on an individual. This contrast, though, has faded over time as the director has emerged within film theory as more central to the artistic process than all others involved in filmmaking.

Another interesting finding is that the majority of book reviews interpret the meaning of the books in every time period. Film reviews, however, offer an interpretation in a minority of cases in 1935, 1940, and 1960, although the proportion is highest in 1960. In 1970 69 percent of film reviews interpret the films, a proportion that is similar to that for book reviews (67 percent).

The content analysis as a whole, then, paints a picture of initial differences followed by convergence between the characteristics of film review and book review. There are two important points to be made regarding these results. First, it appears that insofar as literature is representative of high art[28], *the observed trends in film review reflect a movement toward a high art mode of review.* This is reassuring—we have more confidence that we are drawing the right conclusions about the film review results. Second, *the data do not support the idea that the observed trends in film review are a result of more widespread changes in artistic reviewing.* Again, this is reassuring. It helps to discredit a major alternative interpretation of the film-review findings.

1960s Advertisements Incorporate Film Review

This chapter has so far been concerned with demonstrating that U.S. film discourse changed during the 1960s. The changes in discourse reveal a new attitude on the part of critics, an attitude that it was correct and appropriate to analyze, interpret, and evaluate films as art. The objective of this book, however, is to explain how this perception became widespread among a portion of the American public. Critical discourse, therefore, is only relevant if a case can be made that it resonated with and was adopted by a wider segment of the public. I turn now to the second major goal of this chapter, which is to provide empirical support for the assertion that the critics' legitimating ideology for film was received and taken up by a wider audience.

This argument rests on a key observation concerning the nature of advertisements, which, because strategically designed to be appealing to audiences, necessarily incorporate characteristics that are important and of interest to audiences concerning what is being advertised. In the case of film, then, by examining changes in film advertisements over many years, we can see what has become more or less important to and interesting for audiences regarding film.[29] In this way, advertisements embody the changing expectations and preferences of audiences. With respect to the incorporation of film review as a fundamental characteristic of film advertisements, we have compelling empirical evidence regarding how much weight film audiences have given to critics. The primary empirical result presented in this section is that critical success increasingly served as a selling point for films in newspaper advertisements, with a large increase occurring in the late 1960s.

The sample consists of advertisements, between 1935 and 1985,[30] from the first Tuesday and Friday in January for every fifth year from the *New York Times* and the *Los Angeles Times*, and from the first Tuesday and Friday in July for every fifth year from the *Detroit News*, the *Washington Post*, and the *Louisville* (Kentucky) *Courier-Journal.*[31] All tables in this section are based on the resulting N of 2,553. These periodicals serve a diverse set of audiences; any advertising trends that emerge can be assumed to represent the expectations and preferences of a diverse population. In addition, advertisements come from summer and winter, and weekends and weekdays. Through a strictly objective manifest coding scheme, I recorded several variables. Beginning with the date and source of the advertisement, I then recorded whether there was at least one "critic-quote pair" (e.g., "A magnificent film"—*New York Times*). Unattributed quotes are indistinguishable from the general self-promotion that is advertisement, and were therefore not counted. Next, I recorded the total number of critic-quote pairs in the advertisement, the number of words quoted in each critic-quote pair, and the length and width of each advertisement, rounded to the nearest quarter inch, used to calculate the area of each advertisement. Finally, I coded for references to the direction of the film and the use of the word "master" or its variants in the critic-quote pairs. The content analysis as a whole provides an indication of the changing value of critical discourse as a tool for creating a positive impression of films.

Trends in the Use of Criticism in Advertisements

Table 4.7 reports three measurements of the degree to which film review has been incorporated into film advertisements. (These are baseline measures; the changing size of advertisements is dealt with later.) The first column addresses the basic question of what percent of advertisements have at least one critic-quote pair. This measurement can be considered a baseline threshold for the extent to which film reviews are incorporated into advertisements. At the beginning of the time period, the percentage is quite low: only 7 percent of advertisements contain at least one critic-quote pair. This percentage increases gradually with each time period until 1965, when a large increase of nearly 20 percentage points occurs between 1965 and 1970. After a very small decrease, the percentage is stable until another large increase occurs between 1980 and 1985.

Advertisements, then, became more likely to include at least one quote from a film review. To clarify what was happening with film advertisements, and to support this initial finding, we can also look at how many quotes were used in the average advertisement and how long the average quote was. Columns 2 and 3 provide this information and in doing so reinforce the findings of column 1. The mean number of critic-quote pairs per advertisement gradually increases until 1965, when a larger increase occurs, then stabilization until a second jump between 1980 and 1985. As for the mean number of words per quote, this measure takes a substantial jump between 1935 and 1940, rises moderately until 1965, and then takes another substantial jump between 1965 and 1970, after which time it appears to plateau.

TABLE 4.7.
Three Measures of the Incorporation of Film Review: Percentage of
Advertisements with at Least One Quote, Mean Number of Quotes,
and Number of Words per Quote in Film Advertisements: 1935–1985

Year	Percentage of Advertisements with at Least One Quote	Mean Number of Quotes per Advertisement	Mean Number of Words per Quote
1935	7	0.1	2.8
1940	9	0.1	6.1
1945	14	0.2	5.6
1950	15	0.3	6.4
1955	22	0.4	7.1
1960	25	0.4	9.6
1965	27	0.5	8.1
1970	46	1.1	12.6
1975	44	1.2	11.3
1980	47	1.3	13.3
1985	70	2.2	13.5
Spearman's rho	.99***	1.00***	.97***

*** $p < .001$ (one-tailed tests)

Columns 2 and 3 add to our understanding of the trends in the incorporation of film review. While column 1 shows that an increasing proportion of advertisements utilized critical commentary, columns 2 and 3 show that those advertisements using critical commentary did so more and more intensively. Among those advertisements quoting critics, there was a statistically significant increase in the use of multiple critic-quote pairs and to quote larger passages from film reviews.[32]

The increases in the 1965–70 period clearly stand out and are consistent with the larger explanation of changes in film discourse. However, the increases in the 1980–85 period are somewhat puzzling. A plausible explanation is to point to a technological development that caused the film industry grave concern at that time: the growth in home video players. When the home video market began, the film industry believed that the theatrical market for films was critically threatened. The initial industry reaction was to take legal action against manufacturers of home video players, based on copyright concerns, in order to preserve the theatrical market. It is possible that another industry reaction was to heighten the appeal to audiences for seeing films in theaters. Thus, the intensification of the incorporation of critical commentary in film reviews might have been a marketing strategy to ensure against a downturn in theater admissions. Interestingly, the measure of the mean number of words per quote does not substantially increase between 1980 and 1985. It could be that advertisers recognized that excerpts are ideally not too long, as readers might be less likely to read longer excerpts or to remember them.[33]

By several measures, then, *advertisements increasingly relied on critical discourse as a way to market movies.* It was especially in the late 1960s that studios decided that what critics were saying was important enough to audiences that this discourse could function as a marketing technique.[34] Without audience interest in critical commentary, there would have been no point in including excerpts from reviews.[35]

A natural question to pose at this point concerns the content of the excerpts. Just what kinds of critical commentary did studios think resonated with audiences? It is difficult to summarize quantitatively the nature of these excerpts, but before we move on to a more qualitative assessment we can look at two measures that provide a small window. The percentage of advertisements containing at least one mention of the "direction"[36] or using the word "master" or its variants is portrayed in figure 4.5. References to both increase over time at statistically significant levels. So when excerpts in general became more common, with big increases in the late 1960s, the *kinds* of excerpts chosen also increasingly reflected concern about the artistic nature of film.

These two measures alone do not give a complete depiction of the nature of the critical commentary that was being incorporated into film review. However, these findings are consistent with the changing nature of film review itself, and they support the larger argument of this chapter. Naming the director and using the term "master" and its variants were two features of film review that became more common in the 1960s. Discussion of the direction of films and the identification of "masters" (or "masterpieces," etc.) appear to have resonated with film audiences. Furthermore, the largest increases in these two measures coincide with the period of greatest change in film reviews and film advertisements in general. As film discourse changed to legitimate film as art in the 1960s, it was reaching the reading U.S. public and it meant something to them.[37]

These tables quantify trends that are readily apparent to an observer who reads even a small number of advertisements from the time periods in question. The overall appearance of advertisements for films was continuously changing. However, the advertisements of the 1930s, 1940s, and, for the most part, 1950s, employed a format that appears quite dated from today's perspective. During the 1960s and into the 1970s, though, advertisements adopted a format that is essentially similar to current

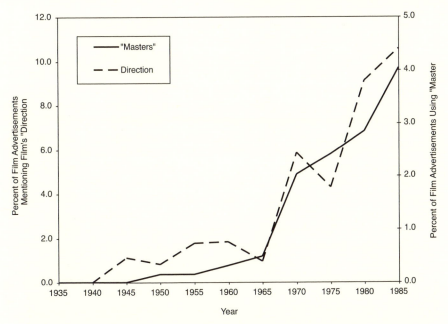

Figure 4.5. Percentage of Film Advertisements Referring to "Masters," etc., and to Direction: 1935–1985

trends. Extensive listing of credits was one feature that became standard. And whereas in earlier time only the lead actors were consistently named, it became commonplace during the 1960s to list the director, producer, screenwriter, and others, usually grouped at the bottom of the advertisement. Also during this time critics' reviews began to be incorporated, resembling current practice. We see a great increase in the reliance on critical success to market films between 1960 and 1970.

A close look at a series of advertisements for famous films provides a clear illustration of the change. Take, for instance, the advertisements for *Casablanca* (1942) and for *The Grapes of Wrath* (1940) that appeared in the *New York Times* shortly after their respective premieres. By today's standards, when quotes from critics are eagerly incorporated whenever possible, the advertisements for *Casablanca* and *The Grapes of Wrath* are startlingly barren. Both are relatively small and include no quotes from critics. These are films that were well received. Studios wishing to find quotes to put in the advertisements could have easily done so. And the films were major productions that warranted substantial promotion. Moreover, the advertisement for *The Grapes of Wrath* mentions the producer but not the director, John Ford, who has since been canonized as one of the greatest American directors. *Gone with the Wind* was an enormous cinematic event in 1939, and the advertisements that appeared in the *New York Times* following its premiere in December of 1939 are quite revealing. The advertisements for this film evolved in format and content in the weeks following the premiere, but the various versions have in common an absence of quotes from critics—all the more striking because the advertisements for *Gone with the Wind* were quite large, sometimes a quarter the size of the page, with a great deal of blank space.

In contrast to these earlier films, advertisements for *The Godfather* (1972) and *Chinatown* (1974) are composed *primarily* of critics' quotes. Admittedly, these films were exceptionally well received, and so the advertisements are above average for their period in the number of words they quote from critics. However, *Casablanca, The Grapes of Wrath*, and *Gone with the Wind* had all received positive reviews as well, and yet the *New York Times* advertisements for these films quoted no critics.

The contrast between the advertisements for *Gone with the Wind* and *The Godfather* and *Chinatown* shows that there is flexibility in the choice of how to fill a given amount of space. *Gone with the Wind*'s advertisement contains open space and information about show times and prices, whereas advertisements for *The Godfather* and *Chinatown* contain almost no open space or information about show time or prices. Furthermore, the font size of title and names of actors is generally larger in earlier advertisements and therefore occupies a greater proportion of the available space. The greater available space in more recent periods, generated by omitting nonessential information, shrinking the typesetting, and increasing the total size of advertisements, is filled with critical opinions. Many of the excerpts are not concerned with evaluating the films on the level of art. However, many are. Moreover, the often lengthy excerpts found in many advertisements in the late 1960s and throughout the 1970s are strikingly serious and weighty from a contemporary perspective.

Rather than merely telling audiences whether a film was worth the price of admission, the quotes offered comparisons with other films, directors, and actors, and opinions about many different components of the films. Most important, the increase during the 1960s in the presence of critical opinion is evidence that critics had begun to play a larger role in the reception and appreciation of film among American audiences.

Controlling for Changes in Advertising Space

Before turning to an analysis of the trends, it is necessary to consider the possibility that the observed increases in the incorporation of film reviews into advertisements is nothing more than the result of an increase in advertising space. If there is empirical support for this alternative explanation of the observed trends, then the interpretation of advertisements as indicative of a link between critics and the reading public loses credibility. There

TABLE 4.8.
Coefficients for Three Regression Models of the Incorporation of Film Review into Advertisements on Square Inches of Advertising Space and Year

Independent Variable	At Least One Quote	Number of Quotes	Number of Words
	Dependent Variable		
Advertising space	.06 ***	.07 ***	1.17 ***
	(.01)	(.00)	(.05)
Year 1940	.24	.07	.83
	(.48)	(.18)	(2.44)
Year 1945	.84 *	.14	1.47
	(.42)	(.17)	(2.24)
Year 1950	.88 *	.21	1.79
	(.41)	(.16)	(2.14)
Year 1955	1.38 **	.30	2.37
	(.40)	(.16)	(2.16)
Year 1960	1.53 ***	.32 *	3.57
	(.40)	(.16)	(2.17)
Year 1965	1.57 ***	.35 *	2.55
	(.40)	(.16)	(2.18)
Year 1970	2.21 ***	.65 ***	7.54 ***
	(.39)	(.16)	(2.16)
Year 1975	2.08 ***	.74 ***	6.76 **
	(.40)	(.17)	(2.25)
Year 1980	2.12 ***	.76 ***	9.36 ***
	(.39)	(.16)	(2.20)
Year 1985	3.14 ***	1.57 ***	20.14 ***
	(.40)	(.17)	(2.26)
Number of cases	2553	2553	2553
	.1553[a]	.2364[b]	.2875

Notes: Coefficients for the measure of whether there was at least one quote were obtained through logistic regression. Standard errors are in parentheses. The 1935 time period is the omitted category.
  * $p < .05$ ** $p < .01$ *** $p < .001$ (one-tailed tests)
  [a] Pseudo R-squared
  [b] Adjusted R-Squared

is indeed an increase in the average size of an advertisement, from 2.86 square inches in 1935 to 10.84 square inches in 1985. However, *changes in advertising space cannot account for changes in the content of film advertisements*, with respect to the incorporation of critical commentary.

Table 4.8 reports the coefficients for regressions of the three measures of the incorporation of film review into advertisements on advertising space and dummy variables for time periods, omitting the first period. By including the size (in square inches) of each advertisement in the regres-

Table 4.9.
Coefficients from the Regression of Three Measures of Incorporation
of Film Review on Advertising Space and Time Period

Independent Variables	Measurement of Incorporation of Film Review		
	At Least One Quote	Number of Quotes	Number of Words
Advertisement size	.64***	.07***	.29***
	(.01)	(.00)	(.02)
1970–1985	1.20***	.66***	3.61***
	(.42)	(.06)	(.30)
Number of cases	2553	2553	2553
	.1283[a]	.2150[b]	.2061[b]

Notes: Coefficients for the measure of whether there was at least one quote were obtained through logistic regression. Standard errors are in parentheses. The 1935–65 time period is the omitted category.
*** p < .001 (one-tailed tests)
[a] Pseudo R-squared
[b] Adjusted R-squared

sions, we can detect whether there was a tendency to incorporate film review that was *independent* of the tendency to place larger advertisements.[38] The first column of coefficients was obtained through logistic regression. The second and third columns were obtained through OLS regression. The three analyses provide very similar results. Controlling for advertising space, the coefficients for the time periods increase fairly steadily from earliest to most recent. In each case, there is a noticeable jump between 1965 and 1970. The statistical significance of the coefficients varies between the three columns. However, the overall pattern is for coefficients for more recent time periods to enjoy greater statistical significance. For each measure, the coefficients for the time periods from 1970 and beyond are significant at the .001 level. These results strongly suggest that the incorporation of film review into advertisements is not an artifact of the tendency for studios to purchase more advertising space.

In order to test more directly the hypothesis that there is an important discontinuity in the late 1960s, table 4.9 presents the same three regressions with the dummy variables for each time period replaced by one dummy variable for the 1970–80 period. The results show the comparison of this later period with the pre-1970 time period. For each film-review measure, while controlling for advertising space, the post-1970 group differs from the pre-1970 group at the .001 level of statistical sig-

TABLE 4.10.
Three Measures of the Incorporation of Film Review: Percentage of Advertisements with at Least One Quote, Mean Number of Quotes, and Number of Words per Quote in Film Advertisements at Least Four Square Inches: 1935–1985

Year	Percentage of Advertisements with at Least One Quote	Mean Number of Quotes per Advertisement	Mean Number of Words per Quote
1935	14	0.1	4.0
1940	5	0.2	5.3
1945	3	0.1	3.5
1950	28	0.9	8.1
1955	36	1.0	8.6
1960	37	0.8	17.9
1965	36	1.0	9.6
1970	55	1.6	13.8
1975	60	1.9	11.9
1980	52	1.7	14.7
1985	80	2.8	14.6
Spearman's rho	.92***	.92***	.82***

*** $p < .001$ (one-tailed tests)

nificance. These results clearly justify the identification of the late 1960s as a turning point in the practice of using film reviews to market films.

A Minimum Threshold

In any given advertisement, a number of requirements must be met. The title of the film must be stated, and nearly every advertisement tells the audience who the stars of the film are. Other features are also often included, such as a picture or drawing of the stars, or the names of the people who produced, directed, and were otherwise involved in the film. Because advertisements cannot consist only of quotes, the inclusion of such necessarily occurs less often in smaller advertisements. The obvious question then becomes, do the same trends obtain when looking only at advertisements big enough to easily have room for quotes?

To answer this we can measure the incorporation of film review into those advertisements in the sample that are four square inches or larger in size (N = 884).[39] Table 4.10 reports the same three measurements of incorporation of film review into advertisements as table 4.7, now re-

TABLE 4.11.
Coefficients from the Regression of Three Measures of Incorporation
of Film Review on Advertising Space and Time Period

Independent Variables	Measurement of Incorporation of Film Review		
	At Least One Quote	Number of Quotes	Number of Words
1970–1985	1.43***	1.27***	6.42***
	(.16)	(.17)	(.75)
Number of cases	884	884	884
	.0754[a]	.0601[b]	.0751[b]

Notes: Coefficient for the measure of whether there was at least one quote was obtained through logistic regression. Standard errors are in parentheses. The 1935–65 time period is the omitted category.
*** p < .001 (one-tailed tests)
[a] Pseudo R-squared
[b] Adjusted R-squared

stricted to large advertisements. The results here are quite similar to those for all advertisements. The presence of at least one quote in an advertisement steadily increases, peaking with 80 percent in 1985. The high percentage of advertisements with quotes in later periods provides assurance that the threshold of four square inches was not set too low. The results for the mean number of quotes per advertisement and the mean number of words per quote are also similar to the results for all advertisements. Large advertisements increasingly incorporated more film review.

The three regressions performed on the entire sample for table 4.8 were run on this sample of large advertisements, this time omitting the variable of advertising space. These regressions tell us whether the post-1960s time period is, on the whole, different from the pre-1970s time period. Once again, the findings reinforce those for all advertisements.

In sum, tables 4.10 and 4.11 demonstrate that *even among only larger-sized advertisements, film review was utilized as a marketing technique in the post-1960s era more extensively than before.* Although advertising space is an important variable, it cannot explain the change in the nature of film advertisements in the late 1960s.

Controlling for General Trends in the Incorporation of Reviews in Advertisements: A Comparison with Fiction Book Advertisements

One further possible explanation for the observed increase in the use of critical commentary in film advertisements is that this trend merely reflects a more general turn toward critics in advertising. In this explanation, film advertisements used critics' quotes not because of the growth in an art world for film, but rather because advertising in general was becoming more reliant on experts as a marketing technique. Perhaps expert opinion was increasingly sought by the American public for consumption in a variety of contexts.

Data on advertisements for novels, however, suggests this was not the case. Rather, just as happened with book reviews and film reviews, the trends for book and film advertisements converge in the late 1960s.

The data on book advertisements come from two sources, the *New York Times Book Review* and the *New Yorker*. All advertisements for novels from the first two weeks of January and the first two weeks in July in the *New York Times Book Review* were coded. Because the *New Yorker* contains far fewer book advertisements, a greater number of issues was selected.[40] All advertisements from every second month were coded, beginning with February. The same four time periods for which reviews were compared were chosen to illustrate how the two sets of advertisements compare initially, just prior to the major changes in the film world, and immediately following the major changes in the film world.

Table 4.12 reports four measures of the incorporation of book reviews in advertisements. Two findings are evident. First, there seems to be a tendency for advertisements for both books and films to increasingly rely on critical success as a selling point. Critical success is more relevant for both genres in 1970 than in 1935.

However, the second and more salient finding is that the trends are primarily characterized by their convergence. Book advertisements incorporated critical commentary from the earliest periods in the sample, at a time when the practice was extremely uncommon in film reviews. All three measures show great disparities between book and film advertisements in 1935 and 1940. These disparities are greatly reduced or, in the case of the mean number of critic-quote pairs per advertisement, reversed by 1970. While book advertisements were more than 6 times more likely to include at least one quote in 1935, they were only 1.37 times more likely to do so in 1970. Moreover, the average quote in a book advertisement contained almost 4 times as many words as a quote in a film advertisement in 1935. In 1970 the quotes in book advertisements contained 1.46 times as many words. The relevance of film critics, as reflected in advertisements, while initially muted, increased by 1970 to resemble the relevance of literary critics. Book advertisements changed over time to more extensively incorporate book reviews in 1970 than in 1935, and substantial differences with film reviews remained. However, film advertisements changed to a greater degree over time, and they came to resemble book advertisements in the extent to which they quoted critics far

TABLE 4.12.
Trends in the Incorporation of Critics' Quotes: Comparison of Advertisements
for Books and for Films: 1935, 1940, 1960, 1970

	1935	1940	1960	1970
Percentage of advertisements containing at least one quote				
Books	45	44	53	63
Films	7	9	25	46
Mean number of quotes per advertisement				
Books	1.00	0.70	0.76	1.06
Films	0.07	0.13	0.39	1.11
Mean number of words per quote				
Books	10.89	17.4	14.73	18.44
Films	2.75	6.11	9.56	12.56
Number of cases				
Books	83	180	147	87
Films	116	141	262	287

more in 1970 than in 1935. Just as publishers believed that reading
audiences were interested in what book critics thought about books and
in what those critics thought books had to say, so studios believed
that filmgoing audiences were concerned with what film critics thought
about films.

The convergence of trends in book and film advertisements supports
the argument that the function of critics in the film world was coming to
resemble the function of critics in other art worlds.

FOREIGN FILM: A PATHWAY TO HIGH ART FOR HOLLYWOOD

> It reminds one not so much of other movies about movie-
> making as it does of those blends of action and philosophy
> that the French intellectual adventurers used to put out. It may
> not be Andre Malraux, but it certainly is on the level of Romain
> Gary—and all the more remarkable and amusing for bearing a
> MADE IN U.S.A. stamp.   (*Time*, September 1, 1980, 58)

This chapter has so far elided the distinction that was emphasized in previous chapters between Hollywood and non-Hollywood films. Because the
aim of this book is to explain how Hollywood films in particular became

accepted as art, this distinction must be addressed in this chapter. This section empirically demonstrates that film discourse served to consecrate Hollywood films in particular, separately from foreign films. In so doing, the data also reveal an intriguing facet of the historical reception of films. Just as with other forms of art, domestic production has traditionally been devalued relative to foreign production. European productions, especially, were more readily legitimated as art for the simple reason that they were European. This prejudice in favor of Europe worked to soften the prejudice against the medium of film. The data strongly suggest that foreign films were a pathway for the consecration of Hollywood films as art.

Although the genre of "film" maintains a large degree of coherence, there is nonetheless widespread recognition of important divisions within it, for instance the extent to which they emphasize "artistic" versus "commercial" qualities. Films are commonly classified according to whether they are "Hollywood" products or "independent" films.

At first glance, this distinction seems to contradict the premise of this book. The contradiction, however, is not as substantial as it first appears for two reasons. First, it is not the premise of this book that all Hollywood films are art, but, rather, that all Hollywood films are eligible to be perceived as art, and that a certain body of them are widely acknowledged as such. To claim that all Hollywood films are accepted as art would be to unwisely expand the conception of art to refer to all things cultural. Fortunately, that is not necessary.

Second, as implied by the first reason, the seeming contradiction arises out of confusion about what people mean when they use the label "Hollywood films." In the strictest of terms, it applies to *Citizen Kane, The Godfather, Psycho, 2001: A Space Odyssey*, and hundreds of classics of the early decades of cinema. These are all "Hollywood films," and are also broadly accepted as real works of art. When most people draw a contrast between "Hollywood" and "art" films, they are using sloppy shorthand to refer to the least respected Hollywood productions. If there is any contradiction, it resides in the term "Hollywood films" itself, for it carries conflicting meanings. The pejorative sense coexists with recognition of the legitimacy of Hollywood artistry. "Hollywood" and "art" are by no means mutually exclusive categories.

Furthermore, there is an argument to be made that the distinction between Hollywood and art films that currently signifies a denigration of the former has become sharper and more corrosive since the early 1970s. The late 1960s and early 1970s are widely viewed by film historians as the golden days of art in Hollywood, when the mode of production most closely resembled the auteur conditions in Europe. Since then, as the blockbuster mode came to predominate (Stringer 2003), the dichotomization between the terms "Hollywood" and "art" has increased. Nonetheless, contemporary usage should not obscure the fact of the premise—that "Hollywood" is not antonymous with "art."

To further muddle the supposed distinctions, just as there is art in Hollywood, there is schlock in Europe. It's just that it is almost never distributed in the United States. And then there is also the independent American film industry, thought to be more artistic than Hollywood. Despite these complexities, there is a long-standing understanding of European films as being artistic (see chapter 3). And, as the excerpt from the review of *The Stunt Man* at the beginning of this section shows, there is a long-standing sense of inferiority regarding Hollywood productions.

Foreign-Language and English-Language Productions: Data from Reviews and Advertisements

In addition to describing how film discourse historically treated foreign-language films apart from English-language films, data on film review and advertisements can help to answer an important empirical question: Are the observed trends in reviews and advertisements an artifact of an increase in the American market for foreign films? This question is important because film history scholarship shows that foreign films gained in popularity in the United States in the 1960s. It is possible, therefore, that a legitimating ideology for film did not first develop in the United States in the 1960s. Instead, it is possible that foreign films had always been discussed at the level of art in the United States, and that the data do not document the development of a legitimating ideology for all film, but rather reflect the fact that foreign films became more popular in the 1960s. In order to assess this explanation, then, we need to examine the data for foreign-language films separately from those for English-language films. It turns out that *this comparison provides powerful evidence that the growth of a discourse of foreign film as art served to legitimate Hollywood film as art.*

The first row of table 4.13 reports the number of reviews of English-language and foreign-language films,[41] pooled across three time periods to generate sufficiently large bases for comparison. As expected, the number of reviews of foreign-language films relative to English-language films does indeed increase over time. Are the trends reported for reviews overall driven by the increased representation of reviews of foreign-language films? A comparison between time periods of English-language film reviews alone, however, undermines the argument that the overall trends in film review are a result of a greater number of foreign films in the sample.

By every measure, we can see that *reviews of English-language films evolved as drastically, or even more so, than did reviews of foreign-language films.* The comparison of the use of "high art" and "critical" terms

TABLE 4.13.
Number of "High Art" and "Critical" Terms and Three or More Critical Techniques:
Reviews of English-Language versus Foreign-Language Films: 1925–1985

	1925–40		1945–60		1965–85	
	English	Foreign	English	Foreign	English	Foreign
Number of reviews	125	19	212	40	209	79
Number of words	47241	6258	79977	15694	158360	49983
Mean number of words per review	378	329	377	392	758	633
"High art" and "critical" terms	44	9	69	29	392	103
"High art" and "critical" terms / Total review words	0.0009	0.0014	0.0009	0.0018	0.0025	0.0021
Percentage of reviews with three or more techniques	6	5	19	30	62	63

in reviews for English-language and foreign-language films shows that foreign-language films were somewhat more likely to use this specialized vocabulary in the 1925–40 period. We need to look at the number of these terms divided by total review words, as there were nearly eight times as many words written about English-language films as about foreign-language films. In the 1945–60 period, the density of the vocabulary in foreign-language film reviews increased, while it remained constant in English-language film reviews. In the 1965–85 period, the density for both types of reviews increased, but much more for English-language film reviews, so that these contained more of the specialized vocabulary on a per-word basis.

The percent of reviews with three or more of the critical techniques (refer back to table 4.3 for a list of the eight critical techniques in film reviews) was quite low for both English-language and foreign-language film reviews in 1925–40. There is a slightly different pattern here in the following period insofar as there is an increase for English-language film reviews. However, there is a similarity insofar as there is an even sharper increase for foreign-language film reviews. And there is a further similarity in the sharp increase observed for both types of reviews in the final period.[42]

Finally, it is worth noting that the increase in the mean number of words per review is small between the first two time periods and then large between the final two time periods. It is interesting that English-language film reviews are even longer than foreign-language film reviews. For the most part, this pattern reflects the other patterns found in this table.

In addition to the striking changes in reviews of English-language films, the table also reveals a key difference between the two types of reviews. The differences between English-language and foreign-language films are greatest in the 1945–60 time period. The patterns described here suggest that foreign-language films were intellectualized earlier than were English-language films.

Data from advertisements are consistent with the finding that foreign films were reviewed differently, more in line with art, from an earlier time. Just as they were intellectualized earlier, so it appears that critical opinion was relevant to the marketing of foreign films before this was the case for English-language films. Table 4.14 breaks down the measures of the incorporation of reviews into advertisements according to whether the film advertised was English language or foreign language.

Before 1970, in no year did more than 20 percent of advertisements for English language films contain at least one critic's quote. Thereafter, the proportion jumps sharply, rising to 72 percent in 1985. In contrast, the proportion of advertisements for foreign-language films with at least one critic's quote begins at 67 percent in 1935 (although that year's result is based on a very small N) and fluctuates between 35 percent and 65 percent throughout the rest of the time span. In comparing the two trends, we see that advertisements for English-language films rise to and converge with advertisements for foreign language films in the late 1960s.[43]

Nearly the same pattern prevails when measuring the mean number of quotes per advertisement. The main difference is that advertisements for foreign-language films experience an increase over time in this measure. Otherwise we see a basic similarity: the measure is higher for foreign-language films until the 1960s, when advertisements for English-language films experience a sharp increase. Thereafter there is a convergence in the trends, followed by English-language films actually surpassing foreign-language films in the final time period.

The final measure of the mean number of words per quote is less telling about the relationship between the advertisement of foreign-language and English-language films. For this measure, both increase consistently, although the jump for English-language films between 1965 and 1970 is greater.

The overall picture that emerges from the data on reviews and advertisements is that a legitimating ideology for film developed first for foreign-language films, most strongly in the period 1945–60.

One interpretation of these data is that *foreign film provided a pathway for the intellectualization of American films*. It may have been that foreign films better conformed to preexisting notions of what kind of culture con-

TABLE 4.14.
English-Language versus Foreign-Language: Three Measures of the Incorporation of Film Review: Percentage of Advertisements with at Least One Quote, Mean Number of Quotes, and Number of Words per Quote in Film Advertisements at Least Four Square Inches: 1935–1985

Year	Number of Cases		Percentage of Advertisements with at Least One Quote		Mean Number of Quotes per Advertisement		Mean Number of Words per Quote	
	English	Foreign	English	Foreign	English	Foreign	English	Foreign
1935	110	6	4	67	.04	.67	3.5	2
1940	123	18	2	50	.02	.89	6.0	6.1
1945	197	21	11	38	.13	.52	5.8	5.1
1950	259	31	12	35	.23	.58	6.2	7.2
1955	238	33	16	64	.28	1.00	6.7	7.8
1960	221	41	19	56	.32	.76	9.6	9.4
1965	207	46	18	65	.42	.91	8.2	7.9
1970	259	28	45	54	1.00	1.61	12.9	10.5
1975	196	28	44	43	1.21	1.36	12.0	7.3
1980	227	37	44	62	1.28	1.41	13.7	11.4
1985	210	17	72	53	2.31	.82	13.5	15.1
Spearman's rho			.95***	.00	.99***	.60*	.96***	.89***

*** p < .001 (one-tailed tests)

stitutes art. For instance, foreign films may have been less "accessible" to American audiences because they dealt with less familiar themes and because subtitles or dubbing presented barriers to easy enjoyment. Art is, stereotypically, more difficult than entertainment. In addition, European films may have been intellectualized because of a tendency to more readily recognize all of European culture as high art compared to American productions.[44] Moreover, a distinction between English-language and foreign-language films from an American perspective compares only the best of the latter with nearly the whole body of the former. As is the case today, only the most respected foreign-language films were offered to the American market. Sklar argues that the consequence of the exhibition of only select European films was "[t]hat the art-house audience which developed in the 1950s was convinced that only Europeans understood the cinema as an art. There was very little in daily or weekly film reviewing that could help them think otherwise, and critical writing on American movies was almost nonexistent" (1994:294). It may have therefore been more likely that a legitimating ideology developed around foreign-language films first, and that this was then extended to English-language films, post-1965. In this way we can see how the appreciation of foreign films affected the appreciation of American films.

It should be emphasized, however, that, just as with Hollywood films, the recognition of foreign films as art was a struggle. The prejudice against the medium of film was deeply ingrained in U.S. intellectual norms. The following two examples show how even as late as 1960 there was disagreement among reviewers about whether to approach foreign film as art or entertainment. In 1960 the *New Yorker* (September 10, 80) printed this review of the Argentinean film *La casa del angel*, which was released under the title *End of Innocence* and is now recognized as a "classic" (Chanan 1996:434) of Argentinean cinema.

> "END OF INNOCENCE," an Argentine film, tells of how Ana Castro (Elsa Daniel), the youngest daughter of a wealthy Buenos Aires aristocrat, is infected with Puritanism by her devout Catholic mother and, in her terrible innocence and fear of sin, is raped by a friend of her father's— an experience that reduces her to the mumbles for the rest of her life. The treatment of this fine old seventeenth-century theme is arty: the camera scuttles over the ground, peering down at socks or up at giants; flies over vast courtyards; scrutinizes pores; tilts to the right and left; and, when all else fails, goes out of focus. It appears to be night throughout the picture, and, accordingly, the acting consists largely of highlighted cheekbones, white eyes, and deep-shadowed chins.

That is the entire review. The critic clearly scorns the film's deviation from Hollywood's style of entertaining audiences in straightforward fashion. The artistry is rejected. There is a stark contrast, however, with the review of the same film that was printed in *Time* (1960, September 5, 43). Here are a couple of excerpts from that review:

> The End of Innocence (Argentine Sono Film; Kingsley) is a shadowed, subtle, intense study of purity, sin and degeneracy. . . . Director Nilsson has tried, with considerable success, to express in 76 minutes much more than can be stated explicitly in that time. His film bears a heavy load of symbolism, of scenes such as the one in which swinish revelers set fire to one lavish apartment and then reel off drunkenly to another. Visions of a society's dying past and corrupt present unfold themselves long after the film is over.

The critic for *Time* embraces the film's claim to art at a time when it was still not widely accepted practice, even for foreign films. The contrast between the two reviews makes an important point about the social construction of artistic status. The redefining of film as art happened through contestation and challenge. In writing of films as art, a critic was asserting himself or herself as more knowledgeable than previous critics. To contradict the working assumptions of one's field is to affirm one's own assumptions and perceptions as more valid. Through the discursive acts of the acknowledged experts in the field—those who had the institutional authority of respected publications behind themselves—this new reality was validated and the old invalidated. But this process happens gradually and unevenly, and only after a critical mass of participants in the art world and then the wider society "see" things the same way does the challenge become the conventional point of view.

Cultural Hierarchy, the Relevance of Critics, and the Status of Film as Art

Perhaps as a consequence of a more sophisticated form of reviewing, the generation of film critics that was writing for mass publications in the 1960s became the first film critics to be *known as* film critics. In contrast, their predecessors were primarily journalists who also reviewed films. Consider, for example, the account of one of the first film critics for the *New York Times* about how he arrived at his role:

> In 1915 I was assistant dramatic editor and critic of the *New York Times*. I was on space, which translated means, I was paid for anything I wrote that was published at so much per column, and to add to my income I appointed myself movie critic . . . and so while no one in authority had suggested that I become its motion-picture critic, none told me to desist. (Pemberton 1936:153)

By the 1960s only those with some claim to expertise specifically in film history and analysis were considered qualified to write film columns in major periodicals. These experts on film achieved a degree of influence, prestige and even celebrity that earlier critics never had (Sarris 1968; Wolcott 1997). Blades (1976) notes that in 1973 *Newsweek* published an article entitled "Critic as Superstar." When associated with names such as Pauline Kael, Stanley Kauffmann, and Vincent Canby, film reviews could often play a large part in a film's success or failure. Such stature was granted to film critics only after their reviews became lengthy, analytically sophisticated critiques. The data from film advertisements shows the progression of critics' influence. It cannot be shown whether critics had their own interests in mind when they changed their mode of review although it must be noted that they stood to gain in prestige by being the arbiters not of mass entertainment but of an art form.

Recent work on the relationship between critics and the status of art provides insight into the significance of the increase in the prestige of film critics. In contrast to explanations focusing on audience composition and institutional arrangements, Shrum (1996) develops an argument that specifies a mechanism for critical influence wherein he states that the distinctions between high and popular art exist because our opinions about art forms are shaped by very different modes of consumption. For popular culture, audiences consume, evaluate, and understand cultural products directly, without any recourse to cultural experts. Audiences believe that they understand the "rules" of popular culture, and so are qualified and capable of forming their own opinions. For high art, on the other hand, audiences participate in discursive mediation.

> To participate in high art is to forgo the direct and unmediated perception of the artwork itself. The principal consequence is the dependence of one's own judgment of artistic quality on the judgment of others. ... Participation in high art forms involves a status bargain: giving up partial rights of control of one's own judgment to experts in exchange for the higher status that competent talk about these artworks provides. The status bargain, then, is *an exchange of prestige for opinion rights.* (Shrum 1996:9; italics in original)

The response to evaluation is the crucial factor distinguishing high and popular culture. If an art form is associated with secondary discourse concerning its meaning and quality, it is considered high art. Those art forms not associated with any such discourse, or for which such discourse is disregarded, are considered popular culture. As the providers of the discourse, critics play a role in maintaining the cultural hierarchy.

With some correction for its strict dichotomization, Shrum's argument can be applied quite effectively to the case of film. When film's status as art was increasing in the 1960s, there was a concomitant increase in esteem for film critics whose opinions were newly recognized as valuable and to whom audiences may have ceded their opinion rights. There was, then, an intellectual fit between highly esteemed film critics and the idea that film was a legitimate art form. It would, of course, be an overgeneralization to claim that audiences felt they had to accept critics' opinions wholesale in place of their own, especially for the most devoted and knowledgeable audience members. Rather than argue that film audiences "exchanged" their opinion rights, I would argue that they simply agreed to acknowledge that critical opinions were relevant and should help to inform their own views.

The data on book reviews and advertisements are also supportive of Shrum's argument that critical opinions are relevant for high but not popular art. Because literature's status as an art form has long been established, critical success was relevant to the evaluation of literature in the earliest time periods examined here. Shrum's argument can help us understand the coincidence between the treatment of film as art and the increasing relevance of critics for audiences. Through the provision of a legitimating ideology, critics helped film achieve the status of art. Because there was an available critical commentary to acknowledge, and because film was plausibly categorizable as art, appreciation of film involved reference to critical discourse on the subject.

The skeptical reader might point to today's newspaper and argue that my interpretation of evidence from film advertisements is misguided. Does the fact that the advertisements for *Charlie's Angels: Full Throttle* included quotes from critics mean that the film must be considered art? This question is warranted but off the mark because of its application of a contemporary perspective on a historical phenomenon.

The perspective in question is the common understanding of the meaning of quotes from critics. This understanding has changed a great deal in the last thirty years. In short, reliance on film critics as a marketing technique has been inflated to the point that its meaning and effectiveness has practically vanished. In 2001 Sony Pictures was sued by the state of Connecticut for inventing blurbs and falsely attributing them to an invented critic and then using these fictionalized quotes in film advertisements. This case is emblematic of the current state of affairs regarding the marketing technique of quoting from critics. First, studios believe that every film must have such in order to be effectively marketed. Second, studios apparently believe that audiences do not bother to discriminate between good and bad sources of quotes.

Quoting from critics today is not evidence that audiences are relying on experts to inform their own opinions. Instead, the role of these quotes is more similar to recommendations from *Consumer Reports*—they act as a spending guide. In a sense, movie studios killed the goose that laid the golden egg. By overusing quotes from critics and cheapening the kinds of quotes they use, the studios have rendered quoting an essentially worthless marketing technique.

How can we be so sure that the situation today is so different from that of thirty years ago? We need to know that it was different if we are to accept the evidence from film advertisements as relevant to explaining how Hollywood films became viewed as potential art. There is no decisive measurement for how audiences understood quoting from critics. However, a review of film advertisements from the late 1960s and early 1970s should convince even skeptical readers that the understanding of the inclusion of quotes from critics then had a lot more to do with art than it does now. Going back to the 1972 advertisement for *The Godfather*, for example, the critic from *Newsweek* is quoted lauding Marlon Brando's performance: "Now the king has returned to reclaim his throne. Like all great actors, He shows us what it is to be human. It is his gift to us." This is loftier discourse than is commonly found in today's film advertisements.

Browsing through newspaper archives for film advertisements, one finds countless examples that indicate that the art world for film was more robust in the 1970s than it is now. Here is a quote from *New York* magazine that was featured in the advertisement for the film *The Conversation*:

A MODERN HORROR FILM! "The Conversation" is exactly that, a distillation of the prime horror of the Watergate affair that was yet to come. Under Coppola's direction it succeeds on a variety of levels, as sheer thriller, as psychological study, as social analysis, and as political comment. Gene Hackman gives his best performance in years. Seldom has a professional been so ruthlessly examined on film and brought to such total exposure. "The Conversation" stands not only as a striking and important work but also as a confirmation of its creator's enormous talent! It is a beautifully made film, the rhythm absorbing! (*Washington Post*, April 12, 1974, B10)

In the same advertisement, several more critics are quoted, among them Pauline Kael:

I WAS FASCINATED BY THE FILM! It's a horror film centering on technology, on a man who's so involved in technology that he's forgotten what it's for, and what it's about. And that's a great modern theme, it's a sort of modern Kafka . . . a horror film. Extraordinarily elegantly structured. It's as if Coppola were in control of every single element. I think it's probably the best performance Gene Hackman has ever given. I LOVED THE WAY THIS MOVIE LOOKS! I LOVE THE WAY IT WORKS!

Not all quotes in 1970s film advertisements look so different from today's. The advertisement for *Serpico* (1973) prominently displays the four-star rating it gets from the *Daily News* and quotes from several television reviewers, among them Gene Shalit of WNBC. But unlike now, these quotes were often placed beside, or were themselves quotes that struck an academic tone, such as the following from Vincent Canby of the *New York Times* about the same film:

MOST PROVOCATIVE, A REMARKABLE RECORD OF ONE MAN'S REBELLION AGAINST THE SORT OF SLEAZINESS AND SECOND-RATEDNESS THAT HAS AFFECTED SO MUCH AMERICAN LIFE. "Serpico" is a disquieting and galvanizing film . . . galvanizing because of Al Pacino's splendid performance in the title role and because of the tremendous intensity that Mr. Lumet brings to this sort of subject. It reflects the quality of Detective Serpico's outrage, which in our society comes to look like an obsession bordering on madness.

It is in the content of the quotes, then, that the case can be made for advertisements as evidence for the creation of an art world for Hollywood films. The current marketing of films, with no pretensions for artistic status and with heavy input from reviewers, should not dictate our views of 1960s and 1970s marketing practices. We need to interpret the evidence from a historically informed perspective.

Summary

This chapter has demonstrated the importance of critical discourse in the creation of an art world for Hollywood films in the late 1960s. The greatest challenges in accomplishing this task are, first, collecting data on film discourse over a sixty-year time span, and, second, providing reassurances that the data are correctly interpreted.

Like much social science data, the indicators chosen in this case to measure the dependent variable (film discourse) are not above criticism. On the one hand, film reviews are ideal sources for documenting the changing nature of film discourse. On the other hand, as products tied to organizations that act in accordance with a variety of internal and external constraints and pressures, film reviews might, in fact, reflect more than pure discourse. That is to say, they are influenced by changes in the publications sampled, in the publishing world more generally, and by changes in American society. For this reason, corroborating evidence is required to bolster the favored interpretation of the evidence.

To recount the major findings of this factor, the most important discovery was the increased usage of a specialized vocabulary and critical techniques between 1925 and 1985, especially in the 1960s. Over time, critics adopted a vocabulary and a set of devices that indicate an approach to film as art rather than entertainment. Further analysis strongly suggests that this change was not caused by the changing qualities of films—early films were reviewed with a more artistic discourse in the 1960s than at the time of their release. Furthermore, a comparison with book reviews indicates that the observed changes in film reviewing truly represent a move toward artistic discourse.

These results underpin the primary contribution of this chapter—to provide empirical support for the assertion that cultural experts create an intellectualizing discourse in the formation of an art world. The greater claim that this discourse influenced the perception of Hollywood films among a segment of the public requires another data source. These data are found in film advertisements. During the late 1960s, critical success, as reflected in newspaper advertisements, increased dramatically as a selling point for films. Counts of both the number of quotes from critics and the number of words excerpted from film reviews increase, even when controlling for the total amount of advertising space. The observed trends reflect significant initial differences from the trends observed for literature, an established artistic genre, followed by later convergence. From the finding that critical success became much more important to the marketing of films in the late 1960s, one can infer that audiences were both familiar with and willing to accept the critical discourse that served as a rationale for film's proper status as art.

Finally, the data from reviews and advertisements were analyzed to support a hypothesis that is generated by the historical comparison of the American and various European film industries. The earlier formation of art worlds for film in Europe suggests that European films might have been more readily accepted as art in the United States, and that this legitimation of European film helped to break down prejudices against domestic film production. The final finding of this chapter is support for the idea that foreign films, perhaps as "ideal type" examples, provided a pathway for the intellectualization of Hollywood films. While all films were most strongly intellectualized beginning in the late 1960s, a legitimating ideology of foreign film as art appears to have developed in the 1940s and 1950s in the United States. The extension of this intellectualizing discourse to American films in the late 1960s follows other important developments in the film world and in American society.

As has been the case with other art forms, critics have played an important role in creating a legitimating discourse for film as art. They have influenced how film was viewed and understood, and whether it could appropriately be discussed as art when they began to use a sophisticated, interpretation-centered discourse in film review that employed a vocabulary and techniques resembling those used in other highbrow artistic criticism. These were then available to audiences for their own use in talking about the films they saw. Because the discourse constituted the means for explaining why Hollywood films could be understood as art, talk of Hollywood films as such was the key to making this idea believable, acceptable, and eventually normal, uncontroversial, and utterly conventional.

CHAPTER 5

Mechanisms for Cultural Valuation

THE ACCOUNT OF THE PROCESS through which Hollywood films were accepted as art in the late 1960s has relied on an explanatory framework with three parts—an opportunity space, production and consumption practices, and a legitimizing discourse.

Films were entertainment oddities when first invented, becoming more technologically sophisticated and developing conventional forms during the first two decades of the twentieth century and at the same time becoming part of American popular culture. Before the First World War, many foreign films were shown in the United States, but after that war ruined European film industries, few foreign films were imported while Hollywood films were frequently exhibited in Europe. Filmmaking and filmgoing occurred on a smaller scale in Europe, under economic conditions more distanced from the free market than was the case in the United States. In Europe generally, and in France especially, film as art was a cultural ideal carried out in both filmmaking and filmgoing.

Production and consumption practices in Hollywood, however, were similar to those of other mass culture industries and dissimilar to those of high art worlds. Into the 1940s, the studio system created films through an efficient and standardized production process. And into the 1950s, filmgoing was popular with working-class audiences and shunned by elites.

The 1960s were the time of greatest change for the U.S. film world. It was in this decade that changes within U.S. society altered the opportunity for Hollywood films to be perceived and experienced as an art form. Television's quick ascendancy as the most popular form of dramatic entertainment shrank film's audiences and provided a foil to highlight the artistic advantages of films. The baby-boom generation swelled the pool of people with college educations and made available many highly educated film patrons. At the same time, intellectual currents within U.S. culture, driven in large part by the Pop Art movement, evolved to make the boundaries between high and low culture more permeable. While distinctions between art and entertainment remained, the gulf between traditional high culture and popular culture was greatly diminished.

Many changes from within the U.S. film world likewise contributed to the new view of Hollywood films as genuine art, the most important of which involving the institutionalization of resources dedicated to promoting or experiencing Hollywood films as art. These developments included the establishment of film festivals and the creation of the academic field of film studies. The self-promotion of well-known directors as artists during the 1960s, quite rare in previous decades, also helped to shape public perceptions of Hollywood films as art.

Other film-world changes that made a difference were economic in nature. The economic problems brought about by the shrinking audience for films, in conjunction with an end to the industry's vertical integration in 1948, led to a restructuring of production processes so that the studio system gave way to director-centered production. The smaller audience, with the attendant decrease in the amount of Hollywood output, led many theaters to become exhibitors of high-quality European productions, launching the art-house movement. And it was the censorship of a European film that led to one of the most important legal decisions—the *Miracle* in 1952–and provided movies with First Amendment protection and eventually helped relax governmental censorship powers and end the restrictions of the Production Code in the mid-1960s. Hollywood films gained the freedom to address difficult themes.

Intellectual fields have both an institutional structure and a field-specific discourse. A specialized set of concepts, understandings, and vocabulary is required for discussing a field's products in a highly analytical fashion and for providing the rationales for calling those products art. Between cinema's invention at the turn of the century and the 1960s, the U.S. film world had an impoverished set of tools for analyzing and communicating about film. For decades there were few efforts to develop these tools because few of film's appreciators sought to discuss film as art. In the 1960s, however, U.S. film discourse adopted some of the vocabulary and techniques of other art worlds, along with ideas imported from French film criticism. Through film reviews, the vocabulary and these techniques found their way from film experts to a wider reading public. With the preexisting bias for finding value in European productions, the discourse was first applied to foreign films before being extended to Hollywood films as well.

The preceding chapters have reviewed the relevant history of the U.S. film world. In this chapter we consider how this historical process can be analyzed to address important questions within the sociology of art. In doing so, we can also fine-tune some of the concepts employed thus far as well as some of the conclusions drawn.

Here, we address five main questions raised by the case study of Hollywood films as art. First, where does film stand in the hierarchy of art, and why? The idea of a dichotomy between art and entertainment misrepresents the cultural spectrum in the United States that validates certain genres as more serious or more legitimate forms of art than others. How legitimate an art form are Hollywood films compared to other genres? Second, what role did class interests play? The role of cultural consumption in processes of stratification is a major vein of sociological research. What can the history of film add to our understanding of how the arts are implicated in class politics? Third, how has the empirical study of a legitimating discourse added to previous work on cultural hierarchy? Should the argument for the key role of a legitimating discourse for film revise our views on studies of other art worlds? Fourth, how did the factors leading to the art world for Hollywood film interact, and how does this alter our understanding of the roles these factors played? The factors involved in the evolution of the reception of Hollywood films have been treated as analytically distinct so far for the purposes of explanation. However, the interaction of the factors must be described to correctly understand the causal processes that were at work. Finally, this book is a case study of the creation of an art world. It offers an understanding of how cultural hierarchy is created and maintained for this case. What does the evidence here imply for theories of cultural hierarchy that have been proposed by others? Can it help to reconcile apparent differences between these theories?

WHY A MIDDLEBROW ART?

Despite the recognition of art in Hollywood films, as a class of cultural product they, like film more generally, do not enjoy the same highbrow legitimacy accorded to more established arts such as opera, sculpture, and painting. In fact, there is ambivalence about the proper place of film. The insights of both Becker (1982) and Bourdieu (1990[1965]) on the middle ground between highbrow and lowbrow can clarify our understanding of the current status of Hollywood films.

The uncertainty about whether Hollywood films can truly be art is reflected in the way various members of the film world and the public talk about films. Directors and actors sometimes talk about their "craft." Becker (1982:ch.9) provides an illuminating discussion of the relationship between art worlds and craft worlds and the mobility that sometimes occurs between them for specific kinds of work. The notions of "arts" and "crafts" are broad, varied, and overlap in common usage, so that it is not possible to speak of them as analytically distinct. Nevertheless, by conceiving of the ideal types of art and craft worlds, Becker is able to identify the principal differences between them in the standards according to which each is evaluated. Crafts are evaluated according to their ability to fulfill a function, the virtuoso skill involved in their creation, and their beauty. Arts, however, are evaluated according to the creativity, expressiveness, and uniqueness that they exhibit as well as their ability to engage a relevant set of conventions.

Becker (1982:277–78) explains that sometimes art worlds develop out of segments of craft worlds. His description of that process is worth quoting at length for its applicability to the case of film:

> We might imagine the differentiation of craftsmen and artist-craftsmen as a typical historical sequence. A craft world, whose aesthetic emphasizes utility and virtuoso skill and whose members produce works according to the dictates of clients or employers operating in some extracraft world, develops a new segment (Bucher, 1962; Bucher and Strauss, 1961). The new segment's members add to the basic aesthetic an emphasis on beauty and develop some additional organizations, which free them of the need to satisfy employers so completely. These artist-craftsmen develop a kind of art world around their activities, a "minor art" world. This world contains much of the apparatus of full-fledged major arts: shows, prizes, sales to collectors, teaching positions, and the rest.

In the case of film, I would argue that in addition to an emphasis on beauty per se, an aesthetic of message—expression of the director's personal vision and ideas—was the addition that helped create an art segment. The focus in reviews on messages suggests that this standard was more important than that of beauty, and is possibly related to film's narrative dimension, something not truly present in arts such as painting and sculpture.

In a fascinating case study, Bourdieu (1990[1965]) explains why photography in France in the 1960s was a middlebrow art. Like jazz, cinema, and chansons, photography belonged to the sphere of the legitimizable, between the "sphere of legitimacy" and the "sphere of the arbitrary" (96). Photography was not a legitimate or high art because, unlike the high arts, it was shut out of consideration by the authoritative institutions capable of bestowing the highest symbolic capital. Like jazz, cinema, and chansons, no authoritative institution was teaching audiences in a methodic and systematic manner how to experience photography as a part of legitimate high culture (Bourdieu 1990:96). Without a set of norms of evaluation, audiences do not feel "forced to adopt a dedicated, ceremonial and ritualized attitude" (Bourdieu 1990:95) as they do with legitimate culture.

Bourdieu also notes that there are specific characteristics of photography that worked against its acceptance by the guardians of high culture. For one thing, the mechanical nature of photography was at odds with the nature of legitimate culture. The common perception was that the camera did the work and required little training (Bourdieu 1990:5), and so "the photographic act in every way contradicts the popular representation of artistic creation as effort and toil" (Bourdieu 1990:77). This absence of serious training (at least the perception of it), and the fact that cameras were affordable by most people, meant that photography was not economically exclusive, which further worked against its legitimation (Bourdieu 1990:7).

On the other hand, photography was not at the bottom of the hierarchy either. Unlike the basest of arts, television for example, photography's practitioners and proponents had developed an aesthetic. Certain canons of taste had emerged, from amateur photography clubs and critical writing in magazines, by which photography could be judged separately from it social functions as a recording device (Bourdieu 1990:7–8). Some of the components of a high art world, to use Becker's (1982) terms, were in place for photography. In this way, Bourdieu's theory takes account of the role of agency in explaining the cultural value of photography; the genre had its proponents whose actions elevated it. His theory also incorporates an institutionalist dimension, as he recognizes how cultural legitimacy flows from the authority and resources of institutions.

These analyses are useful for understanding the history and present cultural classification of film. European art worlds for film probably developed independent of a craft phase, and they clearly developed early on. In Hollywood, this phase was provoked by the enduring financial difficulties that had started in the 1940s and had reached a nadir in the 1960s, a crisis that was brought on by the downturn in moviegoing. At the outset of the downturn, studios reacted conservatively, and risk-averse executives retained much control over the creative process. However, after many years it became clear that that strategy was not working as moviegoing continued to decline. The prolonged nature of the crisis made the studios open to a new mode of production, which saw the independence and authority of the director increase, just when auteurism had been imported (see chapter 3). By the 1960s, the long duration of the financial crisis worked to decrease constraints on directors and there was much more room for them to follow their own dictates. Previously their work had been judged by its ability to fulfill the function as defined by the studios—to entertain and to make a profit. The development of an art world for Hollywood films was precisely the assertion of an alternative standard for evaluation—that they be judged by their beauty, by what they had to communicate, and by how they related to a relevant body of work.

Why, then, is film not at or near the top of the cultural hierarchy? And why are Hollywood films yet further from the top? There are several important reasons. Interestingly, the lower ranking of film is not due to a lack of sponsors among intellectuals. At various times certain intellectuals have hailed film as the pinnacle of artistic potential: "More recently, the thesis that all the arts are leading toward one art has been advanced by enthusiasts of the cinema. The candidacy of film is founded on its being so exact and, potentially, so complex—a rigorous combination of music, literature, and the image" (Sontag 1969:119–20).

Yet more common is the argument that film deserves recognition at least alongside the other high arts. Consider the following excerpt from a 1980 *New York Times* film review of *Wise Blood*, and adapted from the novel by Flannery O'Connor:

> Movies aren't a lesser form of art, but because they are decidedly differ-ent, most of us are inclined to be impatient with attempts to translate some piece of great fiction into a form for which it was never intended. It is as foolhardy as an operation designed to turn a Labrador retriever into a Siamese cat. The operation seldom succeeds and because it sel-dom succeeds, even great movies are downgraded and our expectations of all movies are diminished. This is too bad because when the very good, much more than adequate screen adaptation comes along, it often goes, if not unrecognized, not fully appreciated. (March 2, II:19:1)

Given that there is a cadre of cultural experts who would support film's full artistic legitimacy, why, then, do we think of film as still not quite as prestigious or serious a medium as, for instance, painting or literature? Why do even the most legitimated films not enjoy the cultural reverence accorded to *Ulysses*, *Mona Lisa*, or the *Goldberg Variations*? Perhaps the most important reason is that there *has not been a purification of genres* as there has been in, for example, music or musical theater. It is easy to see how without a clear distinction between "opera" and "musicals," two genres that have many similarities, opera might not be so prestigious. Likewise, the segregation of classical from other forms of music serves as a clear example of how music can be art. The popular conception of film is more inclusive and fails to sharply differentiate those productions seeking to belong in the art world and those seeking to belong in the craft world.

To a limited extent there has been purification; for example, foreign films are often set above domestic films, and independent films are often considered different as well. But these distinctions are too often blurred to function as determinants of art and non-art. Many Hollywood produc-tions are self-consciously artistic—even today (e.g., *The Man Who Wasn't There*, *Being John Malkovich*). And many foreign and independent pro-ductions entertain wide audiences and turn a profit (e.g., *Life Is Beautiful*, *The Blair Witch Project*). Moreover, the presentation of "serious" Hollywood dramas in the same theaters with lighter Hollywood productions further inhibits a clear conception of film as art. In order to achieve high art prestige, films like *American Beauty* need to be exclusively exhibited in different locations from films like *American Pie*. In general, this does not happen.[1]

Ironically, the awards that are an integral part of the art world for film add to the genre confusion that works against artistic legitimacy. For the general public, the best-known and most important awards, such as the Academy Awards and those conferred by the New York Film Critics Circle, often go to big-budget, entertainment-oriented Hollywood films. This situation tends to reinforce the inclusive notion of film as a single genre—films may differ in how good they are, but they all belong in the same category. It seems that there is confusion about how to interpret these awards. When *Gladiator* won the best picture Oscar for 2000, was this an affirmation of the film's artistry or its craftsmanship? This ambiguity tempers the effectiveness of film awards as a means for validating film as art.

When art house theaters were more numerous, in the 1960s and 1970s, they facilitated the redefinition of film as art in precisely this way. The distinction, however, was apparently not meant to last. With the availability of classics and limited distribution features first on video and now on DVD as well, today art house theaters are few in number. Many Hollywood films are explicitly entertainment without pretensions to art. The current lack of genre distinction suppresses artistic claims for those Hollywood films that do seek to be seen as art. The category "Hollywood film" includes too many films that do not possess the qualities that audiences believe are characteristic of art, in that they are not challenging, difficult, or innovative.

It is often argued that art benefits from the prestige of its audience (DiMaggio 1982, 1992; Levine 1988). A strong connection to high SES audiences can legitimate culture as art. As filmgoing became increasingly popular with college-educated audiences in the 1960s, this association helped to elevate the film's prestige. However, the confusion surrounding genres again worked to obscure the full potential benefit of prestige by association. So while it might have been true that different kinds of audiences were seeing different films (Gans 1974), the lack of an institutionalized and clearly articulated distinction between serious Hollywood films and lighter material prevented broad acknowledgement of audience segmentation. The status of art is clearly not solely a function of the status of its patrons. However, it is a factor that plays into cultural hierarchy. If there were strong audience segmentation to accompany genre segmentation, as there is with classical and popular music, for example, serious Hollywood films would have a much stronger claim to artistic legitimacy.[2]

Finally, what has damaged the claims of those who would consecrate Hollywood films as art, perhaps more than any other factor, is the pervasive image of film as business—and for good reason. Unlike art that is under the direction of trustee-governed nonprofit organizations, profit-oriented studios and executives are deeply and conspicuously involved in film production and promotion. Even independent filmmakers are often popularly portrayed as vitally concerned with securing large box-office results for minimal financial investments. Artists need to profess a degree of "disinterestedness" in economic matters to enjoy credibility (Bourdieu 1993:39). In the 1960s, the recent shift away from the studio system highlighted the new independence of directors, many of whom were seen as economically disinterested artists. This impression jibed with the predominant romantic ideology of art.

Film scholarship has shown, however, that the mid-1970s were a turning point for Hollywood. It was then that the industry shifted to the "blockbuster strategy," where more financial resources are devoted to fewer films as a gamble that the overall payoff will be higher (Baker and Faulkner 1991; Schatz 2003). It would require a separate study to fully investigate the causes and consequences of the retrenchment of the art world for Hollywood films. Schatz (2003:26–28) argues that various forces acted in concert to bring on the blockbuster era: the increasing number of theaters in shopping malls, "shifting market patterns and [a] changing conception of youth culture," the "increasing influence of Hollywood's top agents and talent agencies," the elimination of tax loopholes and write-offs which had provided incentives for investors, especially those financing independent films, "the introduction of television-based marketing," and the creation of the home video market, which vastly expanded profit potential.

There is no doubt that the blockbuster formula has worked against an ethos of film as art, both in terms of the content it encourages and the publicity it generates through business practices involving hundreds of millions of dollars. This is not to say, however, that the blockbuster strategy has eliminated the potential for film art. Not all Hollywood films are made according to the blockbuster formula, or at least its extreme form, and independent films are exempted by definition. Moreover, there are those who would argue that some blockbuster productions are true art. Nevertheless, the cliché that certain well-regarded films of the 1960s and 1970s would not be made under today's funding priorities certainly holds some truth. This is likely the result of the shift away from targeting young adults toward targeting teenagers who have in recent decades become the mainstay of the theatrical film market.[3]

At the same time that we have moved from the golden era of 1960s and 1970s Hollywood and into the blockbuster era, many argue there has been a shift in the function of film critics. Although still popular and well published, critics in general claim that they no longer have the ability to set the aesthetic agenda for audiences, and they decry their declining relevance for how people think about films (Denby 1998; Wolcott 1997). Haberski (2001) argues that the diminution of the cultural influence of film critics is a result of the decline of cultural authority in general. Because we live in an age of aesthetic relativism, where audience preferences are just as "legitimate" as critics' preferences, the role of critics has been significantly narrowed. In addition, critics were influential for audiences in their championing of an underdog cultural form. Now that the fight for recognition of films as art, especially the Hollywood films that many people actually saw, has been won, there is inherently less interest in what critics have to say (Haberski 2001:189).

If it is true that critics are less relevant, then we have evidence in strong support of Shrum's thesis that the distinction between art and entertainment is correlated with the relevance of expert opinion. Moreover, this helps us better understand the observed trends in the characteristics of film review discussed in chapter 4. For most measures we saw decreases in the final time period—film reviews were using less of an artistic discourse than in the 1970–80 period. In the blockbuster era, since the peak of the art world for Hollywood films, film critics have relinquished the art discourse that was once dominant. In part this is because the films decreasingly lent themselves to that discourse. But in part this is also because audiences no longer looked to critics to expand their perspective on films, to explore meanings and ways in which films built on past work. Instead, they began to look merely for endorsements—critics became the *Consumer Reports* of films, as well as cogs in the Hollywood marketing machine. While some serious criticism still gets written, there are now a great many "hack critics . . . handing out rave quotes like free candy on the streets" (Denby 1998:94).

FILM CONSUMPTION AS CULTURAL CAPITAL

This study has found that the history of film has many similarities to other cultural genres that were legitimated as art. For example, after the introduction of film as an alternative form of dramatic entertainment, theater appeared more artistic because in many ways it was more in line with prevailing conventions concerning the characteristics of real art (DiMaggio 1992). In addition, on the average the audience further experienced an upward shift in socioeconomic status as working-class audiences attended films more often. These developments were paralleled by the changes that occurred in the field of film following the introduction of television.

Another similarity exists between opera and film. The creation of opera houses exclusively for the staging of classical opera helped purify the genre of vaudeville and other musicals, which were more often at odds with notions of high art. The creation of art houses for films functioned in a similar fashion for film, although less effectively so.

In studies of other art forms, the research has drawn strong links between artistic consumption and class politics. Does film consumption have a similar tie to class politics? That is to say, does knowledge about and well-developed taste for films serve as cultural capital?

According to DiMaggio (1982), one of the key features of the creation of the cultural hierarchy in the United States during the last half of the nineteenth century is that it served class interests. DiMaggio (1982:47) argues that the differentiation of fine art (painting and sculpture) and symphonic music from entertainment in Boston was accomplished by "cultural capitalists." These members of the Boston elite took action to symbolically segregate themselves and to bolster their cultural authority at a time of political and economic challenges from the rising middle classes and immigrants. The participation of the Boston Brahmins in an exclusionary high culture transformed them "from an elite into a social class" (DiMaggio 1982:49).

Levine (1988:176) makes a similar argument regarding the impetus for the valorization of Shakespearean drama and other high art genres. Processes of urbanization, industrialization, and immigration were threatening the traditional social order. Elites in major cities developed institutions for creating and exhibiting high culture, along with an etiquette for cultural appreciation. One result of the creation of legitimate high art in the United States was to provide a social space to which elites could retreat: "culture free of intrusion, free of dilution, free of the insistent demands of the people and the marketplace; culture that would ennoble, elevate, purify; culture that would provide a refuge from the turmoil, the feelings of alienation, the sense of impotence that were becoming all too common" (206). DeNora describes another example of the elevation of a culture as a means to defend class privilege (1991). She argues that Viennese aristocrats had traditionally been uniquely able to afford to provide classical music concerts for themselves and one another. When the rising bourgeoisie began to imitate them, they created an ideology of "serious" classical music, a taste for the right composers shared only by them. Without the organizational means for separation, they turned to ideological means to style themselves as "aristocrats of taste" (337). The particular kind of music they selected was then sacralized as "great" music.

The history of film evinces both similarities and differences with these other case studies regarding the use of culture to bolster class differences. On the one hand, the history of film differs in ways that are importantly related to timing. The creation of the art world for film happened much later than the other cases described. In the United States, the contours of social stratification had been clearly established and linked to cultural consumption patterns for many decades by the 1960s. Film as art, therefore, existed in contrast to earlier high arts.

As discussed in chapter 2, the expansion of the boundaries of art to include previously lowbrow and folk genres was an intellectual and aesthetic shift that fully bloomed in the 1960s. This shift, or "attack" (Peterson 1997:85), on highbrow snobbery had important class implications. It occurred in concert with swiftly rising educational levels and the increasing importance of education for occupational outcomes. The college-educated, the core of the new film generation, were on their way to becoming members of the upper-middle class. But rather than merely imitate the high-status consumption patterns of prior classes, they relied on new cultural signals to symbolically set themselves apart from their predecessors (Brooks 2000). Film—good films, the best European and then Hollywood films—served this function. Knowing the current discourse about film became cultural capital—a high-status cultural cue. The corollary of that use of film knowledge is that film became accepted as art. It was thought of as a more democratic, less snobbish art than the stuffy high culture of opera and museumgoing, but it was to some extent put to the same uses—as a status marker.

This function of film was viable only after film audiences shrank and became less clearly working class. In the same way as established high arts, once the products were less "contaminated" through appreciation by low-status audiences, they became useful as markers.

An Emphasis on Intellectualizing Discourse

This study differs from previous studies of artistic legitimation in its heavier emphasis on the role of a legitimating ideology. The reason for this emphasis is well articulated in a 1964 article in the *Journal of Philosophy* by Arthur Danto. The recent emergence of the Pop Art movement, wherein artists inserted everyday objects into artistic contexts and labeled them art, highlighted for Danto the role of theory in creating art.

> What in the end makes the difference between a Brillo box and a work of art consisting of a Brillo Box is a certain theory of art. It is the theory that takes it up into the world of art, and keeps it from collapsing into the real object which it is (in a sense of *is* other than that of artistic identification). Of course, without the theory, one is unlikely to see it as art, and in order to see it as part of the artworld, one must have

mastered a good deal of artistic theory as well as a considerable amount of the history of recent New York painting. It could not have been art fifty years ago. But then there could not have been, everything being equal, flight insurance in the Middle Ages, or Etruscan typewriter erasers. The world has to be ready for certain things, the artworld no less than the real one. It is the role of artistic theories, these days as always, to make the artworld, and art, possible. It would, I should think, never have occurred to the painters of Lascaux that they were producing *art* on those walls. Not unless there were neolithic aestheticians. (581)

The passage makes clear how our perceptions of what is art are influenced by the presence of a theory to apply to particular cultural products. Without a set of conventions to measure films against, there would have been no way to see the art in them, for art is defined by its relation to conventions, adhering to some and playing with others. The legitimating ideology espoused in the film world articulated those conventions in the familiar vocabulary of artistic appreciation and applied them to particular cases so audiences could see for themselves why a film was art.

An acknowledgment of the crucial role of a legitimating ideology permits us to recognize how cultural experts fit into a concept of public legitimacy. As recognized authorities,[4] their pronouncements can influence popular perceptions. Previous authors have not clearly explained how legitimacy among experts relates to legitimacy among the wider public. In the case of film, the marginal idea that film was an art form was entertained by relatively few cultural experts for several decades before the rapid formation of a near consensus on the matter in the 1960s. Previously there had been a fairly high consensus that film was not an art form. Although not the only factor, such consensus among experts contributed to an enhanced view of film as art among the public.

In addition to a greater emphasis on the role of a legitimating ideology, this study differs from previous ones in the provision of data concerning that discourse. While many scholars have pointed to the key role of a legitimating ideology, none has empirically documented and analyzed its emergence. My analysis provides a more general model for the analysis of discourse in other cultural and intellectual fields. When they began to use a sophisticated, interpretation-centered discourse in film review, critics influenced how film was viewed and understood, whether film could appropriately be discussed as art, and vocabulary resembling that used in other highbrow artistic criticism. No critic would claim that all films merit the status of art. However, by devoting serious attention and analyses and a specialized discourse in their writing on film for a popular audience, critics asserted that it was possible to search for, and find, artistic value in films. It is important to note, however, that while they were the primary disseminators of the discourse, they were not its only creators. The legitimating ideology for film as art was the product of a range of film-world participants including critics, academics, filmmakers, and other intellectuals involved with the organization of festivals, programs, and institutes. The focus on film review is justified because its popularity ensured that the discourse of film appreciation was disseminated to the wider public. However, because of the communication between critics, academics, and other thinkers on film, it was not the sole site for the development of this ideology.

INTEGRATION OF FACTORS

In order to assess the role played by the various social forces and factors described here, they have been separated and studied in turn. History, of course, does not progress in analytically distinct units. It would be wrong to present an analysis that discusses each factor in isolation from the others and not to acknowledge the inevitable interaction between them. The strong emphasis here on the 1960s as the turning point in the art world for Hollywood film, and hence the simultaneity of many of the factors, suggests that there were a number of reciprocal relationships occurring.

The various elements of the art world for Hollywood film interacted in ways that increased the momentum of that world. In the most general sense, the creation of a more favorable opportunity space in the 1960s must have been, at some level, perceptible to those who would champion Hollywood films' status as art. This perception, then, would have encouraged the movement to treat film as art. To be more specific, the enormous growth in the number of college-educated people would have been taken into consideration by those who wrote about film. Knowing they had a potential audience with whom they could communicate, film commentators must have been spurred on to take up the task. Similarly, those who were establishing film festivals would have had reasons to be more optimistic about their endeavors. And, most directly, the growth in film studies in the universities themselves would have been greatly facilitated by growing numbers of students to teach.

Further connections can be made between the financial factors cited and the institutionalization of film resources. The financial troubles of American studios caused by the popularity of television and by industry restructuring in the 1950s and 1960s allowed festivals to play a larger role in determining which films and directors succeeded in the United States (Mast 1981:333). Film festivals granted prestige and exposure to many foreign and independent films whose popularity had increased among a more educated audience at a time of decreased Hollywood output.

The growing taste for European films also coincided with Hollywood's business difficulties. Financially troubled Hollywood studios, eager to participate in and profit from the trend, hired many foreign directors to make films for American distribution. The film companies further facilitated a view of film as art by entering festivals and promoting their films as artistic products.

Perhaps the strongest interdependence among the factors mentioned was the link between academic film study and the intellectualization of film in reviews. The growth in the number of academic courses and programs on film not only added legitimacy to the idea of film as art, but also aided in the development of a more sophisticated language and style of reviews. While most of the critics writing for major publications in the 1960s and 1970s (including those writing for the publications sampled here) attended college before the emergence of film programs and so did not have academic backgrounds in film, they had the opportunity to read academic work and communicate with like-minded admirers of film. A developing art world gathers its own momentum; cooperation begets further cooperation, and the seizing of opportunities creates further opportunities.

THE STUDY OF CULTURAL HIERARCHY

Although there have been many excellent case studies of the valorization of cultural objects, I am aware of only one sociologist who has attempted to theorize cultural hierarchy in general terms. Pierre Bourdieu's (1993) analysis of the field of cultural production posits that it operates according to a logic that is inverted relative to the economic logic of society. Unlike the literal currency of the economy, the cultural field's most valuable currency is symbolic. Symbolic capital is bestowed selectively upon works, artists, and genres by legitimate authorities of legitimation, namely universities and artistic academies.

Bourdieu's analysis, illustrated through reference to the French literary field, focuses on the finer distinctions between the most highly legitimized and consecrated genres and works of art (within fields of restricted production) and other forms of middlebrow or bourgeois art (within fields of large-scale production).[5] The principles he posits to account for prestige distinctions can be extended to shed light on the distinction between art and entertainment. For Bourdieu, the defining feature of cultural production is the role permitted for the disavowal of commercial interests, which strongly contrasts with the prevailing mode of operation in the economic field. Disinterest in the accumulation of economic capital is replaced in legitimate art by interest in the accumulation of symbolic capital. This is most true for those genres situated in a field of restricted production, which demonstrate their authenticity as art by clearly showing disinterest in extra-artistic concerns such as money.

This logic also operates in fields of large-scale production, but less so because the pursuit of economic capital is not as taboo. Intellectuals and other cultural producers grant symbolic capital through recognition. Economic success is granted by mass audiences and detracts from the viability of claims to disinterestedness. Artistic legitimacy, then, exists for genres in proportion to the consecration by "symbolic bankers" (1993:77), those with the prestige, reputation, and authority—symbolic capital—to invest in particular works or genres.

The conflict between earning both symbolic and economic capital is historically rooted in the belief that art and commerce are rightly opposed. It is necessary for artists, therefore, to cultivate and maintain an image of disinterestedness in economic success. Only they are eligible for consecration by legitimate authorities. Likewise, the most legitimate genres of art are those that are most fully consecrated by the academic and professional authorities within art worlds: painting, theater, sculpture, music, and literature.

In many ways this study affirms the principles behind Bourdieu's analysis of cultural hierarchy. Bourdieu has not, however, traced the trajectory of a particular art from a low point in the cultural hierarchy to a higher point. There is much to be learned about the nature of cultural hierarchy *as a process* by studying cases of "aesthetic mobility" (Peterson 1994:179). Lopes's (2001) study of the aesthetic mobility of jazz highlights the significance of many of the same art-world features identified by others; the role of cultural entrepreneurs and critics interested in gaining prestige for jazz; the development of publications and clubs and the creation of concerts to institutionalize resources and practices devoted to jazz as art; and the evolving relationship between jazz and the wider worlds of both American music and American society generally. Within these musical and social contexts, the meaning of jazz evolved as its connections to audiences segmented by race and class evolved. Jazz's place within the American cultural hierarchy was influenced by the role it played in the identity politics of high-status audience segments who were able to capitalize on its status as a genre of music not only outside the established high-culture canon but also associated with groups whose outsider status contributed to their authenticity and credibility as artists. This occurred over the course of several decades when the traditional barriers between high and low culture were blurring, with the rise of jazz a contributing factor to the blurring of these boundaries.

The analysis in this book combines the strength of historical analysis with the insights of Bourdieu's analysis of cultural fields and cultural hierarchy in particular. The analysis here also incorporates various insights from an array of prior empirical case studies of cultural hierarchy to build an argument that explains the valorization of Hollywood films in terms that are useful for understanding cultural hierarchy more generally. For any cultural genre, its status within a hierarchy should be analyzed according to the historical features of its opportunity space, its art-world institutions and practices, and the features of the discourse that frame and interpret the genre.

Within this framework, there are several key insights about cultural hierarchy that must be emphasized. First, cultural valorization has much to do with status seeking. Status has associative properties, meaning that people gain status through association with high-status things. It is also a sociological truism that people are status seeking. Both cultural producers and cultural consumers are making decisions that have consequences for their status when they produce and consume. The shape of the cultural hierarchy is influenced by the outcome of cultural politics where different genres are supported by their sponsors. This might seem clearer in the case of the most consecrated artistic genres, but it is equally true in the case of Hollywood films.

Second, cultural hierarchy is always multicausal. It is an academic cliché to posit that two or more seemingly competing theories are in fact complementary. Nevertheless, when it comes to prior research on cultural hierarchy, the cliché is apt. Take, for example, the apparent contradiction between "compositional" and "discursive" approaches to understanding the status of culture. Gans's (1974) influential work on taste cultures and taste publics posits a causal correlation between the status of cultural genres and the status of audience members. At the same time, "the major source of differentiation between taste cultures and publics is socioeconomic level or class" (1974:70). The implicit argument here is that cultural valorization is a result of group solidarity. Elite groups provide high status to the cultural forms with which they are strongly identified. Shrum (1996:ch.10), on the other hand, argues that distinctions between art and popular culture are founded on differences in discursive practices. Unmediated cultural consumption, where critical input is deemed irrelevant, both signals that the culture is popular and is not art and reinforces that classification by leaving no room for a theory of art to play a role. In contrast, those genres for which criticism is deemed relevant are signaled and reinforced as art. It is, of course, unnecessary to view culture only as art or non-art; cultural productions are situated along a spectrum of valorization. This flexibility makes it easy to recognize that there is no need to argue that only one determinant of status may be operating. Cultural valorization is influenced by *both* the existence of "status bargains" *and* other factors such as the status of audience members. A cultural form that has an audience entirely of high socioeconomic status and a tradition of critical mediation will more likely find legitimacy as art than a cultural form with an audience of low or mixed socioeconomic status or lacking a tradition of mediation. The case of film is supportive of Shrum's argument but is also consistent with a compositional approach. It appears that the increase in the relevance of critics closely followed the recognition of film as art. At the same time however, the composition of film's audience shifted to include relatively more members of high socioeconomic status. As discussed, the rise of an educated audience was indispensable for creating a readership for the critics, so the two developments were intimately related to each other as well as to the outcome for film, namely the enhancement of film's legitimacy as art.

Third, the beliefs and values of Western societies deem commercial interests antithetical to the legitimacy of art. The Romantic notion of art prevails, connecting artistic legitimacy with the noble activities of rare geniuses. The case of film conforms to this as well. Unlike the genres studied by DiMaggio (1982, 1992) and Levine (1988)—fine art, opera, drama, modern dance, and theater—film in the United States has almost entirely been created by large, profit-oriented corporations. Yet it also managed to achieve a certain degree of legitimacy as art. It is probably true that it would be even more widely accepted as art if it were solely in the hands of nonprofit organizations. But the history of film still supports the logic behind the argument that nonprofit organizations can legitimate cultural products as art. Production conditions for film in important ways resembled, at least to outsiders, the conditions of nonprofit production and so partially resolved the tension between the opposing exigencies of art and entertainment. Most significant, the director-centered production system placed an emphasis on portraying the director as largely unfettered by commercial interests or constraints. It is probably most accurate to say that a small number of directors were allowed a measured amount of greater creative flexibility during the studios' financial crises in the 1960s. However, the *image* of a director as an autonomous artist was widespread, and it was through this *perception* that the shift to director-centered production most influenced the acceptance of Hollywood films as art. In this way, the director was film's analog to the author in literature, the playwright in theater, and the composer in music and opera. Foreign films, especially, were convincingly noncommercial, most often produced with small budgets and strongly identified with a star auteur director.

Finally, artistic legitimation is an essentially intellectual enterprise requiring cultural authority. Art worlds are, of course, collectively created and institutionalized by everyone from the artist him- or herself to the factory workers who make the chairs the audience members occupy. But there is a special role for cultural experts in artistic fields, where quality and achievement are tremendously difficult to objectively measure. In virtually every cultural field, quality and success almost always involve some subjectivity to their measurement, no matter whether the field is science, sports, law, journalism, or finance. But the degree to which quality and success in art resist objective measurement exceeds that in any other field. Quality and success are therefore more influenced by experts with cultural authority in art than in other fields. Because discourse is the means by which experts participate in art worlds, a special attention to discourse is essential for understanding cultural hierarchy.

Notes

1. The differences between musical genres provide a good example of how some genres are widely seen as art while the artistic status of other is contested. In their analysis of musical tastes as status markers, Peterson and Simkus find "that there is general agreement among Americans that classical music anchors the upper end of the taste hierarchy," while "there is less and less consensus on the ranking as one moves down the hierarchy of taste" (1992:168). The ranking of musical genres begins with classical, followed by folk, jazz, "middle-of-the-road," big band, rock, religious, soul, and finally country. While Peterson and Simkus were looking at prestige rather than artistic status per se, because art is an honored category, those genres that are more prestigious are also more readily viewed as art.

2. Two of the best known proponents of proceduralist viewpoints are George Dickie (1974), who proposed an institutional theory of art, and Arthur Danto (1964), who focused on art's relationship to the theory of an art world.

3. Much has been written about the quality of Hollywood production between the late 1960s and the late 1970s. Among film scholars there is debate about the extent to which the films of this era were literally better and more deserving of being called art (King 2002:13). Even if one were to agree that the films were better, the question remains as to why recognition of these films as art became widespread. After all, not all culture that could conceivably qualify as good art is widely seen as such. Moreover, the quality of films in the 1960s and 1970s does not explain how many forgotten classics of the 1920s, 1930s, and 1940s were reinterpreted as art during that period after having been dismissed.

4. Competing histories give more credit to the Lumière brothers of France for some of the key inventions involved in the creation and exhibition of motion pictures.

5. In addition, while the first and second factors are both helpful for understanding how a product, idea, or practice can become popular or commonplace, the third is needed to explain the creation of legitimacy—the shifting of a boundary between categories.

6. In recent work Ferguson (1998) has argued for a distinction between the similar notions of "field," elaborated by Bourdieu (1993), and "world," developed by Becker (1982), as they pertain to cultural production. She characterizes an art world by its "cooperative networks," which "can exist only in fairly circumscribed social or geographical settings endowed with mechanisms that promote connection" (635–36). A field, on the other hand, offers "the acute consciousness of positions and possibilities for social mobility in a circumscribed social space" (634), and is "structured by a largely textual discourse that continually (re)negoti-

ates the systemic tensions between production and consumption" (637). I contend that the differences between field and world are of degree rather than type. For instance, Bourdieu (1993) illustrates his concept of field through a study of the *French* literary field—fields, too, need to be bounded geographically and socially to be analytically useful. Moreover, Becker (1982) identifies the role that reputation (ch. 11) and "critical discussions" (339) play in art worlds. While they are not central, they are nonetheless important to the dynamics of an art world. Ferguson seems to emphasize the ideological foundation of a field and the organizational foundation of a world. However, in their original formulations both field and world allow for both ideological and organizational elements, albeit to varying degrees. I use both terms interchangeably. Ferguson argues that we know relatively little about how cultural fields originate. I would argue that if we accept the analogy between an art world and a cultural field , we know more than Ferguson claims about the origins of cultural fields. Some of the literature reviewed here can be interpreted as explaining antecedents of cultural fields.

CHAPTER 2
THE CHANGING OPPORTUNITY SPACE: DEVELOPMENTS
IN THE WIDER SOCIAL CONTEXT

1. In discussing opportunity space, DiMaggio (1992) also places a heavy emphasis on the imitation of cultural genres. In the cases he studies, the institutional support for the genres was modeled on existing organizational forms of high-art sponsorship. Therefore, the timing of the transformation in prestige for those cultural genres is significant precisely because it allows for imitation. For DiMaggio, the concept of an opportunity space takes into account the existence of models available for imitation. I argue that actors in the film world likewise created institutions and organizational forms that were sometimes based on existing high-art models. However, these actions are analytically separate from the influences connected with the opportunity space as defined by the existence of competitors or substitutes and the availability of patrons. The influence of institutionalized resources and practices is discussed in the following chapter.

2. There is a partial analogy between my analysis of the legitimation of Hollywood film and Stinchcombe's explanation of the relationship between social structure and the founding of organizations: "The organizational inventions that can be made at a particular time in history depend on the social technology available" (1965:153). As an example, Stinchcombe writes that "railroads perhaps could not be 'invented' until the social forms appropriate to an inherently very large-scale enterprise had been invented" (1965:160). The variables that determine the state of "social technology" that Stinchome focuses on are literacy and advanced schooling, urbanization, a money economy, political revolution, and density of social life (1965:150). Similarly, if one views the creation of an art world for film as a much dispersed type of organization, one can argue that its creation awaited the appropriate "social technology" discussed in this chapter.

3. There is a large degree of similarity between the concept of an opportunity space and that of a "niche," as it has been developed in the population ecology

paradigm by biologists studying plants and animals. It has since been applied to the study of organizations (see e.g., Hannan and Freeman 1988; Hannan and Freeman 1987; Hannan and Freeman 1977). If this case is conceptualized as a competition between different "species" of cultural products for Americans, the development of television can be seen as having "crowded out" the niche for popular dramatic entertainment. Film was not sufficiently competitive for the resources (audience members) within that niche. Similarly, if this case is conceptualized as a competition between different "species" of leisure-time options, then the increase in the birth rate can be seen as having greatly limited the availability of resources (audience members) necessary for the survival of film within the niche of America's dominant leisure-time activity. The increase in the number of highly educated audience members, on the other hand, can be seen as having "opened up" a niche by making available resources (audience members) within a niche for film as art. The concept of an opportunity space is meant to refer to both the competitors and the availability of patrons as resources.

4. An observant reader might notice that the class breakdown of this audience was probably not so far off from the general population. Although it is not clear from the source how "leisure class" is defined, it is most likely only meant to describe a small proportion of the population, the high end of the socioeconomic scale. Nevertheless, the breakdown provides an interesting contrast with the case of an established high-culture activity, opera attendance. While only a minority of the upper or upper-middle class attend opera, audiences for opera are nonetheless almost entirely elite (Blau 1986). Other high-culture audiences are disproportionately elite. It would seem that, insofar as association with the status of audience members matters, the status of culture is quite sensitive to "class contamination." High culture is associated with a "purification" of audiences, not merely a representative sample of high SES members.

5. Sklar finds evidence for a difference in the class character of American and British film audiences from a very early period. He quotes from a 1910 handbook for theater managers and operators in the United States that states that working-class neighborhoods are ideal locations, and wealthy neighborhoods or neighborhoods with many churchgoers would not provide business or would interfere with business. In contrast, a similar handbook from the same period in Great Britain advised that a location among the "artizan or middle classes" was advantageous relative to working-class areas (1994:16). In the main, there appears to be more evidence that film audiences in Great Britain were primarily working class until at least the 1930s.

6. Kracauer was, ultimately, pointing to the distinctions between high art and the cinema, including the differences in the acts of high-art reception and "distraction" of mass art for which the new "palaces" were created. Nevertheless, what is significant here is the phenomenon of a high-art sheen on film theaters in Berlin in the 1920s.

7. Since filmgoing is more common among youth, inclusion of all teenagers may boost the annual attendance rate. However, supposing that the inclusion of those aged thirteen to seventeen doubled overall attendance, however unlikely, German annual per capita attendance would still lag far behind American attendance.

8. See Adler (1976) for a discussion of the relationship between moments of social or political change and aesthetic innovation.

9. The German film industry was the exception. Uricchio (1996:66) notes that through centralized authority and the work of leading industrialists, the German industry strengthened. However, U.S. market penetration in Germany remained high through much of the war (Uricchio 1996:70).

10. See Schluepmann (1986) for a discussion of a 1913 attempt by German filmmakers to link film with highbrow literature.

11. Crisp, in writing about the French audience for film after the development of television, provides a way to characterize the behavior of the American audience for film. Crisp writes that filmgoing became the provenance of "that bourgeois audience still willing to 'go out to the cinema,' as it expected to go out to the opera, to a concert, or to a play" (1993:73). This feature of filmgoing, namely leaving the home and making an occasion out of a film, likewise may have contributed to a culture of filmgoing as artistic experience among certain audiences in the United States.

12. It is also possible that young people in the 1960s became the film generation in part because they had acquired a familiarity with a large number of old films through television broadcasts. Such exposure would not have been possible for earlier audiences. It is true that film studios initially resisted broadcasts of old movies because they were concerned about the negative effects of television on cinema attendance. They eventually, however, permitted the networks access to their archives once they had established that the financial benefits outweighed the costs.

13. Although data correlating college plans and cinema attendance are not readily available, one doubts that a similar comment could be made today.

14. Richard Maltby (2003) reviews data on film audiences from several decades. Interestingly, he finds that in addition to changing educational levels, audiences that were originally majority female were either no longer so or were majority male by the 1960s. He writes that

> [s]urveys in the 1920s and early 1930s supported the industry assumption that women formed the dominant part of its audience, and all the evidence from the trade press and other industry sources makes clear that during those decades the motion picture industry assumed that women were its primary market, both through their own attendance and through their roles as opinion leaders, influencing the males with whom they attended. (20)

However, "[i]n the 1960s, the movie industry gradually came to the conclusion that its principal target viewer had changed gender" (21). The gender association is interesting as a matter of symbolic contamination (Lieberson et al. 2000:1285). In such an analysis, film may have initially been accorded lower status through association with women, much the same way that feminized occupations have lower status. Regarding education levels, Maltby notes the following:

> Audience research in the 1950s began to suggest that as Hollywood's audience declined, its social composition also changed. In 1941 Gallup had suggested that the great majority of movie tickets were purchased by people on

low or average incomes. Surveys in the 1950s, by contrast, indicated that people in higher socioeconomic brackets attended more frequently than did others. Not until the early 1960s, however, did the industry begin to reconsider its idea of its principal target viewer, and the process was not complete until the late 1960s. (21)

15. Shrum refers to this argument as the "compositional approach" (1996:8). As will be discussed in greater depth in chapter 4, Shrum contends that cultural hierarchy cannot be explained by the status of the patrons of art.

16. For further reference on sources documenting the size of early film audiences, see Ross (1998:283, n.7).

17. Crisp notes the connection in France and Germany, citing studies that find that in the Lille region of France and the Ruhr area of Germany, where television penetrated more households earlier than elsewhere in the respective countries, cinema attendances shrank even earlier (1993:72). Data similarly based on a natural experiment are cited by Solomon: "Figures did not lie, and a Singlinger survey showed that when *The Wizard of Oz* (1939) was aired on television for the first time on November 1, 1956, national box-office receipts dropped by $2 million" (1988:119).

18. Gomery (2001:123) also notes that working-class people who could not afford televisions began to go to taverns and bars where they could watch. This period was rather short-lived, however, as prices dropped further and even the working class could afford to have televisions in their homes.

19. Changing residential patterns brought on by suburbanization are another consideration and are discussed in chapter 3.

20. The first year for which a statistic is reported for radio ownership by *International Historical Statistics: The Americas 1750–1993* is 1922. That year 60,000 radios are reported in use.

21. While it is somewhat surprising that radio appears to have had no effect on cinema attendance, this finding—that an additional narrative and dramatic medium could be accommodated by filmgoers—is consistent with the argument that television alone did not cause the drop in filmgoing.

22. As indicated by the Durbin-Watson statistic, there is first-order serial correlation in this time series: a good predictor for any given year's cinema attendance is the attendance in the previous year. Because this condition violates an assumption under which generalized least-squares regression operates, a correction is needed (Prais-Winsten).

23. There is an interesting parallel here to the role of tastes as explored by Lieberson et alia (2000). In an examination of first-name selection, the authors tap into pure taste mechanisms to demonstrate how concerns over symbolic contamination can influence tastes. The authors find that tastes in names that are used for both boys and girls reflect a pattern of avoidance—as a name becomes increasingly common for girls, parents often stop using that name for their boys. The motivation is simple: "the advantaged have a greater incentive to avoid having their status confused with the disadvantaged" (Lieberson et al.:2000:1285). Taste patterns in names reflect society's gender biases. Furthermore, status concerns result in taste segregation that can be modeled in the same way as residential

segregation. Whereas residential patterns are shaped by collective behavior that conforms to group norms about race and status, naming, in the case of androgynous names, is collective behavior that conforms to group norms about gender and status.

24. German intellectuals and academics took a serious approach toward film from an early point in film's history, and so the disdain of the Frankfurt School—being German—seems curious. This disparity results from Horkheimer and Adorno's condemnation specifically of Hollywood and the studio system, as part of the entertainment industry, while early German scholars were more welcoming of early German filmmaking, which was less profit driven and formulaic than the studio system.

25. There is a lack of consensus over the distinction between postmodernism and postmodernity, and also over which ideas are represented by those terms. For example, the idea that postmodernity is the era that has followed the modern era has been criticized for overstating the differences between these time periods; many aspects of modernity are still with us, and the very label of postmodernity elides this overlap. For my purposes, I adopt Harrington's (2004:177) distinction of postmodernity as "the thesis of the end of modernity's ideals, struggles, problems and 'grand narratives' of historical development. 'Postmodernism' may be defined as the articulation of this thesis in a diffuse body of motifs, images and discursive constructions in late twentieth-century culture."

26. Similarly, Peterson (1997:85) argues that the blurring of brow levels was facilitated by broader social change: "The social dislocations, flirtations with Communism, and cultural mixing driven by the Great Depression of the 1930s and the Second World War of the 1940s increased the elite's fascination with folk and working class-based popular culture forms."

27. Sandler makes the case for Pop Art's legitimation of photography as a fine art:

> In fact, one of the most important innovations of Warhol was to make commercial photography and print-making central to his art, ushering in the use of media that became central to art in the sixties. (This led to the elevation of fine photography, long considered a minor art, to the "high art" status of painting and sculpture). (1988:145)

CHAPTER 3
CHANGE FROM WITHIN: NEW PRODUCTION AND CONSUMPTION PRACTICES

1. The Motion Picture Association of America introduces itself in the following way:

> Founded in 1922 as the trade association of the American film industry, the MPAA has broadened its mandate over the years to reflect the diversity of an expanding industry. The initial task assigned to the association was to stem the waves of criticism of American movies, then silent, while sometimes rambunctious and rowdy, and to restore a more favorable image for the motion

picture business. (http://www.mpaa.org/AboutUs.asp) (last accessed December 19, 2006)

2. The post-1985 data come from three sources—*Compact Variety*, a CD-ROM entertainment database published by *Variety*, which is the leading trade publication of the entertainment industry; that same publication's online listing of film festivals; and a list supplied by the American Film Institute. The 1970 directory—*Film and TV Directory* (Zwerdling 1970)—attempted to comprehensively catalog all film festivals (as well as television festivals) and provided their founding dates and stated purposes. It billed itself as "the first complete compilation that has ever been attempted" (Zwerdling 1970:vii), based on two years of research.

3. On its Web site, the festival describes its founding:

Since its inception, the object of the Film Council has been to encourage and promote the use of 16mm motion pictures and, subsequently, video tape in all forms of education and communication, not only in the local community but throughout the world. During these many years of continuous operation, the Festival has honored thousands of film and video producers. The Festival has grown in scope, becoming international in 1972, in the late 80's adding video, and in 1997 adding the CD ROM format. (*www.chrisawards.org/* pages/about/about.html) (accessed December 19, 2006)

4. The directory included information about film festivals that bear little resemblance to the kind of festivals of interest here. For example, the Annual National Safety Film Contest was established in 1937 with the stated purpose, "To select the outstanding films on Accident Prevention and to recognize film excellence through an awards program" (Zwerdling 1970:3) Festivals that were solely concerned with narrowly defined, nonartistic goals (e.g., educational films, business communication films, and public service films) were excluded from my accounting of festivals.

5. This characterization of the time when film festivals grew in number and importance in the United States is consistent with the retrospective impressions conveyed in film scholarship (e.g., Chin 1997:61).

6. It makes sense to focus only on the most renowned directors from both the studio and "New Hollywood" periods. Not only is more evidence available for such directors, but those with the most renown will have had the greatest potential influence on public perceptions.

7. Hitchcock does not quite fit the same pattern as the other directors because he had been making films since the 1920s. His self-promotion as an artist, however, mainly occurred in the 1960s.

8. Kapsis (1992:70) finds that, although Hitchcock's reputational development was in part a result of self-promotion, it was in fact multicausal, and the adoption of auteurism by U.S. critics was the key factor: "More important than either individual sponsorship or self-promotion, this broad shift in film aesthetics proved to be the deciding factor in reshaping Hitchcock's reputation."

9. John Cassavetes is less well known than some of his peers because his films were less commercially successful. He did not win an Oscar and his films do not

appear on the AFI's 100 best list. Nonetheless, his fame and status among film scholars (for films such as *Husbands* [1970] and *A Woman under the Influence* [1974]) are sufficient that his self-presentation is worth noting. Carney (1985:9) relays the following anecdote that qualifies as a high-art cliché:

> What other director, while being interviewed by Pauline Kael for *The New Yorker* and its half-million influential, ticket-buying readers, would have dared to break off the interview halfway through (actually throwing Kael out of the restaurant where they were talking) because, according to him, she showed insufficient appreciation of the "artistic side" of his work?

It can also be expected that great artists will speak somewhat cryptically about their art. Carney (1985:17) quotes from a 1971 interview in which Cassavetes said, "I had fallen in love with the camera, with technique, with beautiful shots, with experimentation for its own sake. . . . It was a totally intellectual film, and therefore less than human." And great artists also damn the marketplace. Carney (1985:63) quotes Cassavetes from the introduction to the published (1970) screenplay of his film *Faces* (1968): "I looked back at my accomplishments and I could find only two that I considered worthwhile, *Shadows* and *Edge of the City*. All the rest of my time had been spent playing games—painful and stupid, falsely satisfying and economically rewarding."

10. In addition, in order to explain those few early directors who did conceive of themselves as artists we can point to the fact that many of them came from Europe or the New York theater world, rather than having worked their way up within Hollywood. Willingness to self-promote as an artist, then, would be linked to the director's occupational origins. In European film and in New York theater, the director as artist would have been an unproblematic concept.

11. The organization of the *Blue Book* changed over time, making it difficult to confirm this. Furthermore, the categorization of different programs under a common rubric can be troublesome. Grouping film studies with media studies or with visual arts makes it difficult to get an accurate count.

12. Decherney's (2000) work reveals the details of the process by which film "studies" made its way into Columbia's curriculum. In the 1910s and 1920s, film executives who were eager to boost the social standing of film lobbied Columbia to maintain a collection of film scripts and to teach courses on screenwriting. Columbia did so, but in the adult education division of Columbia's Extension School. As Decherney shows, Columbia was careful to segregate courses on film. While the film executives achieved a boost in legitimacy through an Ivy League affiliation, Columbia was able to achieve several goals. The courses on film formed part of a larger, populist and practical curriculum within the Extension School, through which Columbia could serve the public interest by educating immigrants and others who lacked a postsecondary education. But this particular model for doing so protected the prestige of the elite college and was profitable as well. Belief in the artistic value of film was not a serious consideration.

13. *U.S. News & World Report* no longer rates film programs, and so the programs investigated come from the list it compiled in the late 1990s.

14. Information on these departments comes from their Web sites or from correspondence with departmental administrators. Among the departments on the

U.S. News & World Report list, of which there were nineteen in total, those whose founding date was not listed on their respective Web sites were contacted. The departments not listed above either were not able to provide the information or did not respond to a written inquiry.

15. It should be noted that Morrison relies in part on unpublished data from another author.

16. Other institutions that can help to shape the film canon in the United States include libraries and the American Film Institute. Among libraries, the MOMA in New York has probably been most influential in canonizing films, due to the early start of its film collection (1935) and to that museum's strong reputation. See Allen and Lincoln (2004) for an in-depth discussion of the role of the AFI in creating a canon for American film.

17. The catalog contains over 62 million records and allows users to extensively tailor their searches. In general, searches in WorldCat returned a larger number of records than searches in the catalog of the Library of Congress, the largest single library collection in the world, and a larger number of records than searches in the catalog of the Harvard University library system, the largest university library in the world. The data on books about film were collected using the following limits: format = books; language = English; keyword in subject = (motion pictures) and (aesthetics or criticism); publication date = year. This search distinguishes books that were concerned with the analysis of films from more general-interest film books.

18. Data from the two sources overlap for the period 1950–1970. During this period the figures match exactly between the two sources. The data include both new books and new editions with substantial changes. The inclusion of new editions does not present a problem for comparison with the data from the library catalog. In the library data, new editions are listed as separate records.

19. Tebbel does not make it clear what specific effects this technology had or whether they were direct or indirect.

20. Detailed data on theater are not reported for the sake of parsimony but are available from the author on request.

21. Bourdieu distinguishes between types of cultural production. For some cultural production, the pursuit of economic success is explicit and legitimate. This distinction, between restricted and large-scale fields of production, is discussed in more depth later in this section.

22. Film in the United States has evolved to incorporate both standing as art and commercial success. However, as will be discussed below in this chapter and in chapter 5, this combination results in a compromised degree of artistic legitimacy.

23. Such a difference in the backgrounds of French and American directors can perhaps explain a great deal about the different perceptions of film in each country. The typical American director was not likely to have had formal artistic training. Consequently, the backgrounds of French and American directors were likely not only to have found distinct forms of expression in the films that they made, but were also likely to have influenced the degree to which each sought recognition as an artist. Further research on systematic differences between the two groups of directors is warranted.

24. How much control directors had under the studio system and whether they truly gained from its collapse is debatable (see, e.g., Sklar and Zagarrio 1998). While they surely gained some amount of autonomy, it is equally important that directors now enjoyed the *appearance* of a significant amount of freedom and autonomy.

25. Pauline Kael, for example, was a well-known detractor of auteurism, and the complex question of authorship still inspires academic debate. For many interesting investigations on the theme of authorship, see Gerstner and Staiger (2003). The following review, of the film *While the Sun Shines*, published in the *New York Times* in 1950 (July 1, 9:2) provides a clear example of how the credit for filmmaking was attributed prior to the adoption of auteurism, namely by elevating the contribution of the writer:

One of those curiously likable British pictures—meaning a film that plays poorly most of its length, but still has a certain amount of charm which can't be ignored—arrived yesterday at the Trans-Lux Theater in East Seventy-second Street. It is called "While the Sun Shines" and, as a play, had a brief run on Broadway back in 1944. Terence Rattigan is the author, and he is a man who can write some very funny dialogue when the spirit moves him. Unfortunately his pen was only spasmodically inspired in composing this treatise on romantic misunderstandings.

The principal characters in "While the Sun Shines" are a young Earl who is just a plain jack-tar in His Majesty's Navy; his titled fiancée, who has been demoted from sergeant to corporal in the W.A.A.F for having misplaced some important document; a breezy American entertainer; a meddlesome, romantic French youth; a worldly little blonde and an impoverished duke. They are all nice people in their way and when the occasion permits, quite entertaining.

After Lady Elisabeth meets the Yankee acrobat she isn't quite sure that she wants to go through with her marriage to the Earl of Harpenden and this disturbs her titled father no end, since he is looking forward to embracing a rich son-in-law. The Earl takes the bad news quite casually—he still has the blonde on the string, you see—and Mr. Rattigan skillfully maneuvers the relationship of all concerned from that point through a series of complications aimed for both visual and oral amusement. The fun may not be consistent enough to add up to more than halting divertissement, but the author does come up with some cute tricks, including a scene where the three men in Lady Elisabeth's tangled love life shoot a game of craps to decide who will be first to propose to her.

Ronald Howard is very likable as the Earl, Bonar Colleano Jr. is aggressive as the American, Brenda Bruce is bouncy as the blonde, Barbara White is attractive as Lady Elisabeth, Ronald Squire is dryly amusing as her perplexed father and Michael Allan is effusive as the Frenchman. Anatole de Grunwald joined Mr. Rattigan in writing the screenplay of "While the Sun Shines," but he apparently was not able to help out very much when Mr. Rattigan, who was the sole author of the play, ran out of bright dialogue. As the director, Anthony Asquith saw to it that the actors kept moving about, which was helpful anyway.

26. In the case of the few major movie moguls who were high-ranking studio executives and simultaneously actively involved in producing films, the producer was sometimes identified as the artistic force behind a film. Behlmer presents an example from a 1945 memo from Darryl Zanuck, who was vice president in charge of production at Twentieth Century-Fox for approximately thirty years. The memo is to director George Cukor (an established director who would later win an Academy Award for best director) conerning a proposed adaptation of Somerset Maugham's *The Razor's Edge*:

> This is the only picture that I am going to put my name on as an individual producer this year. . . . I feel justified in saying that if something goes wrong with it I will be primarily the one who is left holding the bag. They may complain about Maugham's dialogue, and they may criticize [Lamar] Trotti's adaptation, or lambast your direction, but in the final analysis if it turns out to be a dud I know that I will be the one whom the critics and the industry will pounce on and hold primarily responsible. (1993:95)

A producer's assertion that the critics will hold him primarily responsible for the film's quality is in sharp contrast with contemporary notions of how films should be evaluated.

27. As will be discussed in greater depth in chapter 4, the changing perceptions of film within the United States were affected by distinct attitudes toward foreign films. It would be instructive to compare the perceptions within European countries of differences in artistic status between European and American films.

28. Elsaesser makes the claim in the opposite direction for an earlier time period. He writes of the 1930s,

> the decade which witnessed an unprecedented economic expansion of the film-industries in Europe and America also saw critics only too willing to conclude that popularity automatically spelled aesthetic nullity. The new art of the talking picture came to be written off as irredeemably "commercial," peddling to nothing but escapist entertainment, or worse still, pernicious demagogy. (1975:201)

29. Moreover, previous claims about the commonality or banality of film had obscured the artistic potential of films. But in the 1960s one had only to point to television to highlight film's relative artistic value. As Dick (1992:23) and Solomon (1988:158) write, television fulfilled the function of providing the "B" material that film studios ceased producing in the late 1950s. Patrice Petro (1986:6) argues that the prestige of film has benefited from the introduction of television and notes the irony of this situation: "What is surprising is that some film scholars assign a place to television outside the domain of legitimate culture, outside the arena of academic respectability, particularly since this was (and in some cases, continues to be) precisely the 'place' assigned to cinema by educators, intellectuals, and artists." Only after economic capital in film was overtaken in television could the act of bestowing symbolic capital assume a central role.

30. See Orbach (2004) for a thorough review of the details of the case.

31. There are discrepancies in the estimates of the number of art houses in the United States. Stones reports that in 1952 there were 470 art houses, and 600 by

1966. Sklar cites a figure of four or five dozen art houses, in the early 1950s (1994:293), Gomery reports 200 in 1956 and over 1,000 in the late 1960s (1992:181), while Balio states that there were 83 art-house theaters in 1950 and 664 in 1966 (1987:224). These discrepancies likely result from variance in the definition of an art-house theater. The higher estimates of the 1950s likely count theaters that were independent (neither owned by studios nor part of a theater chain) and that devoted some of their screen time to non-Hollywood films. The lower estimates likely count only those independent theaters that exhibited foreign and/or small budget, non-Hollywood films exclusively. Regardless of the exact number, film historians agree that the number grew during the 1950s, peaked in the 1960s, and was never more than a small proportion of all theaters. Moreover, there is agreement that art houses were small, neighborhood theaters located in university towns or large cities (Balio 1987:224; Sklar 1994:293; Stones 1993:200).

32. Although there was likely a great deal of variation in the characteristics of art-house theaters, Gomery draws a general picture of the art house as a place where the food was more refined than popcorn, where proper audience etiquette was observed, and where prices could be higher than in regular theaters (1992:186).

33. Over time the film industry became heavily dependent on "pre-tested" material, both literary and theatrical. Maltby notes that by the end of the 1920s studios relied on adaptations for more than half of their productions (1996:103). While not all of this "pre-tested" material was meant to elevate the status of film, prestige productions were based on literary and theatrical work that had gained critical approbation and had high art connotations that could elevate those particular productions.

34. The strategy of elevating an art form's status by juxtaposing it with classical music had been employed for dance several decades earlier by Isadora Duncan.

35. Randall puts it concisely: "If there is a touchstone of the art film it is probably that of a modest budget and a director of originality" (1968:219).

36. It is perhaps true that genuine aesthetes would have preferred that film remain junk before picking it up as high art. Nevertheless, the general public would have found that more difficult to swallow. In general, good art is expected to show technical proficiency. While theorists would expect more, namely for art to show experimentation with convention, they are not the crowd whose acceptance of Hollywood films as art we are trying to explain.

37. The Board's name was changed in 1915 to the National Board of Review (Jowett cites a date of 1916 [1989:66]), which exists today although it was to lose its censorship functions by the end of that decade. It lost its power because (1) it had been closely tied to and supported by the Motion Pictures Patent Company (composed of the ten major film manufacturers holding important film and camera patents) (Mast 1982:102), which was dissolved by 1917 due to a string antitrust and other lawsuits (Sklar 1994:144), and (2) Hollywood replaced New York as the heart of the film industry (Czitrom 1996:37).

38. Maltby offers an alternative view on the determinants of motion picture content during the period of heavy self-censorship from the early 1920s to the mid-1960s (1996). He maintains that the film industry did not have to be actively

censored in the 1920s and 1930s because the studio executives did not want to make controversial movies. Through the consensus of the film studios, moral entrepreneurs, and audiences alike, controversy was agreed to be the provenance of books and plays. Movies were made to entertain and to affirm traditional American values. It was easy for film studios to uphold this idea because adherence to it brought in the largest audiences. From this perspective, the Hays Office and the Production Code were merely safety mechanisms to ensure that there were no mistakes.

39. This disparity between film, and the other visual medium of television, continues today. Film industry and television network self-censorship has no real analog in radio, print, theater, or on the Internet.

40. Doherty (1999) argues that the lax application of the Production Code between 1930 and 1934 resulted in a relatively free and open American cinema, containing far more risqué elements than what was to come between 1934 and the mid-1960s. While Doherty provides convincing evidence that many films in this four-year period invoke themes that were later censored, the extent to which they do so is minimal compared to the cinema of the 1960s.

41. Dick writes of the Production Code, "Under such a system, it would seem that art would wither; yet the 1930s and 1940s were the glory years of the American film" (1993:145). Whether this is true or not is debatable. Nevertheless it is clearly revisionist, as the prevailing views during the 1930s and 1940s held that the Production Code was appropriate precisely because film was not an art. Real art would have been freer from such strict regulations.

42. These data may be misleading if there were a systematic bias in the kind of American films that were selected for import to France. Just as American distributors import only those European films that they believe to be of highest quality, it is possible that French distributors were selecting American films in a way that made them less objectionable to the Catholic Church. Such a dynamic would, however, function in the opposite way from the case in the United States, where imports were clearly more risqué than the domestic product. It is more likely that the data represent the more "sanitized" nature of American films, although without information concerning how films were selected for import, this conclusion is speculative.

43. This stifling effect of censorship on the development of film as art in the United States was recognized in a 1936 book chapter by William Allen White:

> Given ten or twenty million dollars—no large sum when one considers what it would achieve in American life—a theater would be chartered in every country town of more than twenty-five thousand inhabitants where the minority that loves truth in art could find it in the movie. . . . That does not mean "clean, wholesome plays"—nothing like it. That means, rather, a selective reality in the presentation of life that makes truth rise and shine in a picture. It does not mean salacious plays—quite the contrary. It means sex would not be snubbed or repressed, but also neither emphasized nor exploited, but take its place candidly as a part of life and its motives. . . . This all means that the motion-picture industry might develop an art, as writing and painting and sculpture and the drama have developed arts, without

the accursed censorship of the aesthetically lame and the halt and the blind forever snuffing out the fire of truth in the movie as ignorance puts out the divine fire. (9)

44. The following three paragraphs on the evolution of the legality of film censorship draw on the account of Jowett (1996).

45. Roth, citing legal scholar Angela Campbell, recounts five primary causes behind the erosion of the Production Code: (1) a post–World War II increase in the demand for realism in film; (2) competition from television; (3) a decrease in the major studios' control over the industry following the antitrust decision of 1948; (4) an increase in independent film production; and (5) the conferral of First Amendment protection to filmmakers in 1952 (2000:10). To this, Roth adds the "cultural revolution of the 1960s" and the economic pressure from falling theater admissions as reasons why the Production Code was abandoned (2000:10). This reasoning is consistent with all the arguments of this book.

46. In addition to the financial imperatives encouraging experimentation, another source for experimentation can probably be found in the cultural milieu of the 1960s. As a period of more general cultural rebellion in the popular culture industries, confidence among decision-makers waned as cultural currents flowed quickly and in unforeseeable directions. This was particularly true in the field of popular music, where artists (who previously had to follow the instructions of record-company artists and repertoire men as to what they recorded and how they recorded it) experienced several years of unprecedented creative autonomy. This might also have been true to an extent in the film world as well.

CHAPTER 4
THE INTELLECTUALIZATION OF FILM

1. The search for an instructive discourse that shaped the thoughts of audience members necessarily leads to the field of social constructionism. As has been argued in the first chapter, the process whereby the view of Hollywood films gained legitimacy as art is more social than aesthetic. The socially constructed nature of legitimacy has been explored with regard to a variety of phenomena, including professional jurisdictions (Abbott 1988; Zhou 1993), the authority of physicians (Starr 1982), legal order and change (Stryker 1994), gender roles (Lorber 1991), corporate takeovers (Hirsch 1986), illnesses (Hacking 1995; Hepworth 1999), scientific knowledge (Latour and Woolgar 1986), and informal interpersonal hierarchies (Ridgeway et al. 1995). Such studies are investigations into the social construction of the very categories used for talking about social phenomena as well as into the application of those categories. Building on prior work in the sociology of knowledge, Berger and Luckmann helped to make social constructionism more widely known and examined in sociology with their book *The Social Construction of Reality* (1967 [first published in 1966]), in which they explain how all the social institutions upon which societies are based emerge, consolidate, and are legitimated as objective reality. For them, all "the institutional world requires le-

gitimation, that is, ways by which it can be 'explained' and justified" (1967:61). Berger and Luckmann distinguish between four levels of legitimation.

> Incipient legitimation is present as soon as a system of linguistic objectifications of human experience is transmitted. For example, the transmission of a kinship vocabulary *ipso facto* legitimates the kinship structure. The fundamental legitimating "explanations" are, so to speak, built into the vocabulary. (94)

> The second level of legitimation contains theoretical propositions in a rudimentary form. Here may be found various explanatory schemes relating sets of objective meanings. These schemes are highly pragmatic, directly related to concrete actions. Proverbs, moral maxims and wise sayings are common on this level. (94)

> The third level of legitimation contains explicit theories by which an institutional sector is legitimated in terms of a differentiated body of knowledge. Such legitimations provide fairly comprehensive frames of reference for the respective sectors of institutionalized conduct. Because of their complexity and differentiation, they are frequently entrusted to specialized personnel who transmit them through formalized initiation procedures. (94–95)

> Symbolic universes constitute the fourth level of legitimation. These are bodies of theoretical tradition that integrate different provinces of meaning and encompass the institutional order in a symbolic totality (95). . . . In this way, the symbolic universe order [*sic*] and thereby legitimates everyday roles, priorities, and operating procedures by placing them sub specie universi, that is, in the context of the most general frame of reference conceivable. (99)

Any social institution may be legitimated at each of these levels. Legitimation, however, must emerge and be maintained over time, and it is possible to identify who performs this function.

> Reality is defined. But the definitions are always *embodied*, that is, concrete individuals and groups of individuals serve as definers of reality. To understand the state of the socially constructed universe at any given time, or its change over time, one must understand the social organization that permits the definers to do their defining. (116)

Although this study does not explain the creation and maintenance of artistic status in the terms employed by Berger and Luckmann, the analysis here is consistent with their analysis of social institutions in general. As this chapter will discuss, legitimation of the experience of film as art involved explicit theories that explained film, as such, by critics and other intellectuals.

2. Despite the acceptance of Chaplin among a portion of the intellectual elite, Maland (1989:179) notes that in general the place of film in the cultural hierarchy effectively limited what even Chaplin could do cinematically. He writes,

> Although the critics respected and were intrigued by what he attempted in [*The Great Dictator*], many felt the film engaged too directly with politics.

Because of the ideology and aura of "entertainment" deeply embedded in the classical Hollywood system of filmmaking, overt treatment of controversial political issues was taboo. When a filmmaker violated that taboo, even in order to attack an ideology like fascism that was being widely assailed in the country at the time the film was released, the filmmaker was certain to alienate a substantial number of critics and to make many viewers uneasy.

3. The distinction between critics and criticism on the one hand and reviewers and reviewing on the other has been made before (see, e.g., Engel 1976; Titchener 1998:ch.1). The distinction is usually between the more serious, experienced, specialized critics and the less intellectual, less sophisticated reviewers. The time-sensitive nature of reviewing makes it difficult to maintain the standards to which critics hold themselves. I feel that it is misleading to characterize the work of critics and reviewers as dichotomous; indeed, their work can be classified on a continuum with critics *tending* to write for a more serious and scholarly audience. This tendency coexists, however, with significant overlap between criticism and reviewing. Rather than drawing arbitrary lines, I prefer to use the terms interchangeably while recognizing that there is wide variability in the nature of film reviews/criticism.

4. Discourse analysis is a versatile research method that can effectively extract key concepts and trends from vast amounts of data. See Phillips and Hardy (2002) for an excellent discussion and illustration of the strengths of discourse analysis. Discourse analysis is a necessary first step to performing an insightful content analysis of film reviews. Content analysis involves the counting of manifest and/ or latent elements of texts. However, in order to know what is worth counting, it is first necessary to do the conceptual work of identifying how film reviews embody attitudes about film as art. Film reviewers have only rarely made explicit statements about their perceptions of film as art. Instead, such perceptions needed to be teased out of often complex exegeses on film, which is what discourse analysis achieves. At the same time, the indicators of the reviewers' perceptions needed to be specified with enough precision as to be countable and acceptable to the objective reader as reliable and accurate indicators. Only through reading a vast number of reviews for different kinds of art can one develop a sense of the kinds of words and analyses that these cultural experts employ to engage with culture as art. It is in the use of these words and analyses that a discourse is made and can then demonstrate the artistic worth of the cultural productions under review.

5. The original terms were: "achievement," "amazing, art, beauty, bold, brilliant, composition, delicate, distinction, distinguished, genius, genre, the greatest, important, inspired, intelligent, irony, magnificent, master, masterpiece, metaphor, powerful, remarkable, reveal, satire, school, simple, strength, striking, subtle, suggest, symbol, technique, tone, work, ian/esque."

6. Because not all issues of the *New Yorker* for 1925 were available to me, the sample includes reviews from several of the same months for that year in order to get twelve reviews.

7. In writing longer reviews in more recent periods, reviewers may have avoided using precisely the same words repeatedly for stylistic reasons. Therefore, the measure of the number of terms divided by the total review words may

underestimate the prevalence of an intellectualizing discourse for film present in the reviews.

8. Spearman's rho is a measure of association ranging from -1 to +1, and it is similar to the Pearson product moment correlation, except that the values of the variables are first converted to ranks. There are two popular ways of computing Spearman's rho. The first is to use the formula for Pearson's product moment correlation. This is the method used by the statistical software package Stata, and is the one used in this chapter. The second way to compute Spearman's rho is with the formula $r = 1 - \sum D^2 / N (N^2 - 1)$, where D = (rank x) – (rank y) and N = the number of ranked pairs. The two methods provide similar results. In this chapter I use one-tailed tests of significance as I have a directional hypothesis concerning the relationship between year and rank order of the counts. The specific hypothesis being tested is not whether the ranks are ordered at all, but rather whether they increase over time.

9. Because the sample is based on only three publications, the possibility exists that one of the three is alone driving the increases we observe. The following table reports the results of a comparison of the three publications. Because there are only twelve or twenty-four reviews sampled from a publication in each year, it is necessary to pool several years. The table provides the ratio of "high art" and "critical" terms together to the total number of words in the reviews. The data show that similar increases are experienced in each publication. The rate of terms in the 1945–60 period is only slightly higher for each publication than the rate in the 1925–40 period. In addition, the rate is similar across publications. The rate in the final 1965–85 period more than doubles for each publication. These results show that the overall results are not driven by increases in only one or two of the publications sampled.

Number of "High Art" and "Critical" Terms Divided by Total Review Words, by Source: 1925–1985

Year	New Yorker	Time	New York Times
1925–40	.0009	.0013	.0013
1945–60	.0008	.0012	.0011
1965–85	.0021	.0029	.0026

10. In general, the selection of techniques was based on the assumption that just as the goals and methods of film as art would follow those of other high art forms, so the development of film criticism would be heavily influenced by other forms of high art criticism. Carney (1985:11) notes,

> Up to twenty or thirty years ago . . . American films largely escaped the burden of being High Art, and the best American movies were largely free of such cultural grandiosity. But whether through the influence of European cinema or of film schools on a new generation of writers and directors, that seems to have changed. Film, even American film, has become Art, and the

assumption seems to be that it should emulate the techniques of other major modern art forms.

11. Gomery argues that the development of an interpretive framework for film criticism grew out of the changing nature of films:

> Since the art cinema stressed ambiguity, the meaning of a film was not as explicit as in a straightforward classical Hollywood tale. Some apparatus had to be set up to interpret art films though such publications as the *New York Times* and the *Saturday Review*. The task of the Hollywood reviewer had been to serve as an extension of the industry to promote films and stars. During the 1960s film critics were expected to explain the meaning of films. (1992:189)

This book, of course, disagrees with the idea that the reason reviewers began to interpret films was tied to the nature of films being made in the 1960s. As we will see, the tendency to interpret films has been retrospectively applied to classics of earlier decades, and they are the site of contested meanings. If the classics are available for multiple interpretations, then the argument that reviewers began to interpret films because of the content of 1960s films falls apart.

12. See Verdaasdonk (1983) for a discussion of the importance critics place on the mutual incompatibility of commercial and artistic values and the consequences for aesthetic legitimacy as applied to the literary field. Verdaasdonk refutes the validity of this dichotomy.

13. In 1980 only 50 percent of reviews contained at least three of the techniques. Some of the other measures in the content analysis drop off in the final time period. Although the declines do not bring reviews back in line with the pre-1960 levels, they do warrant discussion and are addressed in the next chapter.

14. There is a contrast between the measurement of the vocabulary and of the techniques. The vocabulary words were counted according to each appearance, so long as each was in the appropriate context. It was important to count each appropriate instance of the vocabulary words because the reviews lengthened over time. The appropriate measure of the specialized vocabulary involves a comparison with the increase in total words used in reviews. It was not possible to do the same with the techniques. For instance, the presence of negative and positive commentary can only be a binary measure. The same is true of the decision to mention the director, and such a decision has much more significance than the decision to mention the director a second or more times. Therefore, the techniques are counted according to whether they were present at least once in a review. For this reason, we must interpret column 10 with caution. The expectations for more techniques to occur in lengthier reviews is tempered by the method of counting not all instances of the use of the techniques but only the first. Therefore, as reviews lengthen, the denominator in the ratio reported in column 10 continues to grow even though the measure of the techniques has plateaued. Therefore, the measure of the percent of reviews having three or more techniques divided by the mean review words may underestimate the prevalence of an intellectualizing discourse for film present in more recent reviews. The declines in the ratio in

the final time periods reflect the fact that reviews are getting very long relative to earlier periods.

15. Logistic regression provides a final test of the value of conceptualizing the 1960s as the turning point in the use of these techniques in film reviews. The dependent (dummy) variable is whether a review has at least three techniques, and the independent variable is whether the review appeared pre-1970, or in 1970 or later. (The N is 684.) The resulting odds ratio is 8.02, with standard error 1.48, and $p < 0.000$. This highly significant result lends credence to the claim that the post–1960s era should be conceived as meaningfully different from what came before.

16. Content analysis relies on quantitative indicators that are designed to be precise and reliable measures of key features rather than to provide an exhaustive representation. The indicators are limited, for example, because they do not measure certain aspects of film discourse—for instance, calling a film a "study," or an "exercise," or an "inquiry"—that could not be a part of the content analysis because they were not present in the 1925 reviews. The indicators, however, do make it clear to all readers exactly what findings the argument is based on. Similarly, the significance tests give us a more objective means for concluding that the differences we find in the numbers really mean something.

17. In order to add to our confidence in the findings, we can look for more assurance that the observed changes are not merely an artifact of the data. Because the sample is composed mostly of lead reviews, one concern a reader might have is that the data are possibly distorted by a tendency for publications to emphasize the importance of the lead review in more recent periods. If so, then the characteristics of the reviews in the sample would not be representative of film review in general. Let us consider again data from 1935 and 1975. Between these two times there does not appear to have been a stronger emphasis on the lead review in the later period. In 1935 the lead review of each month was on average 79 percent longer than the second review published each month. In 1975 the lead review was on average 73 percent longer than the second review published each month. Furthermore, second reviews in 1975 were 37 percent longer than lead reviews in 1935, and 145 percent longer than second reviews in 1935. It does not appear that the data are significantly distorted by the prominence of the lead review. The disparity between the lead and second review seems constant over time. Therefore, there is little danger that the observed change in film review is an artifact of a change in orientation toward lead reviews rather than toward film review as a whole.

18. There are two important impediments to the objective measurement of artistic quality. First, there is far too much disagreement over what constitutes the essential components of art. Second, and equally important, whatever those components are, they are bound to change over time. The reason for this is tied to the very nature of art, which is defined by its relation to a set of field-specific conventions. To be part of an art world, a work of art must engage the appropriate conventions. Engagement entails not only incorporating the conventions but also playing with and changing to some degree those conventions. Art that merely replicates existing conventions is dismissed as uninteresting. Therefore, works of

art at time-2 will exhibit a set of characteristics that differ from those works of art at time-1 because, as art, they have been required to break the conventions.

19. The restriction of second reviews to popular periodicals enforces a stringent standard of comparison. The *Film Review Index* lists a large number of reviews for each film. The comparison was originally executed by taking the first pre-1950 and first post-1960 reviews listed. Most frequently this produced a review from a publication that was film-specific and written by a cinema scholar for consumption by other cinema scholars. The original reviews all came from popular periodicals, as there were virtually no film studies journals before 1950 in the United States. The differences between the two time periods, therefore, were even greater than those reported here between first and later reviews from popular periodicals. However, because I want to provide a stronger test of how reviews changed over time, I have chosen to present only the most closely comparable cases from popular periodical in both time periods.

20. The most recent review in the sample is the one published for *The Rules of the Game*, a 1939 French film that was released, and therefore reviewed, in the United States in 1950.

21. The films that comprise this sample of twenty films are: *A Woman of Paris, Best Years of Our Lives, Casablanca, City Lights, Fantasia, Gone with the Wind, Modern Times, Napoleon, Olympiad, Orphans of the Storm, Snow White and the Seven Dwarfs, That Hamilton Woman, The Birth of a Nation, The Emperor Jones, The Grapes of Wrath, The Great Dictator, The Last Will of Dr. Mabuse, The Rules of the Game, The Ten Commandments,* and *Zero Conduite.*

22. The question of whether critics influence or reflect the opinions of their audience has been addressed as it pertains to whether people see films that are recommended by critics (Eliashberg and Shugan 1997). This is a separate question, however, from whether critics influence or reflect their audience's perception of film as an art form. Influence or reflection in one case does not imply the same function for critics in the other case.

23. Sklar's description of the discrepancy between contemporary reception of silent films and their later reevaluation supports the notion that canonization through reevaluation of older works is part of art-world development:

> The almost undiluted commercialism of motion-picture production was a constant source of exasperation to critics and reviewers in the silent era, who looked, most often vainly, for redeeming aesthetic value in the stream of feature films pouring out of Hollywood at the rate of nearly two a day. . . . Posterity, however, has found it easier to recognize enduring artistry in American silent films. In a world-wide poll of critics published in 1972 by the British Film Institute in its quarterly, *Sight and Sound,* some twenty American silent features were named at least once on the various critics' lists of the top ten motion pictures on world cinema. . . . In all thirty-five silent films received mention. (1994:87)

24. The method of data collection was identical to that used for the film reviews. Using optical character recognition software, the book reviews were scanned and read as Microsoft Word files. Accurate counts were then achieved

using the "find" function and examining each term in context to verify its intended meaning.

25. In order to present a more orderly comparison, the comparison of book and film reviews is based on an equal number of reviews. For those time periods (1960 and 1970) for which there are seventy-two film reviews in the sample, the thirty-six first reviews are used for each. This congruity simplifies the presentation.

26. A difference of proportions test (Agresti and Finley 1986:167–71) reveals that the increase in the density of terms in film reviews between 1935 and 1970 is statistically significant at a 99 percent confidence level. In contrast, the difference in the density of terms in book reviews, which decreases, is not statistically significant at a 95 percent or above confidence level. In 1935 and 1940, the density for film reviews is considerably lower than that for book reviews. After a moderate increase in 1960, the density jumps in 1970 to surpass that for book reviews. It is not clear why film reviews would contain a higher density of the specialized vocabulary, although it is quite possible that the difference is the result of sampling error. Difference of proportions tests show that the difference in the density of "high art" and "critical" terms between film and book reviews is statistically significant at a 99 percent confidence level in 1935 and 1940, while the differences in 1960 and 1970 are not statistically significant at a 95 percent confidence level or above.

27. The same techniques were coded with minor alterations. While mention of the director in film reviews was coded, it was necessary to code for mention of the author in book reviews. In addition, comparisons between authors and between books were coded in lieu of comparisons between directors and between films.

28. There surely is variance in the degree to which the literature in the sample is "artistic." However, a sample that is taken from first reviews seems to be biased toward weightier fiction, albeit consistently throughout the time periods under study. The sample includes at least one book by a Nobel Prize winner from each of the four years (Ivan Bunin in 1935, William Butler Yeats in 1940, Salvatore Quasimodo in 1960, and Nadine Gordimer in 1970).

29. To be precise, advertisements are a measure of what the studios believed to be important to audience members. A better measurement would be survey data of audiences of that time. In the absence of such data, advertisements serve reasonably well because the studios were in the business of knowing and catering to audience preferences.

30. Because the results from the preceding section indicated that the period of change in film discourse was the 1960s, data collection began in 1935 rather than 1925. This economizes on data collection while still allowing for observation of trends prior to the period of interest.

31. Only the first advertisement was coded for films with multiple advertisements. In addition, to be considered an advertisement, it was necessary that more information than merely the title and show time be present. The presence of any additional information, such as the studio, one of the actors, a graphic, was sufficient for inclusion.

32. Because means are sensitive to extreme values, it is useful to verify the trends with a different measurement. The 75th percentile values of each of the three variables have not been reported in order to save space. However, they do

not provide useful new information as they reveal trends in the data that are nearly identical to those reported by the means.

33. This question deserves further historical research; however, one can speculate about other possible reasons why the use of critical commentary increased in the 1980s. For example, an increase in the presence of critical commentary in advertisements might have been the result of increases in advance screenings, in the number of cities in which films were opening, or simply in the number of reviewers working. Such increases would have made more early reviews available for quotations. On the studio side, it is possible that a change in strategy occurred where well-reviewed films received increases in their advertising budgets, thus increasing the likelihood that advertisements would have critical quotes.

34. It is worth noting as well that it appears that change in critical language preceded change in advertising by approximately five years (see figure 4.1). The picture drawn by the two data sets is that the nature of film reviews changed first, and this development of the art world for films was picked up by the Hollywood studios shortly thereafter. Because the data are spaced in five-year intervals, it is not possible to provide a more precise figure for the lag, but the best guess based on these data is about five years.

35. Staiger's (1990) research on the history of film advertising reveals that since the 1930s film advertising has been nationally coordinated by the major studios. Although earlier film advertising was locally controlled by exhibitors, as advertising became more sophisticated and research driven, it fell to the major studios. This is a significant piece of information because it means that the observed incorporation of critical commentary into film advertisements in the 1960s was not a result of a shift in who was arranging the advertising.

36. Only quotes that used the words "direct," "director," "direction," and so forth, or referred to the director by name were counted.

37. One may question whether these two features were used more frequently on a quote-by-quote basis. Controlling for the mean number of quotes per advertisement is not appropriate, however, because there likely is a tendency for an advertisement to have quotes that are relevant to different aspects of the film. It would be a better marketing strategy to emphasize a variety of the film's strengths, not only the direction. Also, overuse of "master" and its variants would detract from the strength of the term's meaning. This latter point is also relevant to understanding why only a very small minority of film advertisements include reference to "master" and its variants. Film reviews themselves employ the terms sparingly, and so were only rarely available for excerpting in advertisements. Nevertheless, later usage is frequent relative to earlier usage.

38. Up to this point, rank order correlations and difference of proportions tests have provided evidence of statistical significance. Regression is more appropriate here because of the need to control for a third variable and to take advantage of the large sample size.

39. The threshold of four square inches is chosen as a compromise. A comparison of the largest advertisements is preferable. However, because there were few advertisements in the earlier periods of larger sizes, a threshold of five or six square inches would not preserve enough advertisements from early periods for comparison. A size of four square inches is small enough to allow a comparison

of a large number of advertisements and still large enough to easily accommodate critics' quotes.

40. No fiction book advertisements appeared in 1935 in the *New Yorker*. As such, the sample relies on the advertisements from the *New York Review of Books* only for that year. *Time* did not contain a substantial number of advertisements for fiction books.

41. The foreign-language films in the sample come from a variety of European countries as well as Japan, Argentina, Mexico, Senegal, Israel, and China. European films represent the vast majority of the foreign-language films.

42. The measure of the use of these techniques divided by total review words would paint a different picture. However, as explained in footnote 14, dividing by the total number of review words "handicaps" the measure of the presence of these techniques since they were recorded for whether they occurred at least once. Therefore, whether a director is mentioned once is important, but as reviews lengthen, dividing by the total number of words produces a lower ratio. In effect, the practice of measuring these techniques by whether they occurred at least once is incompatible with standardizing by length of review.

43. We might wonder if the reason that advertisements for foreign-language films relied on quotes from critics was that those films lacked well-known (to American audiences) actors and therefore needed to include information from critics as a selling point that was usually provided by the name recognition of the stars. This interpretation cannot be ruled out entirely, but the explanation it puts forth to explain the incorporation of film review into advertisements is not consistent with the bulk of the evidence. For instance, if the role of critics' quotes is to substitute for star power, then we would not expect to see examples such as figures 4.10 and 4.11 which rely heavily on reviews for films with very famous actors. This practice was commonplace in the 1970s. In addition, that view of the role of reviews in advertising cannot explain the drastic change in the late 1960s in advertisements for English-language films. Although the celebrity status of the actors was not coded, it is my impression that the films advertised following the late 1960s were as reliant on big-name actors as the previous productions. Although a quantitative measure of the fame of the actors in the movies advertised is needed, my sense of the correlation between big stars and reliance on critics is that it was strongly positive rather than negative, as this alternative interpretation would imply.

44. Sklar claims that this perspective bore directly on film: "Since it was widely believed in universities and intellectual circles that art came to America from Europe, there was a predisposition to imagine that cinema as art would stem from across the Atlantic, too" (1994:292).

CHAPTER 5
MECHANISMS FOR CULTURAL VALUATION

1. An argument can be made that multiplex theaters have helped to make more artistic films economically feasible. Because theaters with many screens need varied content, they will exhibit films with smaller budgets that would normally lose

out to the exhibition of blockbuster movies. Such a contribution to the economic feasibility of artistic films would help to elevate the artistic status of film overall while also blurring the lines between artistic films and mass entertainment films.

2. The conditions that shape our perception of film as a middlebrow art are largely present for literature as well, and yet they are not nearly as crippling to literature's status. I would argue that the most important reason for this discrepancy is that, for most people, the primary and secondary educational systems inculcate a respect for literature and largely ignore film. The teaching of literature in elementary and high school creates a firm foundation for literature as art in our popular culture.

3. According to Motion Picture Association Worldwide Market Research (2006), younger (12–24 years old) moviegoers account for more admissions than any other age group.

4. It is a separate, though interesting, question to ask why they have authority and how this authority is maintained.

5. In addition, Bourdieu is interested in understanding the qualitative features of cultural genres as products of the demands, cultural capabilities, and social backgrounds of cultural producers and consumers. This aspect of his work is not dealt with here.

References

Abbott, Andrew. 1988. *The System of Professions: An Essay on the Division of Expert Labor.* Chicago: University of Chicago Press.

Abel, Richard. 1988. *French Film Theory and Criticism: A History/Anthology, 1907–1939.* Princeton, NJ: Princeton University Press.

———. 1984. *French Cinema: The First Wave, 1915–1929.* Princeton, NJ: Princeton University Press.

Abrams, Lynn. 1996. "From Control to Commercialization: The Triumph of Mass Entertainment in Germany 1900–1925?," pp. 642–65 in *Perspectives on German Cinema,* edited by Terri Ginsberg and Kristin Moana Thompson. New York: G. K. Hall and Co.

Adler, Judith. 1976. " 'Revolutionary' Art and the 'Art' of Revolution: Aesthetic Work in a Millenarian Period." *Theory and Society,* vol. 3, no. 3:417–35.

Agresti, Alan, and Barbara Finlay. 1986. *Statistical Methods for the Social Sciences.* 2nd ed. San Francisco: Dellen Publishing Company.

Aiken, Nancy E. 1998. *The Biological Origins of Art.* Westport, CT, and London: Praeger.

Allen, Michael Patrick, and Anne Lincoln. 2004. "Critical Discourse and the Cultural Consecration of American Films." *Social Forces* 82:871–94.

Allen, Robert C., and Douglas Gomery. 1985. *Film History Theory and Practice.* New York: McGraw-Hill.

Allyn, John. 1978. "*Double Indemnity*: A Policy That Paid Off." *Literature/Film Quarterly* 6:116–24.

Anderegg, Michael. 1979. *William Wyler.* Boston: Twayne Publishers.

Anderson, Lindsay. 1981. *About John Ford.* London: Plexus.

Ariès, Philippe. 1962. *Centuries of Childhood: A Social History of Family Life.* Translated by Robert Baldick. *New York*: Knopf.

Armes, Roy. 1985. *French Cinema.* London: Secker and Warburg.

———. 1979. *A Critical History of the British Cinema.* London: Secker and Warburg.

Arnheim, Rudolf. 1986. *New Essays on the Psychology of Art.* Berkeley, Los Angeles, and London: University of California Press.

Baker, Wayne E., and Robert R. Faulkner. 1991. "Role as Resource in the Hollywood Film Industry." *American Journal of Sociology* 97:279–09.

Balio, Tino. 1987. *United Artists: The Company That Changed the Film Industry.* Madison: The University of Wisconsin Press.

Bardeche, Maurice, and Robert Brassilach. 1938. *The History of Motion Pictures.* Translated by Iris Barry. New York: W. W. Norton and Company.

Basinger, Jeanine. 1994. *American Cinema: One Hundred Years of Filmmaking.* New York: Rizzoli Press.

Baxter, Peter. 1993. *Just Watch! Sternberg, Paramount and America.* London: British Film Institute Publishing.

Becker, Howard. 1982. *Art Worlds*. Berkeley: University of California Press.

Behlmer, Rudy. 1993. *Memo From Darryl F. Zanuck: The Golden Years at Twentieth Century-Fox*. New York: Grove Press.

Beisel, Nicola. 1992. "Constructing a Shifting Moral Boundary: Literature and Obscenity in Nineteenth-Century America," pp. 104–27 in *Cultivating Differences: Symbolic Boundaries and the Making of Inequality*, edited by Michele Lamont and Marcel Fournier. Chicago: University of Chicago Press.

Beman, Lamar T., ed. 1931. *Censorship of the Theater and Moving Pictures*. New York: The H. W. Wilson Company.

Berger, Peter L., and Thomas Luckmann. 1967. *The Social Construction of Reality: A Treatise in the Sociology of Knowledge*. Garden City, New York: Anchor Books.

Bielby, William T., and Denise Bielby. 1994. " 'All Hits Are Flukes': Institutionalized Decision Making and the Rhetoric of Network Prime-Time Program Development." *American Journal of Sociology* 99:1287–1313.

Biskind, Peter. 1998. *Easy Riders, Raging Bulls: How the Sex-Drugs-and-Rock'n'-Roll Generation Saved Hollywood*. New York: Simon and Shuster.

Black, Gregory D. 1994. *Hollywood Censored: Morality Codes, Catholics, and the Movies*. New York: Cambridge University Press.

Blades, Joseph Dalton Jr. 1976. *A Comparative Study of Selected American Film Critics 1958–1974*. New York: Arno Press.

Blau, Judith. 1986. "The Elite Arts, More or Less de Rigeur: A Comparative Analysis of Metropolitan Culture." *Social Forces* 64:875–905.

Blewitt, John. 1993. "Film, Ideology and Bourdieu's Critique of Public Taste." *British Journal of Aesthetics*, 33:367–72.

Bloom, Allan David. 1987. *The Closing of the American Mind*. New York: Simon and Schuster.

Boddy, William. 1998. "The Beginnings of American Television," pp. 23–37 in *Television: An International History*, edited by Anthony Smith with Richard Paterson. New York: Oxford University Press.

Boggs, Joseph. 1978. *The Art of Watching Films: A Guide to Film Analysis*. Menlo Park, CA: The Benjamin/Cummings Publishing Company.

Bordwell, David. 1989. *Making Meaning: Inference and Rhetoric in the Interpretation of Cinema*. Cambridge, MA: Harvard University Press.

Bordwell, David, and Kristin Thompson. 1986. *Film Art*. New York: Alfred A. Knopf.

Bourdieu, Pierre. 1993. *The Field of Cultural Production*. New York: Columbia University Press.

———. 1985. "The Market of Symbolic Goods." *Poetics* 14:13–44.

———. 1984. *Distinction: A Social Critique of the Judgment of Taste*. Richard Nice, trans. Cambridge, MA: Harvard University Press.

———. 1980. "The Production of Belief: Contribution to an Economy of Symbolic Goods." *Media, Culture and Society* 2:261–93.

Brooks, David. 2000. *Bobos in Paradise: The New Upper Class and How They Got There*. New York: Touchstone.

Brown, Gene. 1995. *Movie Time: A Chronology of Hollywood and the Movie Industry from Its Beginnings to the Present*. New York: Macmillan.

Bucher, Rue. 1962. "Pathology: A Study of Social Movements within a Profession." *Social Problems* 10:40–51.

Bucher, Rue, and Anselm Strauss. 1961. "Professions in Process." *American Journal of Sociology* 66:325–34.

Buhle, Paul, ed. 1987. *Popular Culture in America*. Minneapolis, MN: University of Minnesota Press.

Buss, Robin. 1989. *Italian Films*. London: Anchor Press.

Butsch, Richard. 2001. "A History of Research on Movies, Radio, and Television." *Journal of Popular Film and Television* 29(3):112–20.

Bywater, Tim, and Thomas Sobchak. 1989. *An Introduction to Film Criticism: Major Critical Approaches to Narrative Film*. New York: Longman.

Callenbach, Ernest. 1971. "The Unloved One: Crisis at the American Film Institute." *Film Quarterly* Summer, vols. 22–24:42–54.

Canaday, John Edwin. 1980. *What Is Art? An Introduction to Painting, Sculpture, and Architecture*. New York: Knopf.

Canby, Vincent. 1971. "Introduction," *New York Times Film Reviews*, v. 1. New York: New York Times.

Carney, Raymond. 1985. *American Dreaming: The Films of John Cassavetes and the American Experience*. Berkeley, Los Angeles, London: University of California Press.

Carr, Steven Alan. 2001. *Hollywood and Anti-Semitism: A Cultural History Up to World War II*. Cambridge, UK: Cambridge University Press.

Carroll, Noel. 1998. *Interpreting the Moving Image*. New York: Cambridge University Press.

Chanan, Michael. 1996. "Cinema in Latin America," pp. 427–35 in *The Oxford History of World Cinema*, edited by Geoffrey Nowell-Smith. Oxford: Oxford University Press.

Chandler, Raymond. 1948. "Oscar Night in Hollywood." *Atlantic Monthly* vol. 181, no. 3 pp 24–27.

Chin, Daryl. 1997. "Festivals, Markets, Critics: Notes on the State of the Art Film." *Performing Arts Journal* 19, 1:61–75.

Cook, David A.. "Auteur Cinema and the 'Film Generation' in 1970s Hollywood," pp. 11–37, in *The New American Cinema*, edited by Jon Lewis, 1998, Durham, NC, and London: Duke University Press

Corrigan, Philip. 1983. "Film Entertainment as Ideology and Pleature: Towards a History of Audiences," pp. 24–35 in *British Cinema History*, edited by James Curran and Vincent Porter. London: Weidenfeld and Nicolson.

Corse, Sarah M., and Monica D. Griffin. 1997. "Cultural Valorization and African American Literary History: Reconstructing the Canon." *Sociological Forum* 12:173–203.

Coser, Lewis A., Charles Kadushin, and Walter W. Powell. 1982. *Books: The Culture and Commerce of Publishing*. New York: Basic Books.

Couvares, Francis G. 1996. "Introduction," pp. 1–15, in *Movie Censorship and American Culture*, edited by Francis G. Couvares. Washington and London: Smithsonian Institution Press.

Crane, Diana. 1987. *The Transformation of the Avant-Garde: The New York Art World, 1940–1985*. Chicago: University of Chicago Press.

Crisp, Colin. 1993. *The Classic French Cinema, 1930–1960*. Bloomington and Indianapolis: Indiana University Press.

Czitrom, Daniel. 1996. "The Politics of Performance: Theatre Licensing and the Origins of Movie Censorship in New York," pp. 16–42 in *Movie Censorship and American Culture*, edited by Francis G. Couvares. Washington and London: Smithsonian Institution Press.

Danto, Arthur. 1964. "The Artwold." *Journal of Philosophy* 61:571–84.

Davies, Norman. 1996. *Europe: A History*. New York: HarperPerennial.

Davies, Stephen. 1991. *Definitions of Art*. Ithaca, NY: Cornell University Press.

Davis, Ronald L. 1995. *John Ford: Hollywood's Old Master*. Norman: University of Oklahoma Press.

De Grazia, Edward, and Roger K. Newman. 1982. *Banned Films: Movies, Censors and the First Amendment*. New York and London: R. R. Bowker Company.

De Grazia, Victoria. 1998. "European Cinema and the Idea of Europe, 1925–95," pp. 19–33 in *Hollywood and Europe: Economics, Culture, National Identity: 1945–95*, edited by Geoffrey Nowell-Smith and Steven Ricci. London: British Film Institute.

Decherney, Peter. 2000. "Inventing Film Study and Its Object at Columbia University, 1915–1938." *Film History* 12, 4:443–60.

Denby, David. 1998. "The Moviegoers: Why Don't People Love the Right Movies Anymore?" *New Yorker* April 6:94–101.

DeNora, Tia. 1991. "Musical Patronage and Social Change in Beethoven's Vienna." *American Journal of Sociology* 97:310–46.

Dick, Bernard F. 1993. *The Merchant Prince of Poverty Row: Harry Cohn of Columbia Pictures*. Lexington: University Press of Kentucky.

———. 1992. *Columbia Pictures: Portrait of a Studio*. Lexington: The University Press of Kentucky.

Dickie, George. 1974. *Art and the Aesthetic*. Ithaca, NY: Cornell University Press.

DiMaggio, Paul. 1992. "Cultural Boundaries and Structural Change: The Extension of the High Culture Model to Theater, Opera, and the Dance, 1900–1940," pp. 21–57, in *Cultivating Differences: Symbolic Boundaries and the Making of Inequality*, Michele Lamont and Marcel Fournier, eds. Chicago: University of Chicago Press.

———. 1982. "Cultural Entrepreneurship in Nineteenth-Century Boston: The Creation of an Organizational Base for High Culture in America." *Media, Culture and Society* 4:33–50.

DiMaggio, Paul, and Joseph Cohen. 2003. "Information Inequality and Network Externalities: A Comparative Study of the Diffusion of Television and the Internet." Working Paper #31, Center for Arts and Cultural Policy Studies, Woodrow Wilson School, Princeton University.

DiMaggio, Paul, and Michael Useem. 1978. "Social Class and Arts Consumption: The Origins and Consequences of Class Differences in Exposure to the Arts in America." *Theory and Society* 5:141–61.

Doherty, Thomas. 1999. *Pre-Code Hollywood: Sex, Immorality, and Insurrection in American Cinema, 1930–1934*. New York: Columbia University Press.

During, Simon, editor. 1999. *The Cultural Studies Reader*. New York: Routledge.

Eames, John Douglas. 1985. *The Paramount Story*. London: Octopus Books Limited.

Easton, John. 1997. "Reel Scholarship." *University of Chicago Magazine*. 89: 26–31.

Edwards, Jim. 2001. "The Confluence of East and West Coast Pop," pp. 89–109 in *Pop Art: US/UK Connections 1956–1966*, edited by David E. Brauer, Jim Edwards, and Walter Hopps. New York: Hatje Cantz Publishers.

Eitner, Lorenz. 1961. *Introduction to Art: An Illustrated Topical Manual*. Minneapolis: Burgess Publishing Company.

Eliashberg, Jehoshua, and Steven M. Shugan. 1997. "Film Critics: Influencers or Predictors?" *Journal of Marketing* 61:68–78.

Elsaesser, Thomas. 1996. "Germany: The Weimar Years," pp. 136–51 in *The Oxford History of World Cinema*, edited by Geoffrey Nowell-Smith. Oxford: Oxford University Press.

———. 1989. *New German Cinema: A History*. London: Macmillan Education Ltd.

———. 1975. "Two Decades in Another Country: Hollywood and the Cinephiles," pp. 199–216 in *Superculture*, edited by C.W.E. Bigsby. London: Paul Elek.

Emery, Robert J. 2000. *The Directors—Take Two: In Their Own Words*. New York: Media Entertainment.

Engel, Lehman. 1976. *The Critics*. New York: Macmillan.

Epstein, Edward Jay. 2005. *The Big Picture: Money and Power in Hollywood*. New York: Random House Trade Paperbacks.

Ezra, Elizabeth. 2004. "The Cinemising Process: Filmgoing in the Silent Era," pp. 74–81 in *The French Cinema Book*, edited by Michael Temple and Michael Witt. London: British Film Institute Publishing.

Ezra, Elizabeth, and Sue Harris, eds. 2000. *France in Focus: Film and National Identity*. Oxford and New York: Berg.

Ferguson, Priscilla Parkhurst. 1998. "A Cultural Field in the Making: Gastronomy in Nineteenth-Century France." *American Journal of Sociology* 104:597–641.

Freeman, Bernadine. 1926. No title. *Educational Review* 72:115.

Gabler, Neal. 1989. *An Empire of Their Own: How the Jews Invented Hollywood*. New York: Doubleday.

Gans, Herbert. 1999. *Popular Culture and High Culture: An Analysis and Evaluation of Taste*. New York: Basic Books.

Genocchio, Benjamin. 2003. "When 'Delinquents' Infiltrated Art." *New York Times*, May 11, Late Edition (East Coast), p. 14NJ.9

Gerstner, David A., and Janet Staiger (Editors). 2003. *Authorship and Film*. New York and London: Routledge.

Giannetti, Louis. 1981. *Masters of the American Cinema*. Englewood Cliffs, N.J.: Prentice-Hall.

Gomery, Douglas. 2001. "Finding TV's Pioneering Audiences." *Journal of Popular Film and Television* 29, 3:121–29.

———. 1992. *Shared Pleasures: A History of Movie Presentation in the United States*. Madison: University Press of Wisconsin Press.

Haberski, Raymond J. 2001. *It's Only a Movie!: Film and Critics in American Culture*. Lexington, KY: University of Kentucky.

Hacking, Ian. 1995. *Rewriting the Soul: Multiple Personality and the Sciences of Memory*. Princeton, NJ: Princeton University Press.

Hake, Sabine. 2001. *German National Cinema*. London and New York: Routledge.

———. 1990. "Chaplin Reception in Weimar Germany." *New German Critique* Autumn No. 51, 87–111.

Halle, David. 1993. *Inside Culture: Art and Class in the American Home*. Chicago: University of Chicago Press.

Hampton, Benjamin B. 1970 [1931]. *History of the American Film Industry from Its Beginnings to 1931*. New York: Dover Publications.

Hannan, Michael T., and John Freeman. 1988. "The Ecology of Organizational Mortality: American Labor Unions, 1836–1985." *American Journal of Sociology* 94:25–52.

———. 1987. "The Ecology of Organizational Founding: American Labor Unions, 1936–1985." *American Journal of Sociology* 92:910–43.

———. 1977. "The Population Ecology of Organizations." *American Journal of Sociology*. 82:929–64.

Hanson, Patricia King, and Stephen L. Hanson, eds. 1986. *Film Review Index*. Phoenix, Arizona: Oryx Press.

Harrington, Austin. 2004. *Art and Social Theory*. Malden, MA: Polity Press.

Hartog, Simon. 1983. "State Protection of a Beleaguered Industry," pp. 59–73 in *British Cinema History*, edited by James Curran and Vincent Porter. London: Weidenfeld and Nicolson.

Hawkridge, John. 1996. "British Cinema from Hepworth to Hitchcock," pp. 130–36 in *The Oxford History of World Cinema*, edited by Geoffrey Nowell-Smith. Oxford: Oxford University Press.

Hay, James. 1987. *Popular Film Culture in Fascist Italy: The Passing of the Rex*. Bloomington and Indianapolis: Indiana University Press.

Heiss, Ann M. 1973. *An Inventory of Academic Innovation and Reform*. Berkeley, CA: Carnegie Commission on Higher Education.

Hepworth, Julie. 1999. *The Social Construction of Anorexia Nervosa*. London; Thousand Oaks, CA: Sage Publications

Herman, Jan. 1995. *A Talent for Trouble: The Life of Hollywood's Most Acclaimed Director*. New York: G. P. Putnam's Sons.

Hirsch, Paul M. 1986. "From Ambushes to Golden Parachutes: Corporate Takeovers as an Instance of Cultural Framing and Institutional Integration." *American Journal of Sociology* 91:800–37.

———. 1972. "Processing Fads and Fashions: An Organization-Set Analysis of Cultural Industry Systems." *American Journal of Sociology* 77:639–59.

Hirschhorn, Clive. 1983. *The Universal Story*. London: Octopus Books Limited.

Holsti, Ole R. 1969. *Content Analyses for the Social Sciences and Humanities*. Reading, MA: Addison-Wesley.

Horkheimer, Max. 1982. "Art and Mass Culture," pp. 273–90 in *Critical Theory: Selected Essays*, Matthew J. O'Connell, trans. New York: Continuum Publishing.

Horkheimer, Max, and Theodor Adorno. 1972. *Dialectic of Enlightenment*. Translated by John Cumming. New York: Herder and Herder.

Horton, Robert, editor. 2001. *Billy Wilder Interviews: Conversations with Filmmakers Series*. Jackson: University Press of Mississippi.

Jancovich, Mark. 2001. "Genre and the Audience: Genre Classifications and Cultural Distinctions in the Mediation of *The Silence of the Lambs*," pp. 33–45 in *Hollywood Spectatorship: Changing Perceptions of Cinema Audiences*, edited by Melvyn Stokes and Richard Maltby. London: BFI Publishing.

Jowett, Garth. 1996. "'A Significant Medium for the Communication of Ideas:' The *Miracle Decision* and the Decline of Motion Picture Censorship, 1952–1969," pp. 258–76, in *Movie Censorship and American Culture*, edited by Francis G. Couvares. Washington and London: Smithsonian Institution Press.

———. 1989. "A Capacity for Evil: The 1915 Supreme Court Mutual Decision." *Historical Journal of Film, Radio and Television*, 9, 1:59–78.

———. 1976. *Film: The Democratic Art*. Boston: Little, Brown.

Kaes, Anton. 1987. "The Debate about Cinema: Charting a Controversy (1909–1929)." *New German Critique* 40:7–33.

Kammen, Michael. 1996. *The Lively Arts: Gilbert Seldes and the Transformation of Cultural Criticism in the United States*. New York: Oxford University Press.

Kapsis, Robert E. 1992. *Hitchcock: The Making of a Reputation*. Chicago: University of Chicago Press.

King, Geoff. 2002. *New Hollywood Cinema: An Introduction*. London, New York: I. B. Tauris Publishers.

King, Susan. 2002. "Rescuing the Classics: Computers Do the Nitty-Gritty Work; 'Sunset Boulevard' and 'Roman Holiday' Are Stunning on DVD, but the Restorers Came Close to Pulling the Plug." *Los Angeles Times* (home edition). Los Angeles: Nov. 26, p. E.6.

Kinnard, Roy, and R. J. Vitone. 1986. *The American Films of Michael Curtiz*. Metuchen, NJ, and London: The Scarecrow Press.

Kisseloff, Jeff. 1995. *The Box: An Oral History of Television, 1920–1961*. New York: Penguin Books.

Knight, Arthur. 1957. *The Liveliest Art*. New York: New American Library.

Kracauer, Siegfried. 1987 [1926]. "Cult of Distraction: On Berlin's Picture Palaces." Translated by Thomas Y. Levin. *New German Critique* Winter, no. 40, 91–96.

Lang, Gladys Engel, and Kurt Lang. 1988. "Recognition and Renown: The Survival of Artistic Reputation." *American Journal of Sociology* 94:79–109.

Lanzoni, Rémi Fournier. 2002. *French Cinema: From Its Beginnings to the Present*. New York, London: Continuum International Publishing Group.

Latour, Bruno, and Steve Woolgar. 1979. *Laboratory Life: The Social Construction of Scientific Facts*. 2nd ed. Princeton: Princeton University Press.

Leary, Lewis. 1976. *American Literature: A Study and Research Guide*. New York: St. Martin's Press.

Levine, Lawrence W. 1988. *Lowbrow/Highbrow: The Emergence of Cultural Hierarchy in America*. Cambridge, MA: Harvard University Press.

Lewis, Glen. 2003. "The Thai Movie Revival and Thai National Identity." *Journal of Media and Cultural Studies* 17:69–78.

Lieberson, Stanley. 2000. *A Matter of Taste: How Names, Fashions, and Culture Change*. New Haven CT: Yale University Press.

———. 1985. *Making It Count: The Improvement of Social Research and Theory*. Berkeley CA: University of California Press.

Lieberson, Stanley, Susan Dumais, and Shyon Baumann. 2000. "The Instability of Androgynous Names: The Symbolic Maintenance of Gender Boundaries." *American Journal of Sociology* 105:1249–87.

Long, Robert Emmet. 2001. *George Cukor: Interviews*. Jackson, MS: University Press of Mississippi.

Lopes, Paul. 2002. *The Rise of a Jazz Art World*. Cambridge, UK: Cambridge University Press.

Lorber, Judith. 1991. *The Social Construction of Gender*. Newbury Park, CA: Sage Publications.

Lounsbury, Myron Osborn. 1973. *The Origins of American Film Criticism 1909–1939*. New York: Arno Press.

Luckett, Moya. 1994. "*Fantasia*: Cultural Constructions of Disney's 'Masterpiece,' " pp. 214–36, in *Disney Discourse: Producing the Magic Kingdom*, edited by Eric Smoodin. New York: Routledge.

Lynes, Russell. 1973. *Good Old Modern: An Intimate Portrait of the Museum of Modern Art*. New York: Atheneum.

Maland, Charles J. 1989. *Chaplin and American Culture: The Evolution of a Star Image*. Princeton, NJ: Princeton University Press.

Maltby, Richard. 2003. *Hollywood Cinema*, 2nd ed. Malden, MA: Blackwell Publishing.

———. 1996. "To Prevent the Prevalent Type of Book: Censorship and Adaptation in Hollywood, 1924–1934," pp. 97–128, in *Movie Censorship and American Culture*, edited by Francis G. Couvares. Washington and London: Smithsonian Institution Press.

Manly, Lorne. 2005. "Doing the Hollywood Math: What Slump?" *New York Times*. December 11, 2.15.

Mast, Gerald. 1981. *A Short History of the Movies*. 3rd ed. Chicago: University of Chicago Press.

May, Lary. 1980. *Screening Out the Past: The Birth of Mass Culture and the Motion Picture Industry*. New York: Oxford University Press.

McBride, Joseph. 1983. *Filmmakers on Filmmaking: The American Film Institute, Seminars on Motion Pictures and Television*. Los Angeles: J. P. Tarcher.

———. (editor). 1972. *Focus on Howard Hawks*. Englewood Cliffs, NJ: Prentice-Hall.

Monaco, Paul. 1976. *Cinema and Society: France and Germany during the Twenties*. New York: Elsevier.

Mordden, Ethan. 1988. *The Hollywood Studios: House Style in the Golden Age of the Movies*. New York: Alfred A. Knopf.

Morrison, Jack. 1973. *The Rise of the Arts on the American Campus*. New York: McGraw-Hill.

Motion Picture Association Worldwide Market Research. 2006. www.mpaa.org/researchStatistics.asp.

Mueller, John. 1951. *The American Symphony Orchestra: A Social History of Musical Taste*. Bloomington: University Indiana Press.

Murray, Edward. 1975. *Nine American Film Critics: A Study of Theory and Practice*. New York: Frederick Ungar Publishing Co.

Napper, Lawrence. 1997. "A Despicable Tradition? Quota Quickies in the 1930s," pp. 37–47 in *The British Cinema Book*, edited by Robert Murphy. London: BFI Publishing.

Nowell-Smith, Geoffrey, James Hay, and Gianni Volpi. 1996. *The Companion to Italian Cinema*. London: BFI Publishing.

Orbach, Barak. 2004. "Antitrust and Pricing in the Motion Picture Industry." *Yale Journal on Regulation* 21, 2:317–67.

Ott, Frederick W. 1986. *The Great German Films*. Seacaucus, NJ: Citadel Press.

Pearson, Roberta. 1996. "Early Cinema," pp. 13–23, in *The Oxford History of World Cinema*, edited by Geoffrey Nowell-Smith. Oxford, England: Oxford University Press.

Pemberton, Brock. 1936. "A Theatrical Producer's Reaction to the Movies," pp. 153–65 in *The Movies On Trial*, edited by William J. Perlman. New York: The Macmillan Company.

Perren, Alisa. 2001. "sex, lies, and marketing: Miramax and the Development of the Quality, Indie Blockbuster." *Film Quarterly* 55, 2:30–39.

Peterson, Richard A. 1997. "The Rise and Fall of Highbrow Snobbery as a Status Marker." *Poetics* 25, 75–92.

———. 1994. "Cultural Studies through the Production Perspective: Progress and Prospects," pp. 163–89, in *The Sociology of Culture: Emerging Theoretical Perspectives*, Diana Crane, ed. Cambridge, MA: Blackwell Publishers.

———. 1972. "A Process Model of the Folk, Pop and Fine Art Phases of Jazz," pp. 135–51 in *American Music*, edited by Charles Nanry. New Brunswick, NJ: Transaction Books.

Peterson, Richard A., and Albert Simkus. 1992. "How Musical Tastes Mark Occupational Status Groups," pp. 152–86 in *Cultivating Differences: Symbolic Boundaries and the Making of Inequality*, edited by Michele Lamont and Marcel Fournier. Chicago: University of Chicago Press.

Petro, Patrice. 1986. "Mass Culture and the Feminine: The 'Place' of Television in Film Studies." *Cinema Journal* 25(3):5–21.

Phillips, Gene D. (editor). 2001. *Stanley Kubrick: Interviews*. Jackson: University Press of Mississippi.

———. 1990. *Major Film Directors of the American and British Cinema*. London and Toronto: Associated University Presses.

———. 1981. *John Schlesinger*. Boston: Twayne Publishers.

Phillips, Nelson, and Cynthia Hardy. 2002. *Discourse Analysis: Investigating Processes of Social Construction*. Sage University Papers Series on Qualitative Research Methods, vol. 50. Thousand Oaks, CA: Sage.

Phillips, Patrick. 2000. *Understanding Film Texts: Meaning and Experience*. London: British Film Institute.

Poe, G. Tom. 2001. "Historical Spectatorship around and about Stanley Kramer's *On the Beach*," pp. 91–102 in *Hollywood Spectatorship: Changing Perceptions* of *Cinema Audiences*, edited by Melvyn Stokes and Richard Maltby. London: BFI Publishing.

Prigozy, Ruth. 1984. "*Double Indemnity*: Billy Wilder's *Crime and Punishment*." *Literature/Film Quarterly* 12:160–70.

Putnam, Robert D. 2000. *Bowling Alone*. New York: Simon and Shuster.

Puttnam, David. 1997. *The Undeclared War: The Struggle for Control of the World's Film Industry*. London: Harper Collins.

Pye, Michael, and Linda Myles. 1979. *The Movie Brats: How the Film Generation Took Over Hollywood*. London: Faber and Faber.

Quart, Leonard, and Albert Auster. 1984. *American Film and Society Since 1945*. London: Macmillan.

Rachlin, Seth. 1993. "Anatomy of a Film Revolution: The Case of the Nouvelle Vague." *Poetics* 21:429–42.

Randall, Richard. 1968. *Censorship of the Movies: The Social and Political Control of a Mass Medium*. Madison: University of Wisconsin Press.

Rawlings, Craig M. 2001. "'Making Names': The Cutting Edge Renewal of African Art in New York City, 1985–1996." *Poetics* 29:29–54.

Redmonds, I. G., and Reiko Mimura. 1980. *Paramount Pictures and the People Who Made Them*. San Diego, New York: A. S. Barnes.

Reich, Jacqueline. 2002. "Mussolini at the Movies: Fascism, Film, and Culture," pp. 3–29 in *Re-viewing Fascism: Italian Cinema, 1922–1943*, edited by Jacqueline Reich and Piero Garofalo. Bloomington and Indianapolis: Indiana University Press.

Rhode, Eric. 1976. *A History of the Cinema from Its Origins to 1970*. New York: Hill and Wang.

Richards, Jeffrey. 1997. "British Film Censorship," pp. 167–77 in *The British Cinema Book*, edited by Robert Murphy. London: BFI Publishing.

Ridgeway, Cecilia, David Diekema, and Cathryn Johnson. 1995. "Legitimacy, Compliance, and Gender in Peer Groups." *Social Psychology Quarterly* 58:298–311.

Riley, Gail Blasser. 1998. *Censorship*. New York: Facts on File.

Roddick, Nick. 1983. *A New Deal in Entertainment: Warner Brothers in the 1930s*. London: British Film Institute.

Rosenberg, Bernard. 1971 [1968]. "Mass Culture Revisited," pp. 3–12 in *Mass Culture Revisited*, edited by Bernard Rosenberg and David Manning White. New York: Van Nostrand Reinhold Company.

Rosenzweig, Sydney. 1982. *Casablanca and Other Major Films of Michael Curtiz*. Ann Arbor: University of Michigan Research Press.

Ross, Steven J. 1998. *Working-Class Hollywood: Silent Film and the Shaping of Class in America*. Princeton: Princeton University Press.

Roth, Chris. 2000. "Three Decades of Film Censorship . . . Right before Your Eyes." *The Humanist* 60, 1:9–13.

Rudolph, Frederick. 1977. *Curriculum: A History of the American Undergraduate Course of Study since 1636*. San Francisco: Jossey-Bass Publishers.

Ryall, Tom. 1997. "A British Studio System: The Associated British Picture Corporation and the Gaumont-British Picture Corporation in the 1930s," pp.

27–36 in *The British Cinema Book*, edited by Robert Murphy. London: BFI Publishing.

Sandler, Irving. 1988. *American Art of the 1960s*. New York: Harper and Row.

Sarris Andrew. 1968. *The American Cinema: Directors and Directions 1929–1968*. New York: Dutton.

Saunders, Thomas J. 1994. *Hollywood in Berlin: American Cinema and Weimar Germany*. Berkeley: University of California Press.

Schatz, Thomas. 2003. "The New Hollywood," pp. 15–44, in *Movie Blockbusters*, edited by Julian Stringer. London and New York: Routledge.

———. 1996. "Hollywood: The Triumph of the Studio System," pp. 220–234 in *The Oxford History of World Cinema*, edited by Geoffrey Nowell-Smith. Oxford: Oxford University Press.

Schickel, Richard. 1969. "Don't Go to the Movies to Escape—The Movies Are Now High Art." *New York Times Magazine* January 5, pp. 32–44.

Schluepmann, Heide. 1986. "The First German Art Film: Rye's *The Student of Prague* (1913)," pp. 9–24 in *German Film and Literature: Adaptations and Transformations*, edited by Eric Rentschler. New York and London: Methuen.

Seldes, Gilbert. 1924. *The Seven Lively Arts*. New York: Harper & Brothers Publishers.

Shale, Richard. 1993. *The Academy Awards Index: The Complete Categorical and Chronological Record*. Westport, CT: Greenwood Press.

Shrum, Welsey. 1996. *Fringe and Fortune: The Role of Critics in High and Popular Art*. Princeton: Princeton University Press.

Sinyard, Neil. 1985. *Directors: The All-Time Greats*. London: Columbus Books.

Sklar, Robert. 1994. *Movie-Made America*. 2nd ed. New York: Vintage Books.

Sklar, Robert, and Vito Zagarrio. 1998. *Frank Capra: Authorship and the Studio System*. Philadelphia: Temple University Press.

Smith, J. Douglas. 2001. "Patrolling the Boundaries of Race: Motion Picture Censorship and Jim Crow in Virginia, 1922–1932." *Historical Journal of Film, Radio and Television* 21, 3:273–91.

Solomon, Aubrey. 1988. *Twentieth Century-Fox: A Corporate and Financial History*. Metuchen, NJ, and London: Scarecrow Press.

Sontag, Susan. 1969. *Styles of Radical Will*. New York: Farrar, Straus and Giroux.

Staiger, Janet. 1990. "Announcing Wares, Winning Patrons, Voicing Ideals: Thinking about the History and Theory of Film Advertising." *Cinema Journal* 29, 3:3–31.

———. 1985. "The Hollywood Mode of Production to 1930," pp. 85–153 and "The Hollywood Mode of Production, 1930–1960," pp. 309–64 in *The Classical Hollywood Cinema: Film Style and Mode of Production to 1960*, David Bordwell, Janet Staiger, and Kristin Thompson. London: Routledge and Kegan Paul.

Starr, Paul. 1982. *The Social Transformation of American Medicine*. New York: Basic Books.

Stein, Elliott. 2002. "Old Hollywood's Sure Thing." *Village Voice*, New York; Sep. 11–Sep. 17, vol. 47, Iss. 37, p. 110.

Stinchcombe, Arthur L. 1965. "Social Structure and Organizations," pp. 142–93 in *Handbook of Organizations*, edited by James G. March. Chicago: Rand McNally.

Stones, Barbara. 1993. *America Goes to the Movies: One Hundred Years of Motion Picture Exhibition*. North Hollywood, CA: National Association of Theatre Owners.

Stringer, Julian, editor. 2003. *Movie Blockbusters*. London and New York: Routledge.

Stryker, Robin. 1994. "Rules, Resources, and Legitimacy Processes: Some Implications for Social Conflict, Order, and Change." *American Journal of Sociology* 99:847–910.

Sultanik, Aaron. 1986. *Film: A Modern Art*. Cranbury, NJ: Rosemont Publishing and Printing Corporation.

Tebbel, John. 1987. *Between Covers: The Rise and Transformation of Book Publishing in America*. New York: Oxford University Press.

Temple, Michael, and Michael Witt. 2004. "Hello Cinema!" pp. 9–17 in *The French Cinema Book*, edited by Michael Temple and Michael Witt. London: British Film Institute Publishing.

Thompson, Kristin, and David Bordwell. 1994. *Film History: An Introduction*. New York: McGraw-Hill.

Titchener, Campbell B. 1998. *Reviewing the Arts*. 2nd ed. Mahwah, NJ, and London: Lawrence Erlbaum Associates, Publishers.

Tolstoy, Leo. 1995 [1898]. *What Is Art?* Translated by Richard Pevear and Larissa Volokhonsky. London: Penguin Books.

Tuska, Jon. 1991. *Encounters with Filmmakers: Eight Career Studies*. New York: Greenwood Press.

Twomey, John E. 1956. "Some Considerations on the Rise of the Art-Film Theater." *Quarterly of Film, Radio and Television* 10, 3:239–47.

Uricchio, Willam. 1996. "The First World War and the Crisis in Europe," pp. 62–70 in in *The Oxford History of World Cinema,* edited by Geoffrey Nowell-Smith. Oxford: Oxford University Press.

Uricchio, William, and Roberta Pearson. 1993. *Reframing Culture: The Case of the Vitagraph Quality Films*. Princeton: Princeton University Press.

Usai, Paolo Cherchi. 1996. "Italy: Spectacle and Melodrama," pp. 123–30 in *The Oxford History of World Cinema*, edited by Geoffrey Nowell-Smith. Oxford: Oxford University Press.

Vaughn, Steven. 1990. "Morality and Entertainment: The Origins of the Motion Picture Production Code." *The Journal of American History* 77:39–65.

Verdaasdonk, H. 1983. "Social and Economic Factors in the Attribution of Literary Quality." *Poetics* 12:383–95.

Wapshott, Nicholas. 1990. *The Man Between: A Biography of Carol Reed,* London: Chatto and Windus.

Warburton, Nigel. 2003. *The Art Question*. London and New York: Routledge.

Watson, Robert. 1990. Film and Television in Education: An Aesthetic Approach to the Moving Image. London: Falmer Press.

Weinberg, Charles B. 2005. "Profits Out of the Picture: Research Issues and Revenue Sources beyond the North American Box Office," pp. 163–97 in *A Concise*

Handbook of Movie Industry Economics, edited by Charles C. Moul. Cambridge: Cambridge University Press.

Welsh, James M., and Tibbetts, John C. (eds). 1999. *The Cinema of Tony Richardson: Essays and Interviews*. Albany: State University of New York Press.

White, Harrison C., and Cynthia A. White. 1965. *Canvases and Careers: Institutional Change in the French Painting World*. Chicago: University of Chicago Press.

White, William Allen. 1936. "Chewing-Gum Relaxation," pp. 3–12, in *The Movies on Trial*, William J. Perlman, ed. New York: Macmillan Company.

Winship, Michael. 1988. *Television*. New York: Random House.

Wolcott, James. 1997. "Waiting for Goddard." *Vanity Fair* 440:124–34.

Yoffe, Emily. 1983. "Popcorn Politics." *Harper's Magazine* 267:16–22.

Young, Donald. 1926. "Social Standards and the Motion Picture." *Annals of the American Academy of Political and Social Science* 128:146–50.

Zhou, Xueguang. 1993. "Occupational Power, State Capacities, and the Diffusion of Licensing in the American States: 1890 to 1950." *American Sociological Review* 58:536–52.

Zierold, Norman. 1991. *The Moguls: Hollywood's Merchants of Myth*. Los Angeles: Silman-James Press.

Zolberg, Vera. 1990. *Constructing a Sociology of the Arts*. New York: Cambridge University Press.

Zwerdling, Shirley. 1970. *Film and TV Festival Directory*. New York: Back Stage Publications.

Index